The Nuptial Deal

The Nuptial Deal

Same-Sex Marriage and
Neo-Liberal Governance

JAYE CEE WHITEHEAD

UNIVERSITY OF CHICAGO PRESS   CHICAGO AND LONDON

JAYE CEE WHITEHEAD is assistant professor of sociology at Pacific University. This is her first book.

The University of Chicago Press, Chicago 60637
The University of Chicago Press, Ltd., London
© 2012 by The University of Chicago
All rights reserved. Published 2012.
Printed in the United States of America
21 20 19 18 17 16 15 14 13 12   1 2 3 4 5

ISBN-13: 978-0-226-89528-4 (cloth)
ISBN-13: 978-0-226-89529-1 (paper)
ISBN-10: 0-226-89528-9 (cloth)
ISBN-10: 0-226-89529-7 (paper)

Library of Congress Cataloging-in-Publication Data

Whitehead, Jaye Cee.
    The nuptial deal : same-sex marriage and neo-liberal governance / Jaye Cee Whitehead.
        p. cm.
    Includes bibliographical references and index.
    ISBN-13: 978-0-226-89528-4 (cloth : alk. paper)
    ISBN-10: 0-226-89528-9 (cloth : alk. paper)
    ISBN-13: 978-0-226-89529-1 (pbk. : alk. paper)
    ISBN-10: 0-226-89529-7 (pbk. : alk. paper)   1. Same-sex marriage—Political aspects—
United States.   I. Title.
    HQ1034.U5W46 2012
    306.84'80973—dc23

                                                                2011024764

♾ This paper meets the requirements of ANSI/NISO z39.48-1992 (Permanence of Paper).

TO MY PARENTS, JUDY AND STEVE WHITEHEAD

Contents

Acknowledgments

At each stage of the research and writing process, *The Nuptial Deal* benefited from the support and expertise of friends, family, mentors, and colleagues who fundamentally shaped this work. This includes members of the organization that, for reasons of confidentiality, I call Marriage Rights Now (MRN) who graciously invited me into their lives despite the often uncomfortable questions I posed regarding a political project that is so close to their hearts.

I had the great fortune of working with brilliant, relentless, but also emotionally supportive mentors. Dawne Moon spent countless hours on this project, ranging from discussing the big-picture ideas to reading several very rough drafts. I thank Arlie Hochschild for posing incisive intellectual challenges for this work while also nurturing my budding sociological imagination. I have Krista Luker to thank for her innovations in research methodology, which helped form the scaffolding for my project, and Wendy Brown for her personal encouragement and advice.

The Nuptial Deal also benefited from the administrative support of Sarah Phillips and John Hayes at Pacific University. I am appreciative of Aaron Greer and Jules Boykoff, for reading last-minute drafts and being outstanding colleagues, and the efforts of Jennifer Thomas and Leia Franchini, who provided invaluable advice and commentary from an undergraduate perspective.

I extend my gratitude to Doug Mitchell, Tim McGovern, the outside reviewers, and all the staff involved in the production of this book. I could not have asked for a more reassuring and rewarding publication process.

Finally, I want to thank "the inner circle." Your companionship and love inspired the set of questions I ask throughout this book. One of my favorite moments in the history of this project came during our all-night revision "party." Katie, thanks for your attention to the creative form, and Nich for our numerous intellectual rants. Nili Kirschner, I am forever grateful for your endless commitment to this project. You have edited more drafts of this work than any other person on the planet. Shannon "Sug" Perry, I could not have done this without your infectious optimism and unconditional love.

CHAPTER ONE

Marriage Equality Meets Neo-Liberal Inequality

In the fall of 1997, Hazel Butler and Amber McDaniel[1] celebrated their one-year dating anniversary in a secluded grass clearing just large enough to spread a picnic blanket. Much to Amber's surprise, Hazel went down on one knee with an engagement ring in hand and asked Amber to marry her. After a short pause, reflecting on her own desire to make a "lifelong commitment," Amber accepted Hazel's proposal. For Amber and Hazel, their desire to marry, in Amber's words, "was just natural. Of course we love each other, and we want to be with each other forever. We want to get married."

When Amber and Hazel returned from their camping trip and began preparations for their wedding, their feelings that marriage was the commonsense and natural next step for their relationship were met with confusion and hostility from their local community and extended family. Hazel recalled the illegibility[2] she and Amber felt when attempting to buy their wedding cake: "One of the cake places refused. Well, they didn't refuse; they just kept saying, 'You want a birthday cake,' and we were, like, 'No, we want a wedding cake.' 'For two women, you want birthday cake.' 'No,' you know, we kept pointing, 'Wedding cake,' 'Wedding cake,' and it wasn't, you know, making any sense to them." Amber also felt that her "natural" desire to marry Hazel was incomprehensible to her family. When she told her parents that she and Hazel were going to get married, they responded, "So, are you, like, having a commitment ceremony?" They also asked, "How legal is it?" Amber's parents even asked, "Is that really how you want to spend your money? Isn't it just better to spend that money making a down payment on a house? Your marriage is not real." Hazel and

Amber eventually ordered a cake from an establishment that recognized the possibility of making a wedding cake for two women, refused their parents' cost-benefit analysis, and planned a ceremony because they explicitly rejected the assumption that their marriage would not be real without a legal contract.

Given the initial lack of acceptance they felt from their family, Hazel and Amber were "shocked" when every invited relative not only came to their wedding but also publicly recognized the authenticity of Hazel and Amber's commitment.

> Everyone showed up for this event. I think it really transformed them. I think that they came out of curiosity and also knee-jerk reaction, like, "Well, we go to weddings, and this is a family celebration and we need to be there." There was a part of the celebration where we had the family stand and say, "Do you accept [Hazel] into your family as your daughter?" And they all said, "We do." Hazel's family did the same thing. It was really profoundly sacred at that moment. It is very much like, you know, a commitment to us and back and forth. It is so important to have this moment, because it was not validated by any piece of paper. It was something that needed to be witnessed and acknowledged by the people who were there for us.

Hazel and Amber's wedding was "profoundly sacred," not just because of the vows they made to each other but because their families pledged to recognize their relationship as a real marriage that united two families. In addition, their wedding, as a rite of passage, signaled the official entrance of the families' daughters into adulthood. After their wedding, Amber's family no longer referred to Hazel as a "girlfriend." Amber recalls that since their wedding, "the family members who weren't sure about me being gay or lesbian before and what it meant to have a partner understood what [Hazel] meant to me. They now would introduce her as, 'This is [Hazel], Amber's wife, and she is part of the family.'" Both Hazel and Amber describe their wedding as a magical event that made them momentarily forget that their ceremony would have no legal significance. The law considered their marriage meaningless, but Hazel and Amber felt like a married couple, and their families recognized them as such: they had made a public promise to care for, love, and protect each other for the rest of their lives.

After their honeymoon, Hazel and Amber found these promises to love, care for, and protect difficult to fulfill: they began to experience the reality of being excluded from legal marriage in ways they had not thought about before their wedding. Unemployed at the time, Amber could not be covered as a dependent on Hazel's health insurance, unlike other legally married couples at her workplace. Hazel could not name Amber as the beneficiary of her federal pension. Hazel argued with her car insurance company when, in the absence of a legal marriage license, it refused to recognize her and Amber's relationship and grant them the lower insurance rates for which married couples qualify. Even though Hazel made enough money to comfortably cover Amber's insurance premiums, they began to look beyond their own experiences. As Amber puts it, "[Hazel] and I started looking into all of the rights that come with a civil marriage license that we were denied." Broadly grouped, these rights involve issues of taxation, inheritance, medical directives, access to hospital visitation, legal standing to sue for wrongful death, eligibility for Social Security survivors benefits, the ability to claim spousal privilege in a court of law, legal recognition of joint parenting, dissolution and divorce protections, and immigration for foreign partners. Amber and Hazel's experiences of exclusion sharply contrasted with their otherwise privileged social position as white, upper-middle-class Americans.

From Hazel and Amber's point of view, the state was not living up to its end of the deal: on their wedding day, Hazel and Amber had agreed to the *responsibilities* that come with marriage, but the state refused to allow them access to the legal *recognition* that would give them an official identity as a couple and the specific *rights* designed to fulfill their personal commitments without unwarranted government intrusion. Hazel had vowed to love Amber "for richer or poorer," but the state was making it difficult for her to fulfill this promise.

By 1999, Hazel and Amber had become prominent members in the movement for same-sex couples to gain the legal rights of marriage and helped found a national organization for marriage rights that, for the sake of confidentiality, I refer to as Marriage Rights Now (MRN). Since their wedding, Hazel and Amber have tied their own intimate relationship to the broader struggle. They spend their leisure time on the phone, calling on voters to approve measures to secure same-sex couples' marital rights and reject efforts to restrict marriage to different-sex couples. In their local gay and lesbian pride parade each year, Hazel dons her wedding day tuxedo and Amber her wedding dress, both carrying signs that encourage onlookers to support the "equal right to marry." Every year on Valentine's Day, they join a group of gay and lesbian couples who stand in line at the local courthouse and request marriage licenses, only to be met with rejection and disapproval from anxious heterosexual couples standing in the same line and from clerks who feel their time is being wasted by what they see as hopeless applications.

In the pages that follow, I argue that stories like Hazel and Amber's, coming from the front lines of the marriage equality movement, must be contextualized as a struggle to gain access to neo-liberal governing structures. I combine participant observation, in-depth interviews, and a content analysis of the marriage equality movement in the United States to help explain how individuals can find themselves consenting to and ardently fighting for a model of neo-liberal governance that they ideologically oppose.

The gay and lesbian studies and social movement literature includes a number of notable works regarding the social conditions that account for the historical ascendancy of same-sex marriage on the national gay and lesbian rights agenda (Chauncey 2004), reports of the recent history of marriage equality within particular states (Moats 2004; Pinello 2006), legal and constitutional analysis of the prospects for same-sex marriage or alternative legal arrangements of care (Gerstmann 2004; Koppelman 2006; Polikoff 2008), arguments for (Badgett 2009; Graff 2004; Kotulski 2004; Rauch 2004; Shanley 2004; Wolfson 2004) and progressive critiques of (W. Brown 2004; Butler 2002; D'Emilio 2006; Walters 2001; Warner 1999) same-sex marriage, descriptions of same-sex marriage debates (Cahill 2004; Sullivan 2004), personal accounts of the significance of marriage from the perspectives of "ordinary" gay and lesbian couples (Hull 2006), and even empirical evidence considering the social ramifications of legalizing same-sex marriage (Eskridge and Spedale 2006). Surprisingly absent from this growing literature, however, is an ethnographic account of the same-sex marriage movement and a theoretical framework that places the marriage debate in the context of the practice of governance.

By reconceptualizing the same-sex marriage debate in this way, I have three primary objectives. First, in order to understand the current dominance of the marriage equality movement, we must utilize more than historical and legal analyses; we must understand marriage enticements from the viewpoint of those who ardently fight for them. Throughout this book, you will read stories like Amber and Hazel's that explain how and why individuals end up prioritizing their right to tie the knot while setting aside their very genuine desires for national health insurance, economic equality, and, for some, family diversity. Unlike historical analyses of gay and lesbian social movements, it is not my goal to explain the ascendancy of the marriage debate on the national political agenda but to account for the social and political implications of its contemporary resonance.

Second, I demonstrate that the case of marriage equality is important not just for scholars interested in gay, lesbian, and queer studies but also for sociologists of marriage and family who are working toward conceptualizing marriage in general as a project of neo-liberal governance. As sociologists of the family, we must account for how marriage can advance, rather than primarily stymie, the development of neo-liberal capitalism. Drawing from the governmentality tradition allows sociologists of the family to conceptualize marriage as a particular model of social care constructed along with the deconstruction of a national, public social safety net.

Finally, I hope to contribute to the body of social theory concerned with how forms of neo-liberal governance create terms of consent to power arrangements. I enter a long-standing, multivocal conversation in sociology regarding the often fraught concept of ideology by connecting two prominent voices—Foucault's work on governmentality with Bourdieu's concept of symbolic power—to explain how practices of governance can be misrecognized as lifestyle choices. The case of marriage equality vividly illustrates how individuals who are ideologically opposed to neo-liberalism can come to appropriate and solidify these discourses at the same time that they struggle to see themselves as neo-liberal subjects.

What Is Neo-Liberal Governance?

By using the term *governance* rather than *government*, I am drawing from insights developed by theorists of governmentality who see political power as a process that exists beyond formalized systems of political authority.[3] Theorizing governance as a process rather than the action of the state allows one to understand how modern populations are often *managed* without being under the direct, hierarchical control of state apparatuses. I use the term *manage* to denote how governance does not primarily aim to solve the problems of the population but to regulate them; furthermore, framing social actors as managers recognizes subjects' relationship to governance as one of appropriation rather than creation. Like managers in a corporate setting, many social actors do not make the rules but selectively enforce, resist, or reinforce them in the course of fulfilling daily tasks. Essentially, from this perspective, governance is not primarily defined by "what the state does" but by a particular logic and practice for managing the problems of the population that may be housed in multiple social institutions, such as marriage.

This definition of governance may seem so loose and inclusive as to be meaningless, but governance does have a precise meaning defined by its object and strategy (aim or goal) rather than its subject (the institutions or programs that direct action). In other words, governance is not primarily defined by who or what does the governing but by the particular practices and goals of managing human conduct. Thus, understanding governance requires attention to logics and methods of governing that enact and legitimate programs for regulating the problems of populations. Theorists of governmentality refer to these logics and methods as "political rationalities" and "technologies of governance." Political rationalities are forms of knowledge that both define and moralize particular ways of conceptualizing the proper aims and limits of governance (Rose and Miller 1992): a more or less coherent set of logical and ethical principles that delineate and justify the purposes of governance, legitimate programs for achieving these purposes, and the appropriate role of individual subjects.

"Technologies of governance" are particular institutions, agencies, mechanisms, designs, and devices that are "oriented to produce practical outcomes" (Rose 1999, 52) and personal conduct that is aligned with the logic and aims of governance (Lemke 2001). Technologies of governance are not the products of individual intentions but a practical realization of particular political rationalities. Technologies can range from codified institutions to experimental designs that attempt to give political rationalities a practical form by organizing social space, subjectivities, and social interaction in a way that orients individuals toward the particular rationality's logic and ethos. When approaching governance from this perspective, the state is one of many potential subjects that can legitimately imagine and institute techniques for population management, depending on what a particular political rationality calls forth.

From a governmentality perspective, neo-liberalism is a logic and ethic of governing the population according to economic principles of practicality and efficiency. Neo-liberalism is characterized by its ethic of managing poverty, illness, and social order by prioritizing cost-benefit analysis above citizen well-being (Dean 1999a). According to this logic and ethic of governance, it is not only smart, but just, to reform the state's techniques for managing the population in a way that maximizes profit and reduces state spending. Neo-liberalism aims to economize the management of the population through methods of self-governance rather than hierarchical state-based programs. In the neo-liberal model, ethical and effective governance occurs when subjects make responsible choices and utilize profit-maximizing strategies for managing the problems of the population (Dean 1999a; Lemke 2001; Rose 1999).

Neo-liberalism can be distinguished from classical economic liberalism in three primary ways. First, unlike classical liberalism, the role of the state is not in opposition to the aims of capitalism. For neo-liberalism, the market is not a specified zone of liberty that must maintain its freedom from the state to function properly. Instead of the principles of laissez-faire, as Thomas Lemke argues, "The market mechanism and the impact of competition can only arise if they are produced by the practice of government" (2001, 193). Second, neo-liberalism does not legitimize or valorize the market as a fact of nature; instead, it sees the market as a social construction, an institution that requires management and intervention (Lemke 2001). Finally, neo-liberalism describes the diffusion of economic logic to multiple spheres of social life. In classical liberalism, the ethic of market competition and principles of cost-benefit analysis are limited to the proper aims of the economy. In neo-liberalism, these principles are diffused throughout social space, and they become standards by which to evaluate the performance of nonmarket spheres of social life such as the family and the state.

Neo-liberal political rationalities give life to technologies of governance that maximize individuals' opportunities for self-regulation. Nikolas Rose finds in his examination of neo-liberalism, for example, that "the ideal of the 'social state' gives way to that of the 'enabling state.' The state is no longer to be required to answer all of society's needs for order, security, health and productivity. Individuals, firms, organizations, localities, schools, parents, hospitals, housing estates must take on themselves— as 'partners'—a portion of the responsibility for their own well-being" (1999, 142). Neo-liberal technologies aim to bring individuals' concepts of freedom and morality in line with projects for reducing the state's fiscal responsibility for population-level problems. For example, following the logic of neo-liberalism, slogans such as "Welfare to work" become a specific set of workshops and legal provisions, enacted by agencies and acted upon subjects who must learn methods for managing poverty by making "responsible choices." I argue that marriage in the contemporary United States operates as one such technology of neo-liberal governance.

From Liberation to Neo-Liberalism

The fact that legal marriage would even be considered a worthwhile fight for couples like Amber and Hazel is remarkable, as marriage did not seem to be either a viable or laudable goal for mainstream gay or lesbian rights organizations until the 1990s. Historians and social movement theorists largely agree that the ascendancy of marriage can be attributed to a number of specific precipitating factors, which include the nationalization and homogenization of gay and lesbian organizations, the political framing and resources of the religious Right, the AIDS epidemic, and the "lesbian baby boom." In terms of broad political-economic context, these specific triggers parallel the consolidation of neo-liberal strategies for governance in the United States that elevate the importance of marriage in the context of a diminishing public care structure. The central impetus for marriage equality activism stems from the immediate needs for gays and lesbians to gain access to a structure that acts as a gateway to laws and benefits within civil society that allow and obligate couples to manage social problems such as illness and poverty.

The contemporary marriage equality movement often presents same-sex marriage as the next logical—and, for some, inevitable—step in the linear progression of gay and lesbian civil rights; however, far from being the result of a long-standing consensus within the gay and lesbian movement, marriage was treated with suspicion and outright rejection by gay and lesbian liberation movements, whose momentum grew during the American sexual revolution of the 1960s. For many in the "Stonewall generation,"[4] marriage existed as a structure of heterosexual and patriarchal privilege that drove gays and lesbians from the public sphere to underground subcultures and relegated women to the service of men. The Gay Liberation Front (GLF), one of the more radical gay rights organizations born from the New Left social movements of the 1960s, for example, shared a radical vision of cultural revolution and redistributive politics with lesbian rights groups and the Black Panther Party (D'Emilio and Freedman 1988). Unlike their homophile predecessors,[5] the GLF articulated a more antiestablishment philosophy and rejected single-issue politics. For example, rather than direct their efforts toward lifting the ban on homosexuals in the military, the GLF critiqued the military and expressed antiwar sentiments. Similarly, rather than seeking reform of the institution of marriage to allow same-sex couples access, gay liberation struggles of the late sixties called for a complete revolution of traditional family structures. As the GLF's statement of purpose read: "We are a revolutionary homosexual group of men and women formed with the realization that complete sexual liberation for all people cannot come about unless existing social institutions are abolished" (D'Emilio and Freedman 1988, 321). Furthermore, the GLF rejected single-issue politics and argued that sexuality must be contextualized as one of many vectors of oppression (including gender and race) most effectively addressed by revolutionizing capitalism (Armstrong 2002).

The politics of gay liberation, however, was also characterized by tension and dissent from within that would account for the resiliency of the contemporary gay and lesbian movement (Armstrong 2002; Ghaziani 2008). The reformist goals and single-issue strategies of dissident members of the GLF who formed the Gay Activist Alliance (GAA) left room for continued pliability of gay and lesbian demands precisely because they did not rely on the politics of redistribution. As Elizabeth Armstrong explains, "The rapid decline of the New Left eliminated the credibility of a redistributive political logic without undermining the viability of interest group and identity politics" (2002, 82). Marriage was not on the GAA's agenda, but a decisive focus on "gay" as a master identity provided the structural foundation for a consolidated national movement that would later make marriage a cornerstone issue of the gay and lesbian movement.

Even when the radicalism of the 1960s sexual revolution began to wane in the midseventies, many mainstream gay and lesbian rights organizations, which now have marriage on the forefront of their agenda, explicitly rejected marriage as a goal for gay and lesbian rights. For example, the Lambda Legal Defense and Education Fund, the National Gay and Lesbian Task Force (GLTF), and the Gay Rights National Lobby (now known as the Human Rights Campaign [HRC]) rejected marriage as a worthwhile goal and instead maintained a focus on "individual" rights rather than the exclusions faced by same-sex couples (Chauncey 2004; Polikoff 2008). The majority of political funding and activist efforts were directed at ending employment discrimination rather than gaining access to either the military or marriage.

The issue of same-sex marriage did not become a focal concern of major gay and lesbian rights organizations until the early 1990s. The pursuit of the right to marry, far from logically flowing from gay and lesbian activism of the late sixties, actually radically breaks from the key goals and efforts of cultural revolution and economic redistribution (D'Emilio 2006). Instead of being a concrete example of the Left's battle to redefine cultural values, the struggle for same-sex marriage, like the fight for equal access to the military, embodies reformist efforts to fit within existing structures rather than radical attempts to overthrow them.

The consolidation of a national gay and lesbian movement, together with the emphasis on single-issue politics that paved the way for the marriage equality movement, were not merely a product of internal movement dynamics; they were also triggered by the growth of the religious Right. National organizations such as Lambda Legal Defense and Education Fund and HRC were partially created in response to the sheer size of the religious Right movement in the 1980s. In addition, the religious Right's local initiative campaigns in the early 1990s diverted movement resources and attention from developing and elaborating internal movement goals (Fetner 2008). On the national scale, Pat Buchanan's announcement of a "culture war"[6] at the 1992 Republican National Convention provided an interpretive framework for conservatives and gay and lesbian activists alike to see the relevance of gay rights to marriage. But this culture war was about more than sexuality and the family. Just as homosexuals were the target of Buchanan's culture war, the abject subjectivities of a developing neo-liberal state were not far behind. In the same speech, Buchanan cited welfare clients and communists as the defeated enemy of the old "cold war" and fused the defense of marriage from "homosexuals" with Ronald Reagan's defeat of Marxism around the globe. Behind his hyperbole, and by symbolic association the religious Right's culture war discourse in general, is a nascent neo-liberal political philosophy that links sexuality and political-economic projects to the institution of marriage.

It would be a mistake, however, to reduce the ascendancy of marriage on the national gay and lesbian political agenda to mobilization or framing dynamics internal to social movements, as larger structural changes also emerged in a way that fundamentally shaped gay and lesbian politics.[7] The AIDS crisis and "lesbian baby boom" in the 1980s created an immediate need for addressing access to official care structures (Chauncey 2004). The AIDS epidemic of the 1980s revealed the extreme vulnerability that gay men in particular faced because they lacked care structures that are easily accessible to married couples. AIDS brought issues of medical decision making, access to health insurance, unemployment, and inheritance to the forefront of gay and lesbian rights agendas. For the thousands of gay men who were disabled and dying from AIDS, their informal care structures, or "families of choice," lacked official recognition. However, the AIDS epidemic did not immediately bring the issue of marriage to the forefront of gay and lesbian rights. In fact, in the mid- to late 1980s, at the pinnacle of the AIDS crisis, groups such as ACT UP and others were forming coalitions with health care activists to fight for nationalized health insurance and crafting legal arrangements that would provide an alternative to marriage (Chauncey 2004; Polikoff 2008).

During the same time period as the AIDS crisis, the lesbian baby boom in the early 1980s also made the issue of parenting rights for same-sex couples more pressing. The number of custody cases considering the legality or legitimacy of same-sex parenting meant the growth of groups such as Lambda Legal Defense and Gay and Lesbian Advocates and Defenders forging strategies for gays and lesbians to gain legal rights over their children. The AIDS epidemic and the lesbian baby boom "led growing numbers of lesbians and gay men to start thinking about the unthinkable: that lesbians and gay men needed and deserved the rights and protections of marriage" (Chauncey 2004, 110).

The AIDS epidemic and the lesbian baby boom increased awareness of the vulnerability faced by those uninsured due to a lack of marriage protections, but this does not immediately imply that marriage would be the obvious answer to these inequalities. As Nancy Polikoff (2008) points out, feminist legal reforms, such as the legalization of second-parent adoption in many states, were moving in the direction of disentangling legal marriage from parental rights rather than advocating marriage equality. Larger political-economic developments of neo-liberalism solidified marriage as an essential care structure, thus making the legal acceptance of same-sex couples through marriage a more pressing issue (Polikoff 2008).

The institution of marriage also changed in a way that made it more likely to include same-sex couples at the same time that it became the lifeboat for a drowning American social care structure. First, changes in the conceptualization of marriage itself, beginning in the late nineteenth century, as a contract based on the consent of both parties and a series of United States Supreme Court decisions that established a "fundamental right to marry" left room for same-sex couples to argue for inclusion based on equal protection (Chauncey 2004; Cott 2000). At the same time that same-sex marriage appeared to be a constitutional possibility, compared to efforts to deinstitutionalize marriage in the 1960s and 1970s, it also became more essential to gain access to multiple forms of social insurance (Polikoff 2008). Early attempts to secure the "right to marry" in the 1990s paralleled neo-liberal efforts to reduce wages and benefits while also dismantling an already weak social safety net. Unlike any other industrialized country, marriage in the United States remained an essential gateway to retirement and death benefits (without taxation), health insurance, and bereavement and family leave, at a time when welfare reform became synonymous with privatization.

Recently, in gay, lesbian, and queer studies, scholars have turned their attention toward the relationship between neo-liberalism and the marriage equality movement. Many have argued that the fight for same-sex marriage must be conceptualized beyond the culture wars framework, which emphasizes normative motivations for marriage as an assimilation strategy and tends to marginalize questions of citizenship, governance, and neo-liberal economic forces (Duggan 2003; Phelan 2001; Richardson 2004, 2005; Stychin 2003). In the pages that follow, I take up this call by contextualizing arguments from marriage equality activists who ambivalently find themselves articulating neo-liberal political rationalities in order to gain access to an essential technology of governance that grants individuals the social recognition and "freedom" to manage social problems such as illness and poverty.

How Is Marriage a Neo-Liberal Ally?

Developments in historical sociology, governmentality, and feminist political theory have paved the way to reframe the case of marriage equality in terms of the dwindling American welfare state (Duggan 2003; Polikoff 2008). Feminist political theorists and historical sociologists have documented how family has remained central to the distribution of social insurance in accordance with liberal principles of individual rather than universal responsibility. In welfare reform efforts, from the New Deal through the Reagan administration, the family has been an important filtering mechanism, sorting government support according to adherence to the two-parent nuclear family model (Gordon 1994).

Gender, race, and class remained central to the development of the American welfare state, as the family not only provided an important filtering mechanism for social insurance but particular family forms became targets of political leaders who blamed poverty on families headed by single mothers. For example, Senator Patrick Moynihan's 1965 report *The Negro Family: The Case for National Action* blamed poverty on the "pathology" of black families. Moynihan resurrected and misappropriated "culture of poverty" theories in order to focus reform on creating patriarchal black families, which called for reducing work opportunities for black women (Gordon 1994; Quadagno 1994).[8]

American politicians continue to blame "broken" families, rather than political and economic structures, for high rates of unemployment and poverty among African Americans. In the late 1980s, for example, political analysts argued that Democrats and Republicans had a "new consensus" that problems of poverty in black communities were better solved by family planning and "sexual restraint" than by government intervention through welfare programs (Coontz 1992). Ironically, this "new consensus" persists despite plenty of evidence that it is precisely racist government programs and patterns of neo-liberal economic development that have caused unemployment, underemployment, lower rates of marriage, and ghettoization of American blacks.[9]

More recent welfare reforms in the United States embody cultural values of classic liberal individualism that valorize self-sufficiency among poor women while at the same time promoting a form of classical conservatism that posits marriage as the key to social stability and economic well-being (Hays 2003). President Bill Clinton's 1996 Personal Responsibility Work Opportunity Reconciliation Act (PRWORA) marked the first legislation that made work a prerequisite for receiving federal welfare and placed a five-year time limit on receiving entitlements. At the same time PRWORA mandated work requirements, it also contained provisions encouraging states to create programs that would persuade poor women to marry.[10] As the title of Clinton's legislation makes clear, PRWORA aimed to reduce welfare caseloads by "promoting personal responsibility," thereby individualizing the management of poverty.[11] In this significant new turn in welfare policy, the federal government prioritized the economization of its function above the well-being of citizens by calling on individuals to lift themselves out of poverty through employment and marriage.

The perceived role of marriage as a mechanism for the federal government to improve its own bottom line intensified in President George W. Bush's administration. On February 27, 2002, President Bush brought marriage to the forefront of welfare reform with the announcement of his Healthy Marriage Initiative (HMI). HMI grants were subsequently funded in the Deficit Reduction Act of 2005 (DRA), which authorized $150 million each year from 2006 to 2010 for fatherhood and marriage promotion programs.[12] The policy briefs from which the Bush administration draws use social scientific research to argue that marriage is a "wealth-creating institution . . . [that] leaves men, women, children *and* society better off."[13] While this statement may indicate a general desire to reduce poverty in the United States, many of the same authors of this social science research later concluded that marriage promotion programs will not reduce poverty or racial disparities among the poor (Lichter, Roempke, and Brown 2003; Sigle-Rushton and McLanahan 2002). Moreover, these programs actually reinforce class and race-based inequalities and aim to reproduce heterosexuality (Heath 2009). The fact that the Bush administration continues its efforts to promote marriage through welfare legislation indicates that the well-being of poor Americans is not the top priority of welfare reform. Instead, marriage promotion provides a way for the federal government to shift the responsibility for managing poverty from the state to couples without addressing the widening inequality gap in the United States (Smith 2007).

Thus, each administration from 1980 to 2008 has posited marriage (and, similarly, work programs) as a solution to the problems of poverty. According to this logic, because marriage has the potential to reduce welfare caseloads, promoting marriage makes the state more economically efficient. Regardless of its effect on poverty rates, the Bush administration's focus on marriage indicates a clear priority to reduce welfare spending. Often this economizing goal takes priority over the actual effectiveness of social insurance to protect citizens against risks associated with poverty and illness. In this sense, the role of marriage in welfare policy seems to reflect the priorities of neo-liberal forms of governance: to secure the smooth, efficient operation of the state rather than to improve the lives of citizens (Dean 1999a).

Theorists of governmentality argue that the limitation of governmental action provides an impetus for the development of "indirect techniques for leading and controlling individuals without at the same time being responsible for them" (Lemke 2001, 12). Publicly constructed zones of privacy, such as the legal family, become ideal contexts in which subjects can experience freedom as a certain amount of autonomy from hierarchical state regulation that allows them to achieve self-regulation and self-fulfillment. More specifically, this means individuals marry and create legal families not because of a desire to conform to moralized discourses about health and well-being but because they are making a "lifestyle decision . . . seeking to fulfill themselves and gain personal happiness" (Rose 1999, 86). Under a neo-liberal regime of governance, subjects are "obliged to be free" (ibid., 87), compelled to manage social problems because their autonomy from state hierarchies requires governance through responsible decision making. This indirect governance, however, also leaves room for forms of resistance and adaptations to neo-liberal governing regimes.

I argue that marriage is one such project of governance aimed at—but not completely succeeding in—cultivating subjects who become invested in managing social dangers as a couple so that the state does not have to. Thus, the larger question I ask in this book is, why do individuals such as Hazel and Amber become invested in ways of governing that place unrealistic burdens on their own relationships and families? I treat the governmentality perspective as an entry point instead of a comprehensive or sufficient explanation; it offers a paradigm or metatheory that yields a set of questions that are not often asked of marriage, let alone the same-sex marriage debate. It is not my intent to use governmentality as a grand theory that captures the role of marriage in the United States or neo-liberal societies in general, nor do I attempt to trace the origins of the neo-liberal functions of marriage.

In fact, the governmentality perspective is limited in its ability to capture why and how individuals find themselves committed to the project of self-governance and to account for why the state may have an interest in barring same-sex couples from furthering the state's goal of economization through marriage (a question I take up in chapter 6). For this reason, I bring in the work of Pierre Bourdieu and connect the symbolic power of marriage to its governing function. I draw attention to the underlying neo-liberal "mentality" of governing populations that inheres not only in social logics but also in individuals' sense of justice, equality, emotional security, and belonging. Marriage *works* because it provides a context for the state to economize its own function while also offering couples a set of legal provisions that allow them to manage life risks in a way that promises pleasure, autonomy, and freedom; however, marriage is *preferred* because it ennobles its participants with the symbolic profit of normality.

Sociology's Unhappy Family

The sociology of marriage and family is at the center of political debates concerning the resilience and necessity of marriage, about which it could not be more divided. On the one hand, those drawing from the "fragile families" literature continue to idealize neo-liberal marriage by calling it "traditional" and pointing to its numerous economic and cultural advantages. On the other, queer and feminist sociologists draw attention to exclusions inherent in the marriage model and question the logic and methodologies of studies produced from the fragile families perspective.

The fragile families literature often assumes, and at times insists, that marriage is the only family form uniquely designed to facilitate love and care. As with American culture in general, these authors take for granted that marriage is an important basis and foundation for enduring relationships and a stable nation. This often unacknowledged functionalism directs sociologists to ask why marriage seems to be faltering as a social institution in the United States by explaining such trends as increasing divorce rates and the increasing age of first marriage. As a result, many sociologists understand these demographic trends as a social problem (because they tend to be associated with poverty) that demands an explanation and a solution.

One of the most forceful arguments about the necessity of marriage is that it increases the financial and emotional well-being of children. Sara McLanahan and Gary Sandefur (1994), for example, argue that while marriage is only part of the answer to the problems that children face in the United States, the evidence clearly indicates that kids are healthier, better educated, and more stable if a married couple raises them. David Popenoe (1996) distorts this argument in his endorsement of heterosexuality, in which a man and a woman are necessary, as the only healthy family form for the development of normal children. He argues that fathers' declining participation in their children's lives leads to increased levels of juvenile delinquency, teenage pregnancy rates, and violence against women.

Those engaged in this debate are presented with a peculiar problem: if marriage holds so many benefits for children and adults, why are divorce rates increasing? In response to the question, advocates of marriage argue that American culture as a whole is less supportive of marriage because of the rise of the "culture of divorce" (Gallagher 1996; Waite 2000; B. Whitehead 1996). From Barbara Whitehead's (1996) point of view, Hollywood and capitalism create a consciousness that draws people away from marriage by advocating a permissive and irresponsible way of life. She argues that the family must rise up against capitalism and reclaim values of loyalty, commitment, and obligation. The culture of divorce, from Linda Waite's (2000) perspective, explains why, even though marriages work well for individuals (in terms of financial success and overall happiness), there are fewer marriages—because it is easier to get a divorce when couples experience temporary hardships. Maggie Gallagher (1996) argues that the culture of divorce explains why some Americans still desire marriage but are unable to achieve it. From this perspective, it is really difficult to explain how proponents of same-sex marriage might ardently fight for the right to marry in a culture allegedly distracted from commitment.

Gallagher, Waite, Whitehead, and Popenoe are familiar names in the marriage debates. Their work is endlessly circulated in conservative "family values" policy briefs that become the bases for court decisions, policy proposals, and legislative hearings used to justify welfare-to-marriage programs and oppose family diversity.[14] Many of these analyses of marriage are a part of the discourse that constructs marriage as a solution to national and personal problems (which same-sex couples would allegedly threaten) rather than scholarly studies that can account for how marriage has reached this magical status.

At the same time, sociologists have found convincing evidence that marriage is not the magical formula for healthy relationships and emotionally stable children (Stacey 1990, 1996; Stacey and Biblarz 2001). Mainstream politicians and media continue to sideline these voices despite compelling evidence that it is economic and structural support rather than family form that predicts child well-being and healthy relationships (Lichter, Roempke, and Brown 2003; Stacey and Biblarz 2001). In their comprehensive and impeccable overview of sociological and psychological research, for example, Judith Stacey and T. Biblarz found that differences in the well-being of children of unmarried gay and lesbian couples can largely be attributed to the consequences of social and legal inequalities.

I see my work as more of a direct contribution to the alternative families literature because, unlike the fragile families research and its distortions by conservative "family values" campaigns, these authors explore the economic and social rewards of marriage in terms of its ennobled cultural status. This tradition critiques the assumptions implicit in comparing married couples to single people (divorced and never married) by turning attention to alternative families that come with large networks of support from extended family and community (Carrington 1999; Collins 2000; Stacey 1990, 1996; Weeks, Heaphy, and Donovan 2001; Weston 1991). Kath Weston (1991), for example, argues that forms of kinship in African American, Native American, and white working-class communities tend to defy the marriage ideal and reap great advantages from multiple ties of dependency and affection that involve extended families, friends, lovers, and even ex-lovers.

Those sociologists who have conducted research on alternative family forms tend to agree that family diversity rather than conformity to the married ideal will yield the best social outcomes. As a result, Weston; Christopher Carrington; Jeffrey Weeks, Brian Heaphy, and Catherine Donovan; and Judith Stacey are suspicious of calls for marriage equality that compromise social supports for alternative families. Weston argues that the greatest political potential for gays and lesbians rests in showing how the genetic model of family is flawed and rejecting the profamily versus antifamily debate. While some contend that gay families have the potential to be vanguards of social change by eliminating gender inequality in marriage, Carrington finds that gay couples create gender divisions strikingly similar to heterosexual households. He concludes by suggesting that gay marriage poses the risk of expanding the ideology of domesticity to gay couples, and it comes at the expense of other, unmarried gays and lesbians. Instead, he advocates a gay political agenda focused on universal rights for all regardless of sexual behavior and orientation.

The structural possibility and apparent advantages of building "families of choice" with multiple sources of dependency and financial support are not an immediate reality for the proponents of same-sex marriage such as Hazel and Amber. The fact that these alternative models exist should make us wonder why proponents of same-sex marriage are working for inclusion in the marriage model rather than capitalizing on momentum from the sixties and seventies that was working toward deinstitutionalizing marital privilege in the law.[15] The concurrent development of the "right to marry" and assaults on those who fail or refuse to live up to the neoliberal model of the dual-earning couple have been at the forefront of queer, feminist, and gay and lesbian analyses of the family. With my discursive ethnography of same-sex marriage activism, I build on this literature by explaining how marriage can make neo-liberal calls for self-regulation of population-level problems so enticing.

Sociologists of the family have a long-standing concern about the power of neo-liberal market ideologies to dominate family life. Alongside the literatures explicitly in conversation with marriage debates is a general consensus that the values and logic of capitalism have seeped out of the market and into the home. This is a view shared by many in the fragile families and commercialization of family literature. Drawing from Marxist critiques of capitalism (such as Habermas 1984), some sociologists stress that marriage and the family are essential, yet fragile zones of private life currently threatened by what Arlie Hochschild (2003) calls the "commercialization of intimate life." This research focuses on recent transformations in the structure and function of the family from one that fosters intimacy and produces the next generation of citizens to what Jan Dizard and Howard Gadlin (1990) call the "minimal family," characterized by outsourcing of traditional family functions to the market.

Research in this area also draws from Hochschild's (1997, 1989) analysis of the relationship between work and family in the United States since the influx of white middle-class mothers into the workplace. Ilene Philipson (2002), for example, argues that corporate culture has consciously tried to construct the workplace as a family environment. As a result, many women become "married to the job"; the corporation replaces the home as the primary source of women's identification.[16]

These studies place an important emphasis on the power of late capitalism to shape family life and individuals' investment in love and care. With this I am in full agreement. However, the "commercialization of love" perspective tends to tacitly assume or explicitly theorize marriage as the last line of defense against the unfettered growth of capitalism. My evidence shows how marriage is more of a neo-liberal ally; thus, I detail how marriage operates as a site for personal and passionate investment into the very forms of power these authors see it struggling against. Much can be said about theorizing familism and neo-liberalism as antagonistic social values, but we also need work that brings us closer to understanding how neo-liberalism can gain credibility by appropriating family forms for the project of state economization.

In some ways, it makes sense that mainstream sociology of the family does not incorporate insights for theorists of governmentality, who tend to sideline issues of love and belonging. The governmentality literature does not really resonate with what other sociologists of marriage and the family see as defining elements of family life: a place where—at least ideally—care, dependency, love, and belonging are valued above and protected from the goals of profit maximization and competition characteristic of the market and, increasingly, the state. My work, however, shows how our understanding of neo-liberal projects of governance actually *requires* attention to the "married feeling" created and consecrated by the practices of governance. The sense of belonging and love unique to the marriage license is like magic—while we delight in celebrations of love and care, it successfully makes governance seem to disappear.

Feminist legal scholars, political theorists, and historians have done a much better job conceptualizing marriage as a structure implicit in the neo-liberal political economic project. In part, political and legal theorists' primary concern with political economy allows them to see same-sex marriage outside of the "culture war" framework, which tends to limit the case of same-sex marriage to discussions of cultural equality or family diversity. On the other hand, unlike sociologists of marriage and family, political theorists and historians do not generally utilize methodologies—such as ethnography—that allow one entrée to the complicated and fraught processes of interpretation and meaning-making that I argue are essential to explaining why individuals might find an affinity with neo-liberal governing projects.

Discursive Ethnography

Feminist political theory, governmentality, and historical perspectives on the relationship between marriage and neo-liberalism poignantly illustrate the problems inherent in the fight for "marriage equality." However, these perspectives are mostly textual analyses that provide a limited understanding of the often messy process of meaning-making, interpretation, and feeling that ethnographic methods are designed to capture.[17] Textual analysis cannot uncover how discourses can be forged, appropriated, and locally adapted in particular moments that may never leave a historical trace. In the case of the marriage equality debate, I found a number of dissenting and conflicting voices from proponents of same-sex marriage that are intentionally removed from official documents or public speeches.

Rather than disregarding the importance of texts, I see them as one of many entry points to discourse around marriage equality.[18] I consider this work a discursive ethnography, as I combine observations, in-depth interviews, and textual analysis in order to get a well-rounded sense of how and why proponents of same-sex marriage demand access to marriage. I contextualize proponents' everyday experiences in terms of the strategies and goals of governance they embody and, at times, contest. Interactive methods allow researchers another lens to study power's "capillary" ability to bleed its way into seemingly insignificant slices of everyday life and fleeting moments of individuals' feelings and thoughts.

Nina Eliasoph's (1996, 1997) ethnography of everyday political speech, for example, indicates how the very terrain of what constitutes civic discourse is determined in particular interactional settings where groups create boundaries and rules about political speech. Eliasoph (1997) provides convincing evidence that sociologists or political scientists who study democratic politics must shift their methodological focus from tools such as opinion polling to participant observation if they hope to understand how and why individuals form their political beliefs. Because the meanings and boundaries of civic discourse are constructed at the level of everyday interactions, understanding power and governance requires attention to social practices that may leave only a thin and ambiguous historical residue for genealogical or archaeological analysis.

Paying attention to the microlevels of discourse construction also provides a way to see how power can operate unintentionally and without direct policing or hierarchical restrictions (Moon 2004, 2005). As Moon (2004) found in her study of debates over homosexuality in American Protestant churches, attention to the level of everyday life, as opposed to focus on historical analysis through text, is particularly suited for studying nonhierarchical forms of power. Like Moon, I also "see a paradox in attempting to look for a nonhierarchical form of power in something that bears and reproduces authority by being published or archived" (2004, 11–12).

Ethnography provides a way to understand the relationship between power and resistance in a way that cannot be captured with historical analysis. Paying attention to the reasons why individuals would desire marriage has the advantage of allowing one to see how agents' motivations, wishes, and desires interplay with governing structures. The case of activism for same-sex marriage rights uniquely captures all these dynamics of marriage in a way that allows us to also humanize governance. Individuals' hopes, sense of self, pain, and desire for belonging are central to the governing process—not in the sense that governing is about restricting these emotions but in the sense that particular forms of governance cultivate and nourish ways of feeling.

Marriage Rights Now!

My fieldwork centered around same-sex marriage activism in two major cities ("Hamilton" and "Waterford") in one state on the West Coast.[19] For a total of twenty months, I observed one national organization (with multiple regional locations) at the center of most activism for same-sex marriage in the state, "Marriage Rights Now" (MRN).[20] As an organization, MRN is focused on both grassroots organizing and explicit state lobbying.

I gained entrée to MRN by contacting leaders of the organization—Hazel Butler, Amber McDaniel, Jack Kemp, and Steve Kemp—who eagerly invited me to their monthly MRN membership meetings. After attending the first meeting, I quickly found my calendar full of upcoming MRN events. I tagged along to demonstrations, protests, organization expansion activities, public education events, media trainings, and grassroots efforts to increase public support. I caravanned with group members on overnight trips when they traveled to more rural parts of the state in an effort to increase their number of local organizations. I also went door to door with MRN members who hoped to convince the public to vote against a state constitutional amendment that would restrict marriage to different-sex couples. I attended several public protests on street corners where MRN members would appear in full formal wedding attire and urge passing motorists to "honk for marriage equality." In the twenty months that I observed MRN activism, I came into contact with hundreds of individuals who spent hours of their free time to fight for the "equal right to marry."

I found that my previously conceived stereotype of marriage equality activists as white upper-middle-class couples was confirmed when looking at those in leadership positions but contradicted by diversity within the general membership. Over the course of my fieldwork, I came into contact with six local branches of MRN, four of which were headed by white gay and lesbian couples, one by an interracial gay couple (white and Asian American), and the other by an African American woman who left the organization before I ended my fieldwork. I later learned that the organization specifically recommends selecting a gay or lesbian couple to lead local branches because it feels that such leaders make the movement's public face confirm its primary message. I witnessed no such recommendations in regard to increasing the racial diversity of various local branches. This is in stark contrast to my observations of the prison abolition movement (J. Whitehead 2007), which I found to be constantly troubled by the racial homogeneity of the organization and preoccupied with attempts to increase the number of black and Hispanic members.

During group meetings, MRN members never explicitly discouraged talk about race, nor did they redirect or take pains to avoid the topic (Eliasoph 1999); instead, race talk rarely emerged in group meetings, but in the few times that the issue did surface, it was not problematized. For example, MRN members unanimously applauded endorsements from prominent national political organizations such as the NAACP and United Farm Workers without critical discussion about the underlying tensions that a handful of members alluded to in personal interviews when mentioning resistance from "historic black churches" that disagreed with MRN's framing marriage as a "civil rights" issue. I attribute the lack of group discussions about race to MRN's effort to frame marriage as a universal right that crosses class, race, or gender divisions, subsequently framing their own activism as an effort to secure rights for all rather than consolidate privilege for their individual families.

As noted earlier, MRN participants in general are more diverse than those in leadership positions. I came in contact with members who are straight, gay, queer, male, female, and transgender; white, African American, Hispanic, Asian American, and Canadian; second-generation immigrants, permanent residents, and American citizens; Christian, atheist, and Jewish; wealthy, struggling for work, retired, and students fresh from high school.[21] Members of Marriage Rights Now with whom I spoke also differed in terms of their relationship status and desire to marry: members included people in serious relationships, some who do not even want to get married, and others who are still looking for the "right person." One of the few commonalities among MRN members involves political affiliation. The overwhelming majority identify themselves as Democrats, and only a handful are members of the Green Party. I never came across an MRN member who also considered himself or herself a Republican.

I established my role in the organization as more of an observer than a participant (see appendix A). Rather than creating my own signs for street demonstrations, for example, I would stand at a distance and write field notes. During membership meetings, I would sit quietly while others expressed their opinions. When we canvassed neighborhoods, I did not interact with those who answered their doors. I made a deliberate attempt to avoid disrupting MRN's ongoing activities or inserting myself in such a way as to fundamentally change MRN's usual business. I restricted my level of "participation" to helping set up tables and distribute brochures rather than full immersion into all the activities of a regular MRN member.

I explicitly focused on MRN members' arguments and feelings about why marriage was an essential struggle for gay and lesbian rights. I paid particular attention to the moments of agreement among group members as well as moments of ambiguity and direct conflict. At times, departing from my overall "fly on the wall" approach, I would interject questions that would lead members to talk more about disagreements and conflicts with other members' visions of Marriage Rights Now's mission and goals. In this sense, my observations uncovered the process of meaning-making and narrative construction that does not appear in polished texts. While the goals and strategies of marriage equality activism appear clear-cut and uncontested in MRN manuals, pamphlets, and press releases, in my observations I could also see the compromises and ambiguities that preceded these final products. Revealing conflicts among MRN members is not my primary goal; instead, I see contestation as moments that help to clarify the multiple, and sometimes conflicting, assumptions behind proponents' advocacy of marriage.

The areas of contention among proponents of marriage equality most relevant for my purposes, and to which I refer throughout the following chapters, primarily revolve around the following questions: First, to what extent should MRN's official line preempt critics' accusations by explicitly distancing itself from efforts to deinstitutionalize marriage or expand its definition to include more than two spouses? Should MRN appropriate the language of "family values" to assure Americans that gays and lesbians pose no threat to marriage? Should MRN condone domestic partnership laws or only come out in support of "full marriage"? As you will see in the following chapters, discourses generated around these questions speak to the various ways proponents of same-sex marriage reveal the logic behind imagining marriage as a form of ennobled governance.

As a complement to my observations, I also interviewed twenty-four proponents of marriage equality (see appendix B). My interviews were open-ended and ranged from one to two hours in length. Most of these members are active in the Marriage Rights Now organization. I selected my first round of interviewees by inviting MRN members who regularly attended monthly membership meetings or by e-mailing contacts listed on MRN's official website. My second round of interviewees included proponents of same-sex marriage, some of whom were not active in MRN but were referred by MRN members.

The majority of my interviewees reflected MRN's overall Democratic political orientation. My attempts to interview and observe activities among more conservative proponents of same-sex marriage were relatively unsuccessful. The Log Cabin Republicans, for example, have chapters in both Hamilton and Waterford, but most of their efforts are in lobbying, direct mailing, and research, activities that do not necessarily lend themselves to participant observation. Only one member of the Log Cabin Republicans, Craig Shilling, agreed to an interview.

In general, of the twenty-four individuals interviewed, sixteen are official members of MRN. The remaining participants are active proponents of marriage equality in their communities but not officially affiliated with MRN (see appendix B). My interview participants included three individuals who considered themselves "straight," one married, one divorced, and the other single. Twenty participants consider themselves either gay or lesbian, and eighteen of these individuals were in a committed relationship with a person of the same sex at the time of the interview. Of the participants in a same-sex relationship, six are male and twelve are female. One participant, Jorge Caberro, avoided discussing his relationship status or sexual identity.

I conducted all of my interviews in locations chosen by the participants. I interviewed individuals at home, in their office, or at a coffee shop. Although I talked to most participants one on one, in a few cases, and at their request, I interviewed same-sex couples together. I initially thought that one-on-one interviews with participants in couples would yield more candid responses, but I found the interaction generated by having both partners in the same room addressing the same questions particularly revealing. By occasionally interrupting each other, couples would push themselves to clarify and explain their opinions in ways that my lack of familiarity might not have allowed.

I came into each interview with one standard set of open-ended questions. I asked each participant how and why he or she became involved in advocating for same-sex marriage. I urged individuals to explain their personal motivations and to speak freely about how their own experiences brought them to advocate for same-sex couples' right to marry. I also pushed respondents to clarify their opinions by asking them to respond to popular arguments from both conservative opponents of same-sex marriage and queer critics of marriage. On several occasions, I found that taking these "devil's advocate" positions allowed many participants to, as they called it, move beyond the "party line" espoused by mainstream proponents of same-sex marriage and express their own individual motivations.

As a complement to my observations and interviews, I conducted a qualitative content analysis of hundreds of documents centered on the same-sex marriage debate in the United States. I initially decided to analyze these documents as a method of triangulation, to ensure that the patterns I found in my observations and interviews were not unique to MRN activists or the specific local politics in Hamilton and Waterford. In the end, I found that my content analysis not only reflected the patterns I analyzed in my observations and interviews but also revealed more elite and codified justifications and legitimizations that did not often come up in the course of my interviews or observations.

My content analysis included documents from legislative hearings and testimonies, court affidavits and decisions, same-sex marriage activists' manuals, opinion pieces, and policy briefs. On the federal level, I examined the 1996, 2004, and 2005 congressional hearings and testimonies concerning the Defense of Marriage Act and the Federal Marriage Amendment. I also analyzed all court affidavits, amicus briefs, and decisions from state court cases considering the constitutionality of same-sex marriage in California, Connecticut, Massachusetts, Oregon, New Jersey, New York, Washington, West Virginia, and Vermont. In addition to affidavits from same-sex couples, these documents include amicus briefs in support of same-sex marriage and parenting from the American Civil Liberties Union, American Psychological Association, the National Association of Social Workers, and the American Academy of Pediatrics.

I also analyzed opinion pieces, activist manuals, and organizational statements found on the websites of major pro-same-sex-marriage organizations, including Lambda Legal; the National Gay and Lesbian Task Force; the Human Rights Campaign; Gay and Lesbian Advocates and Defenders; Parents, Families, and Friends of Lesbians and Gays; the American Civil Liberty Union's Lesbian, Gay, Bisexual and Transgender Project; Freedom to Marry; Log Cabin Republicans; Basic Rights Oregon; Equality California; the Alliance for Same-Sex Marriage; the National Black Justice Coalition; and the National Organization for Women. In addition, I analyzed conservative opponents' opinion pieces from Your Catholic Voice, Focus on the Family, Alliance Defense Fund, the Traditional Values Coalition, and Concerned Women for America.

My content analysis also includes several policy briefs in support of same-sex marriage. These briefs include research that supports same-sex couples' ability to raise children, evidence that suggests homosexuality is natural and normal, studies that suggest gays and lesbians value monogamy as much as heterosexuals, economic analyses of the advantageous fiscal impact of legalizing same-sex marriage, and studies that detail the disadvantages same-sex couples face because they lack access to civil marriage. In addition, I studied a few oft-cited conservative policy briefs that argue the exact opposite of the above claims made by organizations in support of same-sex marriage.

From Obscurity to Inevitability

By the time I began my fieldwork in the fall of 2004, mainstream gay and lesbian rights organizations, such as the Human Rights Campaign (HRC), Lambda Legal, and the Gay and Lesbian Alliance against Discrimination

(GLAAD) had created specific marriage projects dedicated to winning the right for same-sex couples to marry. In addition, local state organizations and broad coalitions among gay and lesbian rights organizations devoted to winning the right to marry for same-sex couples were firmly established in all states on both coasts. Many within marriage equality circles attributed the ascendancy of the issue of marriage to the successes of Lambda Legal's efforts in the Hawaii State Supreme Court case *Baehr v Miike* (1993).

In the Hawaii case, the court, on equal protection grounds, ruled it unconstitutional for the state to deny same-sex couples marriage licenses. The Hawaii court's decision quickly gained national attention and galvanized both conservative efforts to protect traditional marriage and gay and lesbian rights organizations' efforts to put money and activists' resources into a fight they had previously considered a lost cause (Goldberg-Hiller 2002).

For many gay and lesbian rights organizations, the Hawaii decision was momentous because it left activists feeling that the quest for same-sex marriage was in fact achievable. Lambda Legal attorney Evan Wolfson (widely known as one of the main leaders and founders of the contemporary marriage equality movement), after serving as cocounsel for *Baehr*, worked as the director for Lambda's Marriage Project and helped create the National Freedom to Marry Coalition. Soon after the Hawaii decision, gay and lesbian legal advocacy and lobbying groups such as GLAAD and the HRC had placed marriage at the top of their agendas.

The Hawaii decision also galvanized a nascent conservative gay movement in favor of marriage. In the late eighties and early nineties, Log Cabin Republicans and "neoconservatives" such as Andrew Sullivan were constructing the "conservative argument for marriage" as a way to "civilize" gays and cure the culture of promiscuity that they felt helped account for the spread of AIDS in the gay male community.[22]

Conservative opponents of same-sex marriage were also sparked into action by the Hawaii decision. Conservative "family values" groups such as the Heritage Foundation, Focus on the Family, and Concerned Women of America also devoted more organizational time and efforts to the issue of same-sex marriage. These groups galvanized voters to urge their legislators to pass laws and vote for amendments to federal and state constitutions that would prevent states from recognizing same-sex marriage.

At the federal level, conservative opponents experienced success with the passage of the Defense of Marriage Act (DOMA), eventually signed into law by President Bill Clinton in 1996. DOMA was a victory for conservative opponents because it gave individual states the power to refuse recognition of same-sex marriages legalized in other states. Since 1996, conservative opponents of same-sex marriage have also introduced several versions of a "federal marriage amendment"—a proposed amendment to the Constitution limiting marriage to different-sex couples. As of 2011, DOMA remains on the books, but the proposed federal marriage amendment, despite several attempts, has failed to muster the required two-thirds majority in Congress.

Conservative opponents have been most successful at the state level in passing constitutional amendments and "clarifying" marriage statutes. As of January 2011, twenty-nine states have passed amendments to their constitutions defining marriage as only a union between a man and a woman. For example, before the Hawaii decision could have any legal ramifications, in November of 1998, almost 70 percent of Hawaii voters approved a state constitutional amendment to "'reserve marriage to opposite-sex couples'" (Goldberg-Hiller 2002, 1).

While the Hawaii constitutional amendment was considered a huge setback for a marriage equality movement that was gaining momentum, less than ten years after passage of the amendment (between 1998 and 2008), the movement for marriage equality has gained some successes in state supreme courts. As of May 2008, eight state supreme courts have considered the constitutionality of their states' marriage statutes. Of the eight states, four have ruled it unconstitutional to deny same-sex couples the legal provisions that come with marriage. The Vermont (2000) and New Jersey (2006) courts left room for the state legislature to create parallel licensing schemes that provide legal benefits comparable to heterosexual marriage, which both state legislatures decided to do. Massachusetts (2003) and California (2008) courts, on the other hand, ruled parallel licensing schemes inadequate and demanded that the state grant same-sex couples access to the same marriage licenses offered to different-sex couples.

Aside from the particular legal outcomes, the issue of same-sex marriage gained a great deal of national attention in the spring of 2004 when several cities issued same-sex couples marriage licenses. Leading the way on February 12, 2004, San Francisco mayor Gavin Newsom ordered the city to issue marriage licenses to same-sex couples. By March 11, when the California Supreme Court blocked Newsom's efforts, San Francisco had issued over four thousand marriage licenses to same-sex couples. Newsom heralded his decision as the only decent and appropriate response to President George W. Bush's State of the Union address in which the president scolded "activist judges," presumably those in Vermont and Massachusetts, and earned applause when he declared that "our nation must defend the sanctity of marriage."[23] Newsom told reporters that he was reacting to "the president's decision to use this [same-sex marriage] as a wedge issue to divide people. I think what he's doing is wrong. It's hurtful."[24]

A week after Newsom's decision, in New Mexico, Sandoval County clerk Victoria Dunlap announced that her county would also issue same-sex couples marriage licenses, claiming that her decision "has nothing to do with politics or morals. . . . This office won't say no until shown it's not permissible."[25] After marriage licenses were issued to twenty-six couples, New Mexico attorney general Patricia Madrid declared same-sex marriage illegal in New Mexico and required a halt to issuing same-sex couples marriage licenses. In June 2004, the New Mexico Supreme Court rejected Dunlap's motion to overturn Madrid's decision.

The month after Newsom's action, on March 3, 2004, Multnomah County attorney Agnes Sowle in Portland, Oregon, announced that the county must begin issuing marriage licenses to same-sex couples. Sowle cited the county's "ambiguous" marriage statutes, which did not specifically restrict marriage to different-sex partners and Oregon's refusal to discriminate on the basis of sexual orientation. By April 20, when Judge Mary Ann Bearden of the Multnomah County Circuit Court halted the issuance of marriage licenses, over three thousand same-sex couples had been issued marriage licenses. A year later, Oregon voters passed a constitutional amendment defining marriage as a union between a man and a woman. All marriage licenses issued to same-sex couples, including those issued in San Francisco, have since been voided by each state.

The national furor over same-sex marriage continued into the November 2004 elections. In the vice presidential and presidential debates, the issue of same-sex marriage had gained so much steam that candidates were asked to publicly declare their stance on same-sex marriage. In the vice presidential debate, Republican candidate Dick Cheney, while declaring that individuals' intimate relationships should not be the government's business, ultimately voiced his support for the president's efforts to explicitly define marriage as a union between a man and a woman. Democratic candidates John Kerry and John Edwards also voiced their support for binding the definition of marriage to different-sex couples. It seemed that same-sex marriage was one of the few issues on which the candidates agreed.

In November 2004, there were also eleven states (Arkansas, Georgia, Kentucky, Michigan, Mississippi, Montana, North Dakota, Ohio, Oklahoma, Oregon, and Utah) that approved constitutional amendments restricting marriage to different-sex couples. Despite Kerry and Edwards's explicitly coming out in opposition to same-sex marriage, the day after the elections, several political pundits partially attributed the Democrats' loss to the number of conservative voters motivated to vote by the marriage amendments. This claim was so pervasive that the Gay and Lesbian Task Force felt compelled to release a report pointing to exit poll data suggesting that, overall, voters approved of granting same-sex couples some form of legal protection.[26]

When I began my study of the marriage equality movement in September of 2004, many same-sex marriage activists, unlike gay and lesbian rights groups from the 1960s through the 1980s, believed that same-sex couples' access to marriage was not only possible but inevitable. Recent court decisions in Vermont and Massachusetts and the defeat of the federal marriage amendment generated a feeling that it was only a matter of time before the United States government would have to revise marriage statutes to include same-sex couples.

Throughout this project, even though I have come to oppose legal marriage due to the political rationality it embodies and the marginalization of consensual intimate arrangements it represents, I have also found myself smiling and cheering when marriage equality activists won particular battles. On the other hand, I also felt discouraged by the discursive ground ceded by official MRN discourse in an effort to win these fights. I found this personal ambivalence very indicative of the predicament central to marriage equality activism, inasmuch as activists' efforts to make their own lives more secure also gave credence to the same rationality and technology of governance that had made their struggle necessary.

Chapter Outline

I begin this story by laying out the terms of what I call the "nuptial deal." In the next chapter, I describe how marriage equality activists set aside their desires for national health insurance and economic redistribution and instead appeal to the state's interest in marriage as a neo-liberal technology of governance that shifts responsibility for managing social problems from the state to individual couples. You will see how recent state supreme courts (considering the constitutionality of restricting marriage to different-sex couples) articulate the state's interest in marriage as an institution that promises to reduce state expenditures. In addition to explaining how marriage equality activists in the United States have strategically appropriated the logic of economization, I also point to a sense of ambivalence felt by individual members of MRN and others who go beyond the "official party line" and strive to fuse democratic principles of free choice and equality with neo-liberal values of economic and bureaucratic efficiency.

In chapters 3, 4, and 5, I detail the terms of the nuptial deal that prove necessary and enticing for proponents of marriage equality. I pay particular attention to the political rationalities and symbolic rewards that make marriage look like the most sensible solution to managing social problems and stigmatized identities. First I explain how marriage matters, not simply because it "normalizes" gay and lesbians but because this normalization provides evidence that same-sex couples "deserve" equal access to social structures that alleviate fear. Marriage equality activists appropriate risk-based political rationalities that construct political grievances in terms of personal experiences of anxiety and insecurity. In this sense, marriage equality activists ask to be governed as if they were subjects worthy of self-regulation. Risk-based rationalities resonate with neo-liberal projects to govern from a distance by asking individuals to manage social problems by making good choices; however, most marriage equality activists reject this downsized model of care at the same time that they ask for inclusion in it; activists believe in marriage not because they agree with the terms of neo-liberalism but because marriage promises to alleviate the anxiety they feel in the course of living their everyday lives. This adherence to the terms of neo-liberal forms of governance happens not only at the level of rational calculation and political strategy but also at the level of prereflexive emotional needs. In this sense, the "nuptial deal" is not as mechanistic and rationally calculated as my metaphor may unintentionally imply.

In addition to seeing marriage as a structure that alleviates fear by offering individual couples and the "gay community" as a whole a mechanism to regulate life's risks, many proponents of marriage equality are enticed by the promise of free choice and personal privacy that living within a state-consecrated intimacy affords. From the perspective of many activists, marriage offers subjective rewards that would allow one to "freely choose" a partnership that reflects his or her natural sexual orientation while at the same time promising a zone of privacy free from unwarranted government intrusion. Proponents of marriage equality agree to the terms of the "nuptial deal" both because they are motivated by the threat of living without marriage and because the state bribes them with marriage enticements.

Marriage offers more to same-sex couples than rewards characteristic of neo-liberal governing regimes. In addition to particular legal responsibilities and rights that allow them to manage life's risks and afford distance from direct state surveillance, marriage comes with symbolic returns. The fact that marriage equality activists are not content with parallel licensing schemes, such as domestic partnerships or civil unions, indicates that the importance of marriage extends beyond specific legal provisions. Activists describe marriage as the "gold standard" because it provides a sense of belonging that a bundle of legal entitlements cannot possibly match. I draw from the work of Pierre Bourdieu to argue that this symbolic power of marriage does not spring just from law but also from everyday acts of social recognition that make "spouses" more prized than "partners." It is this promise of social recognition that makes marriage appear as a natural relationship that the state simply legitimates instead of a state-consecrated category essential to the neo-liberal operation of governance. In chapter 5, you will see how rationalities and technologies of neo-liberal rule work along with, rather than in opposition to, intimate and symbolic processes of belonging and recognition.

Given its interest in marriage as an economized form of governance, how do we explain the federal government's resistance to allowing same-sex couples access to marriage? It might be tempting to assume that the state continues to restrict same-sex couples' access precisely because neo-conservative resistance to redefining "traditional marriage" trumps the economizing logic of neo-liberalism. However, neoconservatives are not the only ones who have a stake in "preserving traditional marriage": the neo-liberal perspective also considers it important to carefully patrol the boundaries of marriage in order to preserve its status as a commonsense institution that couples choose for themselves. Thus, same-sex marriage poses a possible threat to neo-liberal governing regimes to the extent that it risks exposing marriage as a form of governance rather than a natural expression of human intimacy. In chapter 6, I explain how marriage equality activists attempt to address this threat and silence MRN members who may question same-sex couples' commitment to monogamy as both a morally superior form of intimacy and a model of care essential to free-market capitalism.

I conclude by explaining the implications of my research for sociologists of marriage and family concerned with the relationship between marriage and neo-liberalism. I then return to social theory in general by exploring logics and practices of consent essential to neo-liberal governing regimes. I end by drawing out the political implications of my analysis.

CHAPTER TWO

The Nuptial Deal

At the time of our interview, Jennifer and Cathy had been together for seventeen years. By all unofficial indicators they were married: they had a commitment ceremony, shared finances, gave birth to their daughter—her parents were, as Opal explained to me, "illegally married." Jennifer and Cathy attended their first rally in support of same-sex marriage in 1993, but they are not the public face of the movement: they never appear in any official policy briefs, nor has MRN featured their story on its official website or in its educational pamphlets. In fact, Jennifer and Cathy do not even consider themselves dedicated activists. They participate in MRN protests and campaigns, but, as Jennifer explained in our interview, "We are not really activists. We are involved by signing petitions and writing letters, and that's about it. I wrote a letter to the governor at four in the morning—" Cathy quickly picked up her wife's sentence: "In a more subversive way, whenever there are forms to fill out and things like that, we scratch out 'father' and write 'mother number two.' . . . With the school, when they ask about my husband, I say, 'You mean my wife?' That's active—like everyday activism."

Jennifer channeled the conversation back to the heated letter she wrote in the early morning:

> One of the things that I wrote to the governor about was that he should make marriage legal because it would save the country money. Because when Cathy first had Opal, she received welfare, and I was making a sufficient salary that had we been married, we would not have qualified. So the government was losing money to us, and we weren't doing anything illegal. You know, there are a number of other situations with the child-care discounts that she has gotten and financial aid and various reasons that financially it has been to our advantage

to not be married up until now. It has been to the state's or government or governor's detriment; he has been paying for us. We know a lot of couples that have done things like this before. So I was trying to point out that he may not realize how many people are taking advantage of the system by not having to be married.

Jennifer and Cathy point to their modest class status and previous experience receiving state assistance as a reason to advocate for marriage equality. As Jennifer shrugged in bewilderment, Cathy interjected, "When we are not married, we can both claim head of household." Cathy clarified this line of reasoning as if she were adding to the letter as we continued the interview: "We have also known married couples who are dual-income couples that say that they were paying more in taxes being married than when they weren't [married]." Cathy and Jennifer were completely baffled: how could the state be so irrational as to exclude them from an institution that would clearly reduce welfare expenditures and increase state revenues? Jennifer wrote this letter to the governor not only out of frustration but also out of confidence that this argument would resonate with the state in a way that appeals to equality and fairness often would not.

Jennifer and Cathy are only two of several supporters of marriage equality who articulate the neo-liberal interest of the downsized state at the same time that they consider themselves progressives: they support state spending for public programs, unemployment insurance, and national health care. Jennifer and Cathy are both white, but unlike the leadership of MRN, they are not middle-class professionals who advocate for marriage from a position of economic stability or privilege. On the other hand, Jennifer's letter clearly articulates a strategy that has become central in arguments for same-sex marriage. At the level of official political strategy, the marriage equality movement is essentially brokering a "nuptial deal" with the state: offering to set aside their progressive desires for economic redistribution and prioritize the economizing goals of governance in exchange for access to the marriage license. The terms of this nuptial deal and the ambivalence it engenders are the subject of this chapter.

The State's Interest in Marriage Equality

Even if Jennifer's letter to the governor ended up in his trash, the cost-benefit analysis she and other proponents of same-sex marriage articulate is resonating in state supreme courts that have ruled on the constitutionality of same-sex marriage. Unlike the legislative debates and voter propositions, state supreme court decisions explicitly reconsider the state's interest in marriage when evaluating constitutional claims.

As of June 2008, state supreme courts had ruled on the constitutionality of denying same-sex couples access to marriage in Hawaii, Vermont, Alaska, Massachusetts, Oregon, New York, New Jersey, and California. Each court based its decision, to some degree, on reconciling the equal protection clause of the federal Constitution's Fourteenth Amendment with the "police powers of the states" interpreted from the Constitution's Tenth Amendment, to promote the general welfare of its citizens.[1] The supreme courts in the states of Hawaii, Alaska, and Oregon decided to overturn the appellate court decisions in favor of same-sex marriage plaintiffs because those states passed constitutional amendments defining marriage as a relationship between a man and a woman before the courts made their rulings.

The California, Vermont, and Massachusetts courts, for example, explicitly outlined the state's interest in marriage in order to consider whether the state can justifiably exclude same-sex couples from marriage. In each decision, the courts argued that marriage is in the state's interest because it preserves a model of care that reduces state expenditures.

The most explicit link between neo-liberal projects and marriage equality came in 2008, when the California Supreme Court ruled that California does not have a "compelling" state interest in excluding same-sex couples from marriage. Instead, the court ruled that same-sex couples pose no threat to the state's interest in marriage because "same-sex couples who choose to marry will be subject to the same obligations and duties that currently are imposed on married opposite-sex couples."[2] What interest does the state have in imposing "obligations and duties" on married couples?

Chief Justice Ronald M. George outlined the state's and society's interest in marriage by defining these obligations and duties as a way to form a stable setting for child rearing and promote emotional and financial stability without relying on state support. According to George's interpretation, "The legal obligations of support that are an integral part of the marital and family relationships relieve society of the obligation of caring for individuals who may become incapacitated or who are otherwise unable to support themselves" (citing *Elisa B. v. Superior Court* 2005).[3] In this formulation, marriage is not just an expression of intimate desires or a religious sacrament; it is also a care structure—one that places the responsibility for financial and emotional support on individual couples rather than the state or society. As socialist feminists have long pointed out, this leaves the responsibilities for care to the unpaid domestic sphere while relieving the state and market of any domestic accountability.

It is this privatized economic obligation for care with which neo-liberals find an affinity—and one that is not simply hypothetical. Justice George explicitly bases his interpretation of this unique role of marriage in a law review article written by Bruce Hafen twenty-five years earlier.[4] In his fascinating consideration of the necessity of marriage, Hafen cites Paul Johnson's "Family as an Emblem of Freedom" to make the following pronouncement:

> The significant place of marriage in the democratic political structure reflects the extent to which marriage has become "an enormously important element in the rise of stable political systems and dynamic economies. . . . As Professor Hayek has rightly pointed out, 'the rise of the West is due in great part to its ability to define the law with certitude, and to up-hold it against all comers—for legal certainty is the basis of investment and capital formation. At the heart of any stable law of property is a clear and universal legal doctrine of marriage, legitimacy and inheritance.' "[5]

Professor Freidrich Hayek, a well known neo-liberal forefather, makes the role of civil marriage in the neo-liberal context very clear: it exists to stabilize financial investment and extend the reach of capital. Hafen elaborates on Hayek's position by arguing that the marriage contract is akin to economic contracts because it provides a "permanent" basis for personal and financial investment. Thus, not only does marriage leave the management of illness, poverty, and disability to individual couples, but it also provides the legal scaffolding for private property and capital accumulation.

The neo-liberal case for marriage also includes appropriating long-held state concerns about illegitimacy.[6] According to this logic, the marriage contract not only outlines mutual responsibility assumed by the couple, but it also includes taking financial responsibility for their children. This argument appears in Vermont's 1999 *Baker* decision, which found exclusion of same-sex couples from the benefits of civil marriage unconstitutional. The Vermont court reiterated the legitimacy of children as one of the most important state interests in marriage and held that extending marriage to same-sex couples would not undermine the state's interest in reducing the number of illegitimate children, stating, "To the extent that the state's purpose in licensing civil marriage was, and is to legitimize children and provide for their security, the statutes plainly exclude many same-sex couples who are no different from opposite-sex couples with respect to these objectives."[7] The Vermont court emphasized the purpose of legitimization as being to improve the security of children; however, as Jacques Donzelot (1979) finds, illegitimacy becomes a concern for the state when it has a negative impact on its budget. After all, this is precisely the logic reflected in the family-planning model of welfare reform, which strictly polices illegitimacy by instituting programs to reduce out-of-wedlock pregnancies (Hays 2003). As Jennifer noted in her letter to the governor, without official marriage, she and Cathy could receive state funding, such as child-care allowances, to help care for Opal.

In the 2003 *Goodridge* case, the first state supreme court decision to rule exclusion of same-sex couples from legal marriage unconstitutional while also rejecting the constitutionality of parallel licensing schemes, the Massachusetts Supreme Court linked concerns about illegitimacy to a more general and explicit interest in reducing state expenditures. "We construe civil marriage to mean the voluntary union of two persons as spouses. . . . This reformulation . . . advances the two legitimate State interests the department has identified: providing a stable setting for child rearing and conserving State resources."[8] The court ruled against excluding same-sex couples from marriage because it found no reliable evidence that same-sex couples could not forward the state's interest in marriage. According to this formulation, the "two legitimate State interests in marriage" are essentially the same—to reduce the state's bottom line. The Massachusetts court's ruling vividly reveals state concerns for utilizing marriage as a way to ensure that couples remain financially obligated to their children. Of course, illegitimate children are a social problem when the state posits marriage as the primary mechanism for ensuring child welfare.

Marriage Equality's End of the Nuptial Deal

Jennifer's letter to the governor is not an idiosyncratic midnight rant; it's an official argument espoused by major marriage equality organizations. Proponents of same-sex marriage regularly appeal to the state to recognize its own interest in legalizing same-sex marriage so it can reduce public spending and increase tax and tourism revenues. Clearly, the best strategy for obtaining the right to marry is to argue that allowing same-sex couples to marry will further the state's interest in marriage; however, the best strategy for marriage equality is inconsistent with support for the kind of state expenditures required for a stable social safety net. In fact, same-sex marriage activists use the same logic that proponents of President Bush's Healthy Marriage Initiative find convincing: marriage helps people take care of themselves so that the government does not have to. Does this mean that marriage equality activists do not support state spending for social insurance? Many of the marriage equality activists with whom I spoke support universal health insurance and economic redistribution. However, by using neo-liberal logics to justify marriage, even those opposed to the downsizing of the social safety net risk foreclosing these options.

Marriage Equality's Direct Appeals to the State's Interest in Marriage

The marriage equality movement makes appeals to the state's economizing proclivities by pointing to projected reductions in welfare expenditures, illegitimacy, and Social Security, along with expected increases in revenues from same-sex marriages. Writing for the Institute for Gay and Lesbian Strategic Studies, Lee Badgett draws from census data to project the potential fiscal impact of same-sex marriage on the state of Vermont. According to her calculations, the state of Vermont would substantially benefit from the legalization of same-sex marriage, in part because it would reduce the number of poor individuals eligible for state welfare benefits. Badgett projects that "1 percent of same-sex marriages—or from 4 to 61 people—would involve someone currently receiving ANFC [Vermont's name for Aid to Families with Dependent Children] who would no longer be eligible after marriage. Thus the total decrease in state expenditures would be $112,906 to $1,850,735 over a five year period."[9] These numbers would certainly bolster Jennifer's letter to the governor. Unlike Jennifer, however, in this statement Badgett shows no concern for the financial well-being of families supported by ANFC. Badgett does not argue that marriage would increase the financial stability of poor Americans but that marriage would alleviate the state's burden to provide for poor same-sex couples. As Badgett claims, "In a family where a committed adult couple is not allowed to marry, no spousal support can be required, increasing the state's potential responsibility."[10] Same-sex marriage would help the state achieve the goal of cost efficiency, regardless of actually providing any kind of adequate social insurance.

Many of those involved in debates about same-sex marriage also appeal to the state's desire to decrease expenditures by considering the very minimal financial losses the state would incur by extending Social Security benefits to same-sex couples. Proponents draw from a report written by the Congressional Budget Office (CBO) that projects that allowing same-sex couples access to Social Security survivors benefits would only slightly increase expenditures. The CBO explains why costs would be minimal:

> First, most same-sex couples include two workers, and on average, their earnings are closer to one another's than is the case for a husband and wife in a two-earner couple [therefore, they are entitled to lower survivors benefits]. Second, same-sex partners would generally collect survivor benefits for a shorter period. On average, such partners are the same age, and statistically they have the same life expectancy. By contrast, husbands are an average of two to three years older than their wives, earn more, and have a shorter life expectancy.[11]

Because same-sex couples are closer to each other in terms of life expectancy, the CBO concludes that in the case of survivors benefits, same-sex marriages would be much cheaper than heterosexual ones. This calculative reasoning, which carefully enumerates possible costs and benefits for the state if it decided to legalize same-sex marriage, fits the neo-liberal concern of modern liberal welfare states about prioritizing economic efficiency over citizen well-being.

In addition to possible fiscal benefits to the state social insurance budget, some proponents of same-sex marriage argue that opening marriage to same-sex couples will increase state funds by boosting tax revenue from tourism and weddings. According to the Williams Institute's report on the economic benefits of marriage for New Mexico's state budget,[12] "If New Mexico permits same-sex marriage, the State will collect $365,000 in sales tax revenue from New Mexico same-sex couples' spending on their weddings. . . . In addition, couples from other states are likely to travel to New Mexico to marry and celebrate their weddings, generating a boost to tourism that will lead to higher tax revenues. . . . Using census data and research on New Mexico's tourism market, we estimate that the State will collect approximately $4.1 million in tax revenue on spending by out-of-state same-sex couples who travel to New Mexico to marry."[13]

Regardless of the accuracy of these figures, the effort to calculate the potential economic benefits same-sex marriage would bring to state budgets indicates that proponents of same-sex marriage are speaking to the neo-liberal values of basing policy decisions on the logic of cost-benefit analysis.

After the California Supreme Court ruling that extended marriage to same-sex couples, the Williams Institute released a June 2008 report projecting that the state would make $63.8 million in a period of three years. In this report, Bradley Sears and Lee Badgett carefully enumerate possible benefits to the state, including employment and local business revenues from the wedding industries, tourism, and even marriage license fees.[14] These figures are widely cited in the national news media, and even Governor Arnold Schwarzenegger appeared to applaud the decision on similar grounds: "You know, I'm wishing everyone good luck with their marriages and I hope that California's economy is booming because everyone is going to come here and get married."[15]

Others, pessimistic about the permanency of marriage, remain optimistic about the economic growth stimulated by divorce. Attorney Daniel Clement, quoted in the *New York Post*, urges folks to consider the bright side of divorce on his website: "Not to jinx any of the nuptials, but, like heterosexual marriages, some of the same sex marriages will not be everlasting and will end in divorce. These same sex divorces will further drive the economy, as the parties will need to employ the services of lawyers, accountants, financial planners, mental health professionals, appraisers and other divorce professionals."[16] Thus, even if marriage fails to create social stability, from the logic of cost-benefit analysis, it can still be considered a success to the extent that it stimulates economic growth.

Even when crafting arguments specifically framed in terms of "immorality" and "discrimination," marriage equality activists occasionally use the logic of cost-benefit analysis. In March 2005, for example, members of the local Waterford branch of MRN crafted this statement as their main argument in a letter to the local board of supervisors considering a local resolution to support the efforts of marriage equality: "Independent studies conclude that ending discrimination against same-sex couples and their children will save the state tens of millions of dollars and pump hundreds of millions of dollars into the . . . [state] economy. As we face severe cuts from the state for essential county services, ending marriage discrimination will provide much needed funding for county governments. At this time of economic crisis . . . [the state] cannot afford the moral or financial costs of discrimination." In a number of membership meetings considering the framing of the preceding statement, MRN members stressed the importance of showing local officials how discrimination imposes financial as well as moral costs on Waterford residents. The statement brilliantly weaves democratic concerns about equality and eliminating discrimination with the state's concern about generating economic growth and increasing the state's bottom line.

The logic of combining financial and moral discrimination must be contextualized according to neo-liberal rationalities of governance. Rather than the classic liberal perspective that differentiates morality from financial achievement, members of MRN conceptualize the immorality of discrimination according to financial losses. As Wendy Brown argues, "In making the individual fully responsible for her- or himself, neoliberalism equates moral responsibility with rational action; it erases the discrepancy between economic and moral behavior by configuring morality as a matter of rational deliberation about costs, benefits, and consequences" (2005, 42). Just as individuals acting on the basis of a cost-benefit rationality would choose marriage because it maximizes one's ability to regulate risk without interference from the state, marriage equality becomes the moral option, the "right thing to do," because it also allows the state to increase the efficiency of its own operation by reducing public spending.

This statement from MRN also demonstrates how the values of democracy—namely, freedom and equality—may not be enough to convince the state that marriage discrimination should be eliminated. By suggesting that the state could end discrimination while simultaneously solving its economic problems, proponents of marriage equality articulate a confluence between democratic and neo-liberal justifications for state-consecrated categories.

It might be tempting to assume that marriage equality discourses justifying state economization are strategic arguments rather than sincere beliefs; however, in the course of my fieldwork, I have found it often difficult, and perhaps irrelevant, to make such a distinction. I focus instead on how MRN activists juggle, manage, and at times silence their own and other members' ambivalent feelings about the nuptial deal. For this reason, the nuptial deal is not mechanistic, nor are its terms unanimous and uncontested.

Marriage Equality Vows and the Ethic of Self-Sufficiency

Reports such as those published by the Williams Institute appeal to the state's interest in marriage as a model of care that reduces state expenditures and increases revenues—the same logic that brought marriage promotion programs to the forefront of welfare reform. This model of care comes with an ethic of self-sufficiency characteristic of calls for reductions in state-funded care structures. Many proponents of same-sex marriage do not directly appeal to state economization efforts; however, they appear to ardently believe in the same ethic of self-sufficiency that tends to mask privilege and stigmatize universal care structures as "state dependency."

Hazel Butler and her wife Amber McDaniel (both founding members of Marriage Rights Now whom you met in chapter 1) support efforts to nationalize health care, and Hazel even sees the advantages of unhooking Social Security survivors benefits from marital relationships, but when espousing the marriage equality position, they articulate an ethic of care that individualizes responsibility for social problems. Hazel, like many other proponents of same-sex marriage with whom I spoke, says that her "blood boils" when she thinks about how "straight people" really do not understand the mutual obligation to care that comes with signing a marriage license. Hazel raised her voice and leaned forward while explaining the outrage she feels: "They should write on the marriage contract, 'Here is what you are signing up for. You are signing up for community property; you're signing up for shared debts; you are signing up for taking care of this person. These are your responsibilities.'" By being denied an opportunity to marry Amber, Hazel feels that the state excludes her from an institution that she, unlike many straight people she knows, would actually take seriously.

Years of studying the obligations and benefits denied to her and Amber have shown Hazel how marriage would operate as a technology to care for herself and her partner. As Amber put it, denying her and Hazel the opportunity to marry only makes the state's job more difficult, because a marriage license "is between two people that love each other, who want to build a family, who want to create an economically stable unit, who will assume the responsibilities for one another so that the state does not have to—and this is a good thing." As Hazel and Amber demonstrate, the marriage license provides a way for couples to take care of themselves, subsequently reducing the state's potential fiscal liability. From Amber's point of view, marriage not only symbolizes love and commitment between two people but also creates an obligation to care. As Amber ends her discussion of the marriage license, she also emphasizes that "this is a good thing." In doing so, she valorizes the ethic undergirding welfare reform's insistence that self-sufficiency is superior to state dependency (Hays 2003).

In the self-sufficiency model, the state's role in caring for the population comes in the form of a license (Valverde 2003), sanctioning particular relationships as qualified for care and providing legal redress in case these relationships fail. As many proponents of same-sex marriage point out, this role of the state in marriage makes couples more stable. The Alliance for Same-Sex Marriage argues that marriage can provide stable protections against life risks because the state ties two people together in a legally binding relationship. One of its pamphlets reads, "Once two people marry in a civil ceremony, they cannot undo their marriage without first obtaining the permission of the state. The commitment to remain married, and the stability and continuity that provides for families and society, is why civil society provides married couples with extensive legal, social and economic protections."[17] In this view, marriage provides stability to society because the state attaches protections to the contract and gets to decide when the contract can be broken. Thus, the marriage license makes couples responsible for their own protection in exchange for a more indirect relationship with the state. The "legal, social and economic protections" that the marriage license offers are not free; they come with an obligation to care, which is essential to the nuptial deal.

These obligations to care that are explicit in the marriage contract (the same ones that Chief Justice George outlined as the state's primary interest in marriage) remain unquestioned in marriage equality discourse. Instead of insisting that couples cannot possibly manage social problems such as illness, disability, and poverty, the marriage equality movement finds itself trying to convince the state that same-sex couples can be much more self-sufficient if only they had access to the legal provisions that marriage provides. In this narrative, MRN members see economic security as an outcome of individual marriages (microlevel) rather than a precondition for marital self-governance (macrolevel). Therefore, rather than critique the economic privilege required for "self-sufficiency," many members of MRN tend to see marriage as a social advantage that crosses class and racial divides.[18] Thus, Amber describes sexual orientation as the "last vestige of discrimination" in marriage law.

Proponents of same-sex marriage realize how the institution of marriage offers a legal structure for couples to take care of themselves. Marriage provides access to a spouse's medical insurance, and married partners can make medical decisions for each other. The United States government considers health care the responsibility of individuals, not the state. In the absence of a national health care system, access to medical insurance in the United States primarily comes from employers or from expensive health plans offered to individuals who do not get insurance from their place of employment.

People in same-sex relationships find themselves at a particular disadvantage because they often cannot add their partner to company medical insurance plans, as married people can. In my time with MRN, I found that many activists for same-sex marriage were motivated by their employers' refusal to provide health insurance for their partners. With a particular concern for the issue of health insurance, the Human Rights Campaign (HRC) produced a policy brief titled *The Cost of Marriage Inequality to Children and Their Same-Sex Parents*. In this report, the HRC does a thorough job of detailing how married people have more options for health coverage than the unmarried; consequently, marriage leaves some same-sex couples and their children without medical insurance. "Same sex couples and their children are at much greater risk of being denied access to medical insurance through their employer. . . . Most employer-sponsored health plans extend coverage to the married spouses and children of their employees but not unmarried partners. . . . Domestic partner benefits, an alternative means of providing access to health insurance for the partners of gay, lesbian and bisexual employees are not offered by the vast majority of employers in the United States. . . . Domestic Partner benefits are offered by only 6,811 out of 114,488,947 private employers."[19] Essentially, barring same-sex couples from marriage means that the state also denies these couples access to mechanisms for self-care.

Many same-sex marriage activists use a slightly different argument: marriage would finally provide an accurate label for the care that same-sex couples already provide for their families. In an affidavit in *Lewis v. Harris*, the New Jersey case questioning the constitutionality of banning same-sex couples from marriage, Dennis Winslow testified to the care his partner Mark gave to Dennis's ill father. "All of us kids got together and decided that we would take turns caring for Dad in our own homes for two-week periods. . . . Mark supported me just as any married spouse should, and likewise helped with the care when Dad was staying with us. . . . Mark's support is one example of what I think of when I consider what the marriage vows mean."[20] In this statement, Dennis uses *should* to connote an ethic of care consistent with the state's interest in marriage. Mark made a *vow*—a moral pledge—to care for and support those who might otherwise have required state assistance. Dennis's testimony encourages the court to call his and Mark's relationship a "marriage" precisely because they experience the institution of marriage as a care structure that reduces the state's responsibility to care for aging members of the population.

Proponents of same-sex marriage also want the public and policy makers to consider how the marriage license would allow them to protect each other from poverty should one partner become unemployed. Same-sex marriage activists clearly demonstrate what many take for granted: marriage offers at least a minimal form of insurance against poverty. Given the dismantled condition of the social safety net in the United States, same-sex couples find marriage insurance particularly important.

Marriage equality activists argue that same-sex couples already operate as an economic unit and that legal marriage would make it much easier for them to care for each other in the event that one partner becomes unemployed. The Williams Institute draws from US census data to argue that same-sex couples need marriage because, like different-sex couples, they economically depend on each other. The authors provide a table that charts nine different aspects of same-sex couples' economic interdependence. One facet includes the percentage of same-sex couples with only one employed partner. According to the report, 26 percent of same-sex couples include a partner who is unemployed or does not participate in the labor force. Thus, the authors assume, "in many of these couples, one person's income supports both individuals."[21] This assertion does not take into account the possibility that many of these unemployed same-sex partners may receive public aid, have informal sources of income, or could be independently wealthy. In fact, as you have already seen, many proponents of same-sex marriage attempt to persuade their conservative opponents to consider the decrease in public benefits that might result from making same-sex partnerships legal marriages. With legal marriage, the state takes a married partner's income into account when establishing financial need for means-tested welfare programs. Regardless of the accuracy of the Williams Project's assertion, the authors clearly present same-sex couples' relationships as ones who share a commitment to downsized care in which couples take care of themselves so that the state need not intervene.

As with health care, proponents of same-sex marriage argue that their relationships deserve the "married" label because they act as married couples do in times of crisis. Thus, the degree of financial interdependence among same-sex couples constitutes evidence that same-sex couples have already taken *vows* of mutual care and thus believe in marriage as an ethical care structure. For example, in their testimony in the New York case

Hernandez v. Robles, Daniel Reyes and his partner Curtis Woolbright argue that they deserve "the protection that marriage offers" because they are financially committed to each other. They write, "We have joint bank accounts . . . and share our income and expenses. . . . There have been periods when Daniel was out of work and I was the only wage earner in the family. I paid the rent, purchased all the groceries, paid all the bills and paid for the care of our dogs."[22] In considering political strategy alone, this argument is slightly tricky: if same-sex couples have already vowed to love and care for each other, and they also can take care of themselves without marriage, then why would the state bother to allow them to marry? But stories like this one from Daniel and Curtis are also sincere and emotionally charged narratives. Beyond appealing to the state's interest in marriage, marriage equality activists also fuse the basic economic argument with an ethic of making a "fair deal."

Daniel, Amber, and other same-sex couples who advocate for marriage are essentially calling foul, exclaiming to the state that "we have lived up to our end of the bargain; now it's your turn." Same-sex marriage activists ask the state for access to the legal structures that would enable them to fulfill their responsibilities as caregivers, so that they do not end up depending on the state. Underlying the ethic of self-sufficiency, however, is an unacknowledged distance from the necessity of public care that comes as a result of the social privilege afforded to those with the prerequisite economic, cultural, and social capital.

Prioritizing the Nuptial Deal or Replacing the New Deal?

When same-sex marriage hit the gay and lesbian political agenda with force in the 1990s, dissent from the Left included suspicion about how the fight for marriage is essentially a middle-class problem. From this perspective, marriage is a prize only for those who actually have property to share, a job that provides health insurance, or enough income to warrant a tax break. By putting so many resources into the marriage equality movement, some argued that gay and lesbian organizations were essentially turning their backs on those without economic or racial privilege. Marriage can reduce state expenditures in part because it does not actually solve anything for couples who have incomes at or below the poverty line (Sigle-Rushton and McLanahan 2002). Central to this critique is the contention that economic and social benefits should not be tied to marriage at all, and that the pursuit of the right to marry essentially lends credibility to an intrinsically unjust institution.

In the late eighties and early nineties, before same-sex marriage became the "obvious" commonsense path for gay equality, Paula Ettelbrick (2004) and Nancy Polikoff (1993) argued that gay and lesbian rights should focus on universal access to health insurance and economic security regardless of marital status. In her widely cited article "Since When Is Marriage a Path to Liberation?" first published in 1989, Ettelbrick warned progressive gays and lesbians that "gay marriage will not topple the system that allows only the privileged few to obtain decent healthcare. Nor will it close the privilege gap between those who are married and those who are not" (2004, 127).

Four years later, Polikoff reminded those quick to support the efforts of lawyers in Hawaii to legalize same-sex marriage that the rhetoric used now to show how gays desire and pose no threat to marriage could undermine progressive efforts to address inequalities between the married and the unmarried: "Advocating lesbian and gay marriage will detract from, even contradict, efforts to unhook economic benefits from marriage and make basic healthcare and other necessities available to all" (1993, 11). Judging from explicit appeals to the state's interest in marriage and vows to preserve the ethic of self-sufficiency, it appears that Polikoff's warning has gone unheeded.

If one were to read only arguments, written testimonies, policy briefs, and the transcripts of legislative hearings, it might seem that proponents of same-sex marriage have completely abandoned the goal of a social safety net and turned their attention to full support of neo-liberal political programs that call for the economization of the state. However, attention to the everyday struggles of people like Jennifer and Cathy reveal an important subtext to what appears to be an agreed-upon strategy. Cathy and Jennifer felt ambivalent about using their own situation as an example of what the state ought to prevent, and they are not motivated by securing personal economic privilege. As if to preserve her wife's dignity, Cathy struggled to explain how Jennifer's use of state resources "evened things out. . . . We weren't really rich, and I wasn't able to claim them on my taxes. . . . If I could claim them, I wouldn't have been paying nearly as much in taxes." But Cathy and Jennifer were not bragging; they really expressed no delight that they had hoodwinked the same system that refused to officially recognize their relationship. Instead, Cathy repeated several times that she "didn't feel proud." Cathy explained, "I don't think it is the right thing to do. It was not the moral high ground or anything. I don't like that the money came out of social services. I am not proud of that." Holding back her laughter long enough to finish a sentence, Jennifer added, "Yeah, it would have been nice if it came out of the military budget, but they didn't ask us." This moment of humor was also a point of clarification: Cathy did not espouse this loophole that she and Jennifer used in order to profit from the state at the expense of social services; rather, she saw her letter to the governor as a strategic argument that the state could not possibly refute. On the other hand, by saying that "she wasn't proud" of using social services, Cathy also revealed her sincere belief in a care ethic essential to neo-liberalism.

Like Cathy and Jennifer, many proponents of same-sex marriage end up setting aside their support for universal, state-sponsored care for what they call a more "practical" pursuit of the right to marry. Proponents explain why they have prioritized marriage equality by fusing democratic principles of free choice with neo-liberal values of efficiency and expedience. However, the freedom to choose dovetails with neo-liberal values of efficiency and expedience in a way that legitimates the inequalities inherent in the marriage classification.

Marriage as a Lifestyle Choice

In response to Polikoff's and Ettelbrick's arguments, Evan Wolfson, lead attorney for the three same-sex couples in the Hawaii case, responded by calling on all those concerned about gay and lesbian rights to unite for the marriage cause. For Wolfson, the marriage equality position is "prioritizing" rather than "marginalizing or silencing." Wolfson sidestepped the issue of the economic inequalities intrinsic to the marriage model and instead argued that the fights for marriage equality and universal health care are not mutually exclusive: "Our demand as gay people for equal choices and recognition with regard to our family relationships does not undermine our demand as conscientious citizens to decouple benefits from arbitrary criteria of any kind. But, equally, our desire to achieve a more just, contextual allocation of marriage should not require us to accept an inferior status with regard to marriage or other choices."[23] In his response, Wolfson dances around the fundamental question that Polikoff and Ettelbrick raise: if same-sex marriage activists convincingly argue for access to marriage, how can they also argue for its abolition? If the problem is not that same-sex couples cannot have marriage but that the institution itself breeds inequality, the marriage equality position sounds more like silencing than prioritizing.

But, in his response, Wolfson sees marriage as a lifestyle choice rather than an institution that acts as a gatekeeper to resources, such as health care, that should be universally available. Many MRN members have multiple ways of arguing a similar position. As Wolfson's official statement suggests, they see no conflict between advocating marriage and universal care, but they have decided to make marriage a priority because they see it as a lifestyle choice.

Patrick Singleton, a minister, MRN supporter, and longtime advocate of social justice issues such as economic equality and a "woman's right to choose," explained his prioritization of same-sex marriage as a "step in the right direction." "Even people that are not sure they want marriage for themselves seem to be pretty convinced that it is the right thing to fight for, that people should have the option. Gay people should be able to make their choices the same way that straight people do about whether or not they want to cohabitate or be single or get married, whatever it is." According to this logic, marriage is essentially a lifestyle choice rather than a state-sanctioned system that privileges particular intimacies and forms of managing the problems of the population. Even though the legalization of same-sex marriage would do nothing to address the inequalities for the unmarried, Patrick and others do not see this as a violation of democratic values because straight people and gay people would be able to enter the institution if they so chose. Thus, the unmarried are considered those who willingly made a lifestyle decision to avoid marriage, and, characteristic of neo-liberal rational actors, it is they and not the state who are responsible for the decision to forgo marriage protections. In this case, the exclusions that the unmarried face are justified because they could choose to enter the institution if they wanted to.

What is particularly ironic about this argument is that it is the same one that many conservative opponents use to justify barring same-sex couples from marriage. In major state court cases and legislative hearings, opponents of same-sex marriage argue that gays and lesbians are not being discriminated against, because they have the choice to enter marriage if they want to. The law, for example, does not bar a self-identified lesbian from marrying a man of her choice. Thus, conservatives reason that same-sex couples are not asking merely to be included in marriage but to essentially change the definition.

Members of MRN make a similar argument: if same-sex couples could marry, then the law would not bar any single people or polyamorous individuals from marrying *one* person of their choice. Amber, for example, assured me that gender restrictions are really the last vestige of discrimination written in marriage law and that once this distinction is removed, "every single person would now have the option whether they seek to enter into that contract or not. Every single person, regardless of if they are straight or gay, will have the opportunity to decide for themselves whether they want to enter into that civil contract or not." Similar to her conservative opponents, Amber essentially argues that the marriage classification is justified when all individuals are allowed access.

When I asked Amber to address Polikoff's and Ettelbrick's argument that gender actually is not the last vestige of discrimination in marriage law, she distinguished her argument from the conservative position on the freedom to choose marriage by using an analogy in which she likened marriage to a hunting license: "I would never pick up a gun in my life, but I would be on the front lines advocating for the elimination of gender discrimination and sexual orientation discrimination in the issuance of hunting licenses." In other words, even if she rejected marriage as a problematic practice, she would continue to advocate for individuals' free choice to enter the institution. For Amber, marriage cannot discriminate against those who reject the institution. In the arguments of both conservative opponents and proponents, marriage is justified when it allows individuals to choose to conform to the benefit structure that marriage provides.

The lifestyle choice narrative has a resonance beyond Wolfson and MRN. The American Civil Liberties Union (ACLU), for example, in the November 2003 document "Message Points on Marriage for Same-Sex Couples," offers a set of arguments that all proponents of same-sex marriage should articulate. One of these "talking points" encourages activists to "talk about marriage as a commitment, sharing, loving relationships, and a personal choice that should not be denied to couples just because they are the same sex. . . . Two adults who make this private personal choice to form a life-long commitment should not be denied the right to marry."[24] In a country that sees itself as the protector of individual freedom over governmental intrusion, it makes strategic sense to argue that marriage is a private matter.

The lifestyle language appeals to Americans' desire for a distant state, and it resonates with personal experiences of marriage as an intimate, familial, and religious institution; however, this argument is difficult to reconcile with proponents' other main points, which frame the state as the primary authority over marriage. Yet, these positions can coexist in the context of a neo-liberal political rationality that finds an affinity between personal autonomy and governance. In other words, marriage can be both an intimate personal, private choice and a state-regulated institution in a paradigm of governance that finds its ultimate expression in the "good" choices that individuals make. As Nikolas Rose argues, "Government works by 'acting at a distance' upon these choices, forging a symmetry between the attempts of individuals to make life worthwhile for themselves, and the political values of consumption, profitability, efficiency and social order" (1990, 10).

The Marriage Choice Is More Practical and Efficient

The fight for marriage equality reveals how the logic of economic and bureaucratic efficiency dovetails with democratic discourses of choice discussed in the previous section in a way that provides justifications for marriage exclusions. In these formulations, the limits of choice and the right to state-sanctioned intimacies are justified in the name of practicality and efficiency. From this reasoning, unlike liberal democratic formulations, rights are based not primarily on "human nature" but on the smooth operation of government. The logic used to explain this prioritization actually parallels the kind of rationality that good "neo-liberal" subjects ought to practice, valuing both efficiency and practicality over general citizen well-being.

Caitlin McCleary, an active member and previous leader of an MRN chapter, describes herself and her wife of two years, Cindy, as progressive Democrats. Caitlin and Cindy, both white and in their early thirties, moved from Idaho shortly after receiving their bachelor's degrees. At the time of our interview, Caitlin was enrolled in graduate school in preparation for her middle-class, professional career in the social services. Caitlin began her work with MRN shortly after settling in the area but had to "hand over her leadership position" as she finished her thesis.

Although Caitlin's thesis work may have diverted her time, it had not eclipsed her passion for marriage equality. When I asked Caitlin why she felt marriage was an important pursuit, she replied after taking a deep breath:

> I think it has to do with rights. . . . There is the social aspect of it, and there is the rights aspect. And it really touches on my sense of injustice when I see that

straight couples have access to these rights and ways of protecting their relationships and same-sex couples don't. People don't really know that they have them until it comes up on a situation that people don't want to think about like death and divorce. And what has happened over time is that society has come up with ways of dealing with those circumstances, that, you know, are harder to plan for. So straight couples have access to these protections, and same-sex couples don't and they can get really screwed. And that I think is the main reason why I am involved.

Caitlin describes the rights that come with marriage as "protections" from which she and other gays and lesbians are wrongly excluded.

When I asked Caitlin to respond to the argument that marriage is an inherently discriminatory institution, she, like Amber, explicitly acknowledged marriage discrimination, but that did not keep her from supporting it:

I think that we should have nationalized health care. I definitely think that it is discrimination for health care to be based on marital status. . . . Other kinds of rights that would become recognized like . . . custody of a child or property or who is it that makes the decision to pull the plug so that you don't become a vegetable—those things cannot be delegated to groups very well. You know, if you have a child, you need to know which person is responsible for him or her. . . . If you actually get into the rights, a lot of things make sense to do with couples rather than groups. . . . It would be practically very difficult for people to do. In a practical sense, it would be difficult, and what would happen in reality is that people just wouldn't do it. . . . Marriage is the way our society has decided to deal with that.

From Caitlin's perspective, marriage is a legitimate state-sanctioned intimacy even if it excludes singles and nonmonogamous sexual cultures because it is a practical and efficient way to distribute rights associated with care such as parenting, end-of-life decisions, and the ownership of property. In this formulation, the freedom to marry can be limited to couples because ideals of justice must be tempered with the efficient management of the population. In this sense, Caitlin and others who share her opinion agree with the conservatives opposed to same-sex marriage who argue that marriage is the key to social stability because it provides a "tried-and-true" mechanism for organizing care.

Like Caitlin, Judy Marshal is a white lesbian in her midthirties, who has been an active member of MRN for about one year. Judy traces her interest in marriage equality to her volunteer work with the local gay and lesbian community center, which included presenting information about sexual diversity to middle school students. Approximately a year before our interview, Judy met an MRN chapter leader at a community center event and volunteered to attend media trainings and help organize fund-raising events. Judy describes her primary motivation for joining MRN:

> Almost everyone involved in [MRN] is in a long-term relationship and has suffered directly for not being allowed to marry. It's harder to explain to people why I am involved, because I don't stand to benefit directly in any tangible way, right at this moment, from getting marriage rights. I guess it just suddenly occurred to me that I was being treated like a second-class citizen, and I wasn't OK with that. I see my friends, and you know the major difficulties they encounter because they can't marry. . . . [Their experiences] kind of opened my eyes to all of these, you know, I didn't know there were all of these 1,138 rights, federal rights that come with marriage plus state rights.

Like all members of MRN whom I encountered, Judy sees marriage as a fundamental right. The issue of marriage equality is important to her, even though she will not benefit from the privilege of marriage directly, because it speaks to her overall passion to fight discrimination against gays and lesbians.

In addition to basic demographic similarities, Judy also shares Caitlin's perspective on the connection between marriage and social stability, and the need to limit rights for some in the name of practical efficiency; however, Judy draws an important distinction between marriage as a form of intimacy and a type of care structure. When I asked Judy if she felt that the institution of marriage privileges some people over others regardless of whom they decide to marry, she distanced herself from the MRN party line. As if offering a confession, she quietly suggested with hesitation, "Um, well, sure. Married couples are privileged over other unmarried couples, whether they are gay or straight, in terms of all of the rights and protections that they get. Some people say that we should just abolish marriage altogether, but I don't know. It sounds good, but it is just not practical, you know? I mean there's all of those rights and protections for people because we need them." In agreement with Caitlin, Judy essentially argues that marriage may not actually embody the principles of equality and freedom so central to the message of marriage equality activists, but the exclusions marriage requires are justified on the grounds that they are practical.

Unlike Caitlin, however, Judy argues that the practicality of marriage does not rest on monogamous coupling but on a state-sanctioned contract between consenting adults that yields social stability. From her perspective, equality, freedom, and efficiency are compatible with a "liberalized" marriage contract that would not be restricted to couples, lovers, or unrelated individuals. From Judy's point of view, the number of people in a marriage and the degree of their sexual fidelity is irrelevant to her and ought to be irrelevant to the state, because social stability is predicated on the existence of legal protections that allow individuals to care for one another so that the state does not have to. She continued:

> The state has a stake in social stability. Our society is organized in family units—people who are there, and they take care of each other, and they support each other, and when one is out of work, the other one helps, and when one is sick, the other one helps. . . . There is a huge benefit to society in having stable family units that are protected, that have a whole network of protections in place to help it stay together and thrive. I don't think it is so much the government saying that you should settle down and have sex with one person. . . . They set up a system that will help you, but you have to take care of each other, you know, as opposed to a socialist system that doesn't work anyway. I mean it sounds good, but it doesn't work.

Judy brilliantly articulates two important trajectories of neo-liberal governance: First, the efficient governance of the population does not require regulating sexuality; rather, it only requires a belief that people are free when they can manage population-level problems themselves. Second, while it would be ideal to have a socialist society based on universal care, not predicated on marital status, this is not a practical system that actually works. In this sense, the neo-liberal political rationality, founded upon the practical and efficient governance of the population, is consistent with democratic values of freedom and equality (Duggan 2003). Moreover, the potential for a universal social safety net, also predicated on values of freedom and equality, is trumped by the additional sense of practical efficiency that comes when families manage the problems of the population so that the state does not have to. According to this logic, neo-liberalism may have some faults, but at least it is a reality—unlike socialism, which can only be a dream or utopia.

Some activists, such as Caitlin, see monogamy as an essential prerequisite to practical efficiency, and others, like Judy, see voluntary contracts, regardless of the number of partners or sexual relationship, as the key to democratic and practical governance. There is a third set of arguments from other MRN members that echoes Wolfson's claim that the fight for the right to marry is compatible with the battle against economic inequality and the struggle for a universal social safety net. From this perspective, it is neither right nor just that the state shift its responsibility for managing population-level concerns such as illness and poverty to individuals or married couples, many of whom cannot afford to take care of themselves. But in the meantime, as Jack Kemp, a longtime MRN member, puts it, "This debate [about economic equality and a universal social safety net] should not be had on the backs of LGBT [lesbian, gay, bisexual, and transgender] people."

From Jack's perspective, and that of other MRN members who share his view, the pursuit of marriage equality is not incompatible with universal social insurance. Using the example of health care, his husband, Steve Kemp, argues, "This is not some kind of a zero-sum thing. Like if you are working for marriage rights, then you don't care about universal health care or you don't care about fair housing or whatever. This couldn't be further from the truth." As if directly responding to Ettelbrick's claims about marriage securing class privilege, Steve explained, "I think that sometimes there might be an idea of rich lesbian moms in the suburbs that want this [marriage], or rich gay men . . . taking designer vacations want this. Neither of those describe our lives. We are living in a very humble . . . apartment. We are just trying to build a life together. And you know sometimes I feel that these arguments [against marriage from the Left] are directed against us as if we were somebody else—somebody that we are not." Steve has a stable full-time professional career and enough wealth to worry about passing it to Jack without taxation, yet he sees himself as an individual of modest means because he compares his situation to that of "rich gay men." Steve sees marriage as a way of "just trying to build a life" rather than an opportunity to amass social advantage at the expense of strengthening a public social safety net in the United States.

Like Steve and Jack, Amber further argued that not only are the fights for marriage equality and economic equality compatible, but the freedom to marry provides a necessary foundation for LGBT people to enter the debate with the "same rights as straight people." From her perspective, the debate over a universal social safety net cannot be truly equal until gays and lesbians have access to the minimal protections that are offered through marriage.

*   *   *

In the process of "prioritizing" marriage equality, proponents appeal to neo-liberal attempts to apply principles of economic efficiency to the operation of the state. Historically, marriage and the family help shift the burden of social insurance from the state to individuals or couples (Donzelot 1979; Rose and Miller 1992). This sleight of hand also explains Sharon Hays's (2003) evidence that the state defines successful cases of welfare reform in terms of removal from state dependency rather than achievement of economic stability and a living wage. According to the neo-liberal model, risks associated with poverty and illness increasingly become defined as personal problems that require private solutions, and marriage emerges as a way to insure problems of indigence privately, without fiscal liability on the part of the state.

Same-sex marriage activists illuminate why the state might prefer marriage as a model of social insurance: it allows population-level problems to be regulated "from a distance" (Rose 1999), thus minimizing the state's efforts at regulation. However, it would be a mistake to conclude that marriage equality activists are simply colluding with neo-liberal interests to support the state's economization efforts. The stories and explanations from MRN activists in this chapter illustrate the ambiguity and struggle behind official marriage equality statements that now, as a larger part of political discourse, cannot be controlled by those who never intended to add credibility to neo-liberal political-economic discourses. But the motivations to leave the ranks of the unmarried and join the only officially sanctioned care structure prove too enticing for MRN activists to refuse. In the chapters that follow, you will hear MRN members explain why they *think and feel* marriage ought to be pursued in spite of their long-term, and in some cases even short-term, interests in subverting neo-liberal logics that excuse the state from its obligation to prioritize citizen well-being over profit making. In the next three chapters, you will see how particular discourses allow marriage to pass as a lifestyle *choice* at a time when it is an *institution* currently charged with furthering the economizing interest of the neo-liberal state. Marriage matters to marriage equality activists precisely because it is not just one of many viable options.

CHAPTER THREE

The Threat

Fear and Insecurity

I met Patrick Singleton and Bryce Kiplinger at an outreach event sponsored by Marriage Rights Now. The purpose of the event was to sign up members in a well-known, "gay-friendly" sports bar. As we waited for potential supporters to enter the bar, Patrick broke the ice by introducing me to his partner, Bryce: "As you can probably guess, when we hold hands, we get a lot of second glances." Patrick is a graying white man who looks as if he must be nearing his sixties. Bryce is a thin black man who has yet to turn thirty. Bryce echoed Patrick's matter-of-fact tone and elaborated: "Who wouldn't look? I mean, it's not enough for us to be gay, but we have to be interracial and intergenerational as well."

Later that evening, Patrick explained how he and Bryce feel a pressing need to have the right to marry. For the past six years, Bryce, a French citizen, has tried unsuccessfully to obtain a work permit that would enable him to legally reside in the United States. Because he does not have a green card, Bryce could be deported at any time, forced to leave Patrick and their two sons to fend for themselves.

If their relationship were federally recognized as a legal marriage, Patrick could sponsor Bryce for US citizenship, thus resolving Bryce's work status and alleviating fears that he could be deported. Not only do Patrick and Bryce feel that the uncertainty about Bryce's residency status puts the stability of their family at risk, but they also worry about the economic insecurities they experience because Bryce cannot find a job without legal residency. Patrick explained how this adds stress and anxiety to their intimate lives: "I have been working two jobs like crazy, just trying to support us, plus we have two sons. It has been a real financial hardship. Even more than that is the emotional hardship, because I don't think anyone that hasn't been through it can really understand what it does to someone's self-esteem to feel that you are dependent on someone else for everything." These emotional and financial hardships are more difficult for Bryce and Patrick because they do not have a legal and socially sanctioned relationship that would provide access to community and family support systems to get them through the hard times.

In an interview several months later, Patrick stressed how marriage would not just address the lack of protections for his own relationship but would also help alleviate discrimination against all gays and lesbians: "To me, the importance of marriage equality is related to the importance of rectifying all forms of discrimination. It is like one symptom of a big disease, and I think that we have to try to address everything about that disease. I think that one of the most public ways to address the disease is by the issue of same-gender marriage because it is so visible." Patrick argued that the "discrimination disease" is particularly harmful for gays and lesbians because it bars them from gaining access to important forms of protection offered by official marriage. For instance, without marriage, it is much more difficult for gay couples to find outside support from the community and family that give relationships their stability. Patrick and Bryce feel this effect of the discrimination disease in their everyday lives because they cannot marry. For them, marriage is important for a variety of reasons, but it is essential to *protect* their relationship from the negative effects of discrimination, financial instability, and emotional uncertainties.

Like Patrick, many proponents of same-sex marriage share the belief that marriage will not only make same-sex couples more stable and secure but also protect the "gay community" as a whole from the negative effects of social stigma. It is through the logic of risk that marriage equality activists like Patrick and Bryce both make sense of their own personal troubles and also help manage marriage as a regulatory ideal (Butler 1993; Foucault 1990) that promises to alleviate anxieties experienced by all gays and lesbians regardless of their personal decision to enter a marriage contract. Given this formulation, risk discourses not only individualize responsibilities of governance—a position essential to neo-liberalism— they also construct gays and lesbians as a vulnerable collectivity whose "health" and survival depend upon marriage. When imagined according to the logic of risk, marriage can appear as a freely chosen "lifestyle" at the same time that it produces the very terms of the subjectivity it purports to indemnify.

Proponents of same-sex marriage are not the only ones who find a language for their vulnerability in a risk-based discourse. In the span of two months (from March 30 to May 30, 2006), the *Washington Post* published over two hundred articles about some type of "at-risk" phenomenon. American women are increasingly "at risk" for heart disease. United States veterans are "at risk" for identity theft. The entire world is "at risk" for contracting the deadly bird flu. Sioux Falls, South Dakota, is the safest driving city because fewer people there are "at risk" for car accidents. The nation is "at risk" for a terrorist attack.

This focus on risk is not just media-fueled sensationalism. According to sociologist Ulrich Beck (1992), we are living in a "risk society": a historical period characterized by an increasing focus on how to deal with the kinds of dangers produced by capitalist industry without giving up on the project of modernity.[1] As Beck (1992) and Iain Wilkinson (2001) argue, a key distinction between a modern industrial society and a risk-based society is that "class societies remain related to the ideal of *equality* in their developmental dynamics. . . . Not so the risk society. Its normative counter project, which is its basis and motive force, is *safety*" (Beck 1992, 49). According to Beck, motives for political action in a class-based society are centered on how to gain access to the rewards of industrialization, as opposed to a risk society, where motives are about how to avoid the consequences.

My evidence suggests that the class-based projects of equality and risk-based motivations of safety actually work together: same-sex marriage activists, such as Patrick and Bryce, articulate marriage as an institution that will give them equal access to safety. In other words, equality matters not just in principle but also because it gives individuals access to social structures that alleviate fears.

Rather than analyzing risk as a distinct historical period, I argue that the concept of risk currently operates in the United States as a political rationality that calls forth marriage as a way to insure populations by providing security and safety in the name of equality.[2] Risk narratives become political rationalities when security and safety are proper aims of governance best achieved when individuals make responsible choices (Dean 1999a, 1999b; Fox 1999; Hacking 1990; Lemke 2004; Lupton 1999). Risk provides a language for the disenfranchised to express their political grievances in terms of being denied access to governmental technologies that enable individuals—or, in the case of marriage, couples—to manage life's risks. Same-sex marriage activists are essentially asking to be governed as if they were subjects worthy of self-regulation.

Risk rationalities construct social problems—such as poverty and illness—as factors or propensities that only individuals and their loved ones
can reduce. Risk is a political rationality in that it calls for governing strategies; it is also one particularly suited for neo-liberalism, as it asks people
to govern themselves by making smart lifestyle choices. These everyday
procedures and programs of governance inhere in institutions not reducible to the state. For example, in terms of governing the health of the
population, social programs that enable and encourage individuals to make
beneficial choices (such as following a healthy diet and exercise routine)
can be found in high school health classes, advice from one's personal ath-
letic trainer, pamphlets in one's doctor's office, nutrition advertisements
at Jamba Juice, and even diet programs for brides found in wedding magazines. Likewise, governing risk often takes more institutionalized forms.

"Insurance" is one such technology particularly suited for managing
social problems without state expenditures. On the one hand, insurance
technologies make safety a profitable economic commodity; on the other
hand, insurance allows the state to put the responsibility for preventing
misfortune on individuals who have the "option" to make smart lifestyle
choices that reduce individual risk factors.

MRN's articulation of risk-based narratives is not as calculated and
logical as the framework of political rationalities and technologies might
suggest. Marriage equality activists at times use rational cost-benefit calculations, but many proponents find an affinity with these narratives because they express the prereflexive vulnerability they feel in attempting
to live their everyday lives. Thus, the terms of adherence to neo-liberal
forms of governance do not primarily arise at the level of rational calculation as discourses of responsibilization might suggest; they take root
in visceral emotional responses. Patrick and Bryce feel as if they have
been cheated—arbitrarily excluded from a form of insurance that straight
couples in similar circumstances can take for granted. From Bryce and
Patrick's perspective, for example, marriage offers a practical solution
to a variety of insecurities and anxieties they feel in their everyday lives.
With marriage, Bryce would not have to worry about deportation; Patrick would not feel overwhelmed by his role as the family breadwinner. In
short, from Patrick's perspective, marriage would insure him and Bryce
against the "discrimination disease."

I do not argue that all aspects of marriage or the fight for same-sex
marriage is reducible to this model; however, risk-based discourses do
allow marriage to seem like a "smart" lifestyle choice when it is also a
central site for projects of self-governance and normative regulation. In

this way, Wolfson's and others' characterization of marriage as a lifestyle choice enables this neo-liberal sleight of hand. Risk-based rationalities give proponents of same-sex marriage a language with which to express their personal fears in a way that resonates with neo-liberal political economic projects to economize the function of the state. More important, risk discourses construct gays and lesbians (not just those who desire marriage) as a particular *collectivity* whose continued existence depends on "marriage protections."

Family Members Only

About three years ago, Sue and Ann Jacman received a phone call at 2:00 a.m. A calming voice on the other line asked for Sue. A receptionist at Hamilton General Hospital apologized for the early-morning call and regretfully informed her that EMTs had just admitted her daughter to the emergency room for serious injuries sustained in a car accident. Ann and Sue dressed in yesterday's clothing and sped to Hamilton General. When they arrived, as Sue put it, "I remember so well, I pushed into the door, and right there was a sign." She pointed to the words in the air as if the sign were hanging in front of her: "Family Members Only." Sue and Ann had loved and cared for each other for thirty-one years and raised a family of four children together. Yet they were not the family members to which this sign was referring. Almost immediately Sue instructed Ann: " 'You are going to have to be my sister.' She [Ann] said, 'What are you talking about? Let's just go.' I said, 'They have every right to kick you out of this room if you don't claim to be my sister, and that's that.' This was so degrading at that moment. I had to stop in this real emergency and think about what I would say our relationship was to strangers." Still unsure about what she would say to any hospital authority, Ann entered the ICU with Sue. In the end, the nurse took them at their word that they were family.

In the United States, civil marriage and blood ties compose the legal definition of the "family" to which the sign referred. Understandably, Ann and Sue also want their relationship, which they consider to be just as loving and stable as any different-sex marriage, to be recognized so they can protect themselves from the insecurity, degradation, and anxiety that comes with being denied access to a family member's hospital room.

The kind of alienation that Sue and Ann felt as they opened the door to the ICU is part of a working narrative that same-sex marriage activists draw on to explain how being denied marriage prevents them from fully protecting themselves and their families in the event of life's inevitable dangers. Almost all of the activists in committed relationships with whom I spent time in Waterford and Hamilton had some kind of story about at least the fear of being barred from their partner's or child's hospital room.

The hospital narrative is not expressed by proponents of same-sex marriage only in Waterford and Hamilton. Many variations on the hospital narrative also appear in court testimonies from same-sex couples across the United States. For example, in my analysis of prominent state court cases considering the constitutionality of same-sex marriage in Washington, New York, Oregon, New Jersey, and California, I found the hospital narrative in 56 percent of the official affidavits from same-sex couples.[3] These affidavits, written by individuals in same-sex relationships requesting the right to marry, included either a personal experience or a feeling of anxiety due to a hospital administration's refusing access to his or her partner's hospital room because of their marital status.

While in most cases, visitation works out in the end, there are a handful of very extreme and dramatic accounts of losing one's partner without having the chance to say good-bye. Lambda Legal Defense and Education Fund uses the following dramatic version of the hospital narrative to drive home the risks of being denied marriage: "Initially the hospital refused to allow Bill to be with Robert because they were not family. By the time the hospital relented, Robert was in a coma. Robert died without regaining consciousness. Because the hospital would not recognize their relationship, Bill and Robert never said goodbye. Robert spent his last waking hours alone."[4] Examples like Bill and Robert's constitute the worst-case scenario for same-sex couples: this could happen to them. Thus, even though many hospital narratives actually have happy endings in which the hospital administration ignored or refused to enforce hospital rules, the real problem is the lack of predictability. What will happen next time? Many same-sex couples feel that they are more subject to luck or chance than married couples, who need not worry about whether they will deal with a sympathetic nurse. Married couples get to feel a sense of security in times of crisis. The hospital narrative is particularly important because it resonates with risk-based political rationalities that find unwarranted subjection to fate unjust (Ewald 1991).

Marriage provides security and safety by creating a predictable structure that tames many aspects of life otherwise left up to chance or fate. With their hospital experience as a backdrop, Sue and Ann Jacman decided to get involved in same-sex marriage activism even though all four of their children had grown and moved out of the house. Sue recalls how her hope for marriage equality changed over time: "When we first [got involved with MRN,] we were not for the 'M' word, but then we came to realize that it is really only marriage that would offer us true equality." They both felt as if they were "getting to the age" at which they would start worrying about how to "protect their family when something happens." From Ann's perspective, straight couples often do not even realize how they are protected from the unknowns in life: "When you get married, you lock into a certain set of laws that go along with marriage. You never really think about them until something happens—until you have a child or get divorced, or somebody gets sick. These are things that we can't get, no matter what we do." What is most revealing about Ann's remark is her understanding of when marriage becomes important. Marriage allows a couple access to predictable and stable legal avenues that protect them when accidents happen. In this sense, marriage is like having a good retirement plan or dependable car insurance. Marriage counts when life's inevitable risks emerge.

Same-sex marriage activists thus argue that they have a legitimate political grievance because they are systematically more at risk if they were to draw one of life's "unlucky numbers" (Ewald 1991, 202). Just as having car insurance will not reduce the risk of the insured's being in an accident, marriage would not reduce the probability of individuals' drawing an unlucky number. However, as is the case with car insurance, marriage does minimize the resulting financial and emotional damages. Specifically, marriage comes with a sense of security that "you are in good hands" if chance strikes.

For same-sex marriage activists, this hope for safety comes by conflating the compensatory with the preventative function of insurance. One particular couple, Jack and Steve, active in MRN, expressed this conflation in terms of protecting each other from the "inevitable ups and downs of life." When I asked Steve what marriage would protect him from, he replied:

> Well, I think that, um, . . . my first answer is protection in the sense that, not that there is a threat, but protection in the sense that anyone . . . wants to take care of their spouse or life partner. I mean, what if I die? I mean, what if I die soon? Will Jack be protected? So I mean protection in that sense.

When I asked, "So what does Jack need to be protected from?" Steve replied:

Well, let me put it in a slightly different way. If you look at the wedding vows themselves, the traditional wedding vows, they embody the vicissitudes of life: for richer or poorer, in sickness and in health, for better or for worse. They are actually speaking of the inevitable ups and downs of life. We don't know which ones are going to hit us, but they very directly, then, are reflected in the protections that marriage tries to give. . . . So the literal answer to your question is protection from the unknown. People who are able to get legally married get to take all of that for granted. You don't have to think about it. Like, oh, shit, I died without making a will. . . . We don't get to have that taken care of.

As evidenced in Steve's statement, marriage does not just minimize potential damages that could come from a "social accident" such as poverty, illness, or other "ups and downs of life"; marriage also captures a utopian vision that legally recognized couples can help each other *prevent* economic hardships. For example, Steve believes that marriage would help prevent Jack from experiencing poverty, as it would make him eligible for Steve's Social Security spousal benefit. This is a key characteristic of political claims in a risk-based society. As Ulrich Beck describes it, "The dream of class society is that everyone wants and ought to have a share of the pie. The utopia of the risk society is that everyone should be spared from poisoning" (1992, 49).

As Anthony Giddens argues, this slippage between compensating and preventing accidents is what allows risk discourses to "colonize the future" by constructing what is yet to come as "a new terrain—a territory of counterfactual possibility" (1991, 111). When the future becomes one potentially manipulated element in a risk calculation, the distinction between preventing accidents and minimizing the impact of ensuing damages becomes less meaningful. In the case of marriage, it is as if the feeling of security that comes with marriage extends beyond particular accidents to include a general sense of future safety—that one has less to fear if provided the protections of marriage.

This utopian fantasy of safety, characteristic of a "risk-based society," obscures a shift of responsibility for population-level problems of poverty and illness from the state to legally recognized couples. As a result, marriage equality activists tend to view marriage as a smart lifestyle choice that provides an immediate set of protections from life's risks. The risk-based rationality model makes it possible to see how anxiety and the desire for safety become foundations for political grievances. With regard to same-sex marriage, this means unmarried couples are left unprotected in a dangerous and unpredictable world. What better way to feel safe than by gaining access to the "legal" home, which historically has been constructed as the "haven in a heartless world" (Lasch 1977)? Marriage provides a stable structure to translate the unpredictable blows of ill fortune into compensable and preventable accidents. In the next section, I show how this sense of future safety is also symbolized by the figure of the child.

The Children, the Future

Children hold a special significance to a political rationality of risk, for they represent the future orientation of "risk-consciousness. . . . We become active today in order to prevent, alleviate or take precautions against the problems and crises of tomorrow" (Beck 1992, 34). Coming to drastically different conclusions about whether same-sex marriage should be legalized, both proponents and conservative opponents of same-sex marriage use the figure of "the child" to articulate why marriage is important for the security of future Americans.

According to the conservative perspective, the institution of marriage secures the future of American society by providing children with a sense of stability and security. On March 30, 2004, Vincent P. McCarthy, of the American Center for Law and Justice, testified before the US Senate Committee on the Judiciary regarding the importance of passing the Defense of Marriage Act (DOMA) in order to protect marriage from same-sex couples. He remarked, "Traditional marriages, in which one man and one woman create a lasting community, transmit the values and contributions of the past to establish the promise of the future."[5] In this statement, McCarthy went on to argue that the Defense of Marriage Act is important for American families because marriage gives children a sense of security and belonging, which directly translates to a functional future society. Maggie Gallagher, president of the Institute for Marriage and Public Policy, in her testimony to the same committee on March 3, 2004, argued that different-sex marriage is not just one of many possible ways to protect children but the only *good* way to "protect children" in order to "insur[e] the future of the society."[6]

For conservatives who oppose same-sex marriage, only heterosexuality can secure the future of American society and only different-sex couples can protect children by providing a sense of biological origin. Gallagher testified that "legal protections for children are no longer tied to marital status of parents. How then does marriage protect children? Primarily by affirming a social ideal: children have a right to know and love both their mother and their father."[7] Gallagher suggests that when we live in a society that does not give children a sense of their own biological roots, "marriage culture" fails, and children are "put at risk [for] higher rates of poverty, welfare dependence, teen motherhood, juvenile delinquency, child abuse, sexual abuse, substance abuse, education failure, physical and mental illness."[8] From this side of the debate, "at-risk" children are a direct result of society's allowing diverse family forms instead of upholding the ideal of the biological, nuclear family. From the conservative, anti-same-sex-marriage perspective, "the children" and the innocence of childhood itself need to be protected from the destruction of the family unit that conservatives find inevitable if same-sex couples are allowed to marry.

Conservative opponents of same-sex marriage are not the only ones worried about protecting children with the institution of marriage. Children also appear as central figures in pro-same-sex-marriage narratives. Grievances expressed in terms of how children will benefit from the protection of same-sex marriage operate in the context of a risk-based political rationality. Like opponents of same-sex marriage, supporters also see children as the symbol of the future. Plainly stated, when you put "innocent children" at risk, you put the future of the population at risk. Childhood represents a state of vulnerability and innocence that marriage allegedly protects. In this way, children emerge as important symbols in narratives expressing forward-looking grievances that follow from a risk-based political rationality.

Given the symbolic importance of children in the expression of political grievances, it makes sense that proponents of same-sex marriage would include children in their political message. Members of Equality California, a pro-same-sex-marriage organization, decided to literally make children the messengers. In September 2005, after the California legislature passed the Religious Freedom and Civil Marriage Protection Act (AB19), which would have made same-sex marriage legal in California, Equality California had children deliver to Governor Schwarzenegger over forty thousand pink cards from voters encouraging him to sign AB19, pulling them in little red wagons.[9] Clearly the mode of delivery was a way of appropriating the "child" from conservative "family values" narratives. As Stevi Jackson and Sue Scott (1999) argue that parents' anxieties about life in general often get projected onto children, in this case, we can see how children also symbolically express the vulnerability of a population of same-sex couples denied access to "marriage protections."

For proponents of same-sex marriage, children are particularly vulnerable to risks stemming from their parents' not having a legal marriage. Unlike conservative arguments against same-sex marriage, this narrative rejects sex essentialism. In this line of argument, it is important for children to be raised in two-parent families, but the sexes of the parents are not significant for the development of children or, by symbolic proxy, the future of society. Children need marriage protection due to practical concerns, such as how to get children the best medical insurance if the nonlegal parent has better coverage. Many same-sex couples who would like to marry also argue that they worry about what will happen to their children if the nonlegal parent dies, leaving the children ineligible for his or her Social Security benefits. On an everyday level, same-sex couples who want marriage also frequently talk about the school as a social context in which it is difficult to be same-sex parents who cannot marry. Nonlegal parents complain about troubles with picking up their children from school or express a sense of irritation and humiliation because they constantly have to explain their relationship to school officials.

About half (46 percent) of same-sex couples' affidavits in the state court cases referred to in the previous section also focused on the fear and vulnerability they feel because their children are growing up with parents who are unmarried. The percentage of affidavits that include arguments about protecting the children of same-sex couples is disproportionate considering that census data projects that only 22 percent of male same-sex couples and 33 percent of female same-sex couples have children.[10] By emphasizing the concerns of couples with children, same-sex marriage activists hope to counter conservatives' claims that heterosexual married couples provide the best environment for rearing them.

Proponents of same-sex marriage argue that same-sex couples are capable of raising children as well as heterosexual couples, but same-sex couples face significant hurdles because they are not allowed the legal protections that come with marriage. Therefore, any difference in parenting comes not from the sex of the parents but from the legal structure that denies same-sex couples access to mechanisms to properly raise children. In an amicus brief to the Oregon Supreme Court in *Li and Kennedy v. State of Oregon*(2005), the Juvenile Rights Project and several social work associations argued that the court should extend marriage to same-sex couples in order to provide their children a sense of security: "The fact that parental breakup can be a difficult, and often destructive, experience for children is not seriously disputed. Marriage will fortify committed relationships between parents of the same sex and thereby enhance the stable caretaking, permanence, and security that comes from having two available parents. . . . To the extent that the legal protections and obligations of civil marriage are designed, in large part, to support and fortify committed relationships[,] same-sex partners, and ultimately the children of their relationships, will benefit similarly from the same protections."[11] In this statement, the Juvenile Rights Project and its associates articulate the benefits of marriage for the children of same-sex couples using a language similar to that of their conservative opponents: marriage protects children by making their lives more stable and secure. Both proponents' and conservative opponents' arguments articulate the insecurity and anxiety about the future that come with living in a society focused on risk (Beck 1992; Wilkinson 2001). For proponents of same-sex marriage, however, it is the legal protections, not the sense of biological origin, that make marriage an essential institution for raising children.

According to the American Academy of Pediatrics (AAP) and the American Psychological Association (APA), this sense of security that comes from having two married parents has essential mental health benefits for same-sex couples and their children. An article in support of co-parenting rights for same-sex couples written by the AAP and submitted as evidence in a federal legislative hearing concerning "threats" to marriage takes the following stance: "Denying legal parent status through adoption to coparents or second parents prevents these children from enjoying the psychologic[al] and legal security that comes from having 2 willing, capable and loving parents."[12]

The APA also used its scientific authority to argue that the importance of marriage extends well beyond the practical, legal protection to also include the psychological and overall mental health benefits that come from eliminating the stigma of having unmarried parents. In an amicus brief filed in *Li v. State of Oregon*, the APA stated:

> Marriage can be expected to benefit the children of gay and lesbian couples by reducing the stigma currently associated with those children's status. . . . When same-sex partners cannot marry, their biological children are born "out of wedlock," by conferring a status that historically has been stigmatized as "illegitimacy" and "bastardy." . . . As a result, children of parents who are not married may be stigmatized by others, such as peers or school staff members.

> This stigma of illegitimacy will not be visited upon the children of same-sex couples when those couples can legally marry.[13]

Notice that the answer here is to solve the problem of stigma for children who have two parents of the same sex, leaving the reader to wonder why we would not try to address the stigma applied to children of the unmarried in general. In this model, the APA draws our attention to how children of same-sex, unmarried parents are exposed to risks that children with married parents never have to bear. Stigmatized children are harassed by peers and treated differently by school officials. The APA's statement also raises the question of whether marital status alone will address the social stigma faced by children of same-sex couples. What about the stigma of having two moms or two dads? In this formulation, risk rationalities perform a normative function: essentially, the APA is suggesting that marital status could normalize same-sex families.

On behalf of the National Sexuality Resource Center, Gilbert Herdt and Robert Kerzner extend the APA's claims about children to future generations: "Marriage supports mental and physical health and therefore . . . the denial of marriage rights to gay men and lesbians not only compromises their well-being, that of their children, and the well-being of future generations but also ultimately undermines the citizenship of these individuals" (2006, 43). Marriage, then, is the ultimate form of insurance. It protects children from mental and physical ailments, it keeps children healthy, it protects generations to come, and it provides individuals with the benefits of belonging in their nation.

Thus, it appears that we have come full circle, starting with McCarthy's belief that the nation's future depends on children raised in married households and ending with the same assertion by many proponents of same-sex marriage. In arguments both for and against marriage, "the child," as Lauren Berlant eloquently suggests, "is a *stand-in* for a complicated and contradictory set of anxieties and desires about national identity" (1997, 6; italics in the original). Proponents of same-sex marriage symbolically struggle to have the child on their side of the debate, because the child represents a vulnerable figure completely worthy of protection from future dangers.

While proponents and conservative opponents of same-sex marriage come to drastically different conclusions, they both articulate marriage as a form of insurance. For conservatives who oppose same-sex marriage, the insurance only protects the health of the nation when it gives children a sense of biological origin. For proponents, on the other hand, marriage protects the health of the nation because it provides a set of legal structures that make it possible to manage life's risks and thus make children feel safe.

Using the political rationality of risk, same-sex marriage activists can make their claims resonate and argue that if marriage is how society manages potential dangers, then they, too, should have access to this institution. Children become a particularly important element of same-sex marriage activists' arguments because they represent the potential for marriage to prevent feelings of insecurity about the future. More important, the debate over the children also indicates how marriage equality activists can appropriate risk discourse in a way that explicitly rejects marriage as a heteronormative institution (predicated on sex essentialism) at the same time that it upholds marriage as a neo-liberal regulatory ideal.

Protecting the "Community": Gay Bashing, Teen Suicide, and Anonymous Sex

For many MRN members, marriage not only allows same-sex couples to manage population-level risks, such as illness and poverty; it also protects all gays and lesbians by making them more valued by society as a whole. Same-sex marriage activists see marriage as a way to insure gays and lesbians in general—not just those who would marry—from three main forms of danger resulting from the stigma of being excluded from marriage: gay bashing, teen suicide, and anonymous sex. By appropriating risk-based political rationalities, same-sex marriage activists actively construct, rather than simply describe, a gay collectivity populated by individuals whose dispositions and everyday lives are allegedly oriented toward marriage.

The unique power of marriage protections, for proponents of marriage equality, is precisely their ability to extend the benefits of normalization to gay and lesbian subjects who do not choose marriage for their own lives. Thus, marriage might be a lifestyle choice for those same-sex couples who desire marriage, but it also operates as a regulatory ideal (Foucault 1990) that "produces the [collectivity] it governs" (Butler 1993) and orients them to practices of neo-liberal governance. MRN discourse frames the "gay community" in general as "at-risk," but nevertheless responsible, subjects that need and deserve the normative regulation and symbolic status that marriage provides.

Defining the "gay and lesbian community" as those who desire marriage has obvious political advantages for the same-sex marriage movement, but its construction cannot be reduced to the long-standing tension within gay and lesbian social movements between assimilationist and separatist models I discuss in chapter 1. Moreover, activists' risk rationalities at times borrow from marriage narratives consistent with the religious Right, but the driving force of this discourse revolves around its ability to fuse activists' feelings of vulnerability with the unique legal and normative protections offered only by the institution of marriage in the United States.

As Joshua Gamson argues, the creation of collective identities in social movements is not a universal necessity but a response to the larger American political context that "makes stable collective identities both necessary and damaging" (1995, 402–3). Gamson focused on minority politics as one type of American political context; I look to neo-liberal models of governance that frame structural vulnerabilities as a product of poor risk calculations on the part of individuals. Given this political-economic framework, it makes perfect sense for same-sex marriage activists to construct gays and lesbians in general as a collectivity invested in the logic of risk management; however, this collective identity is problematic because it rests upon constructing an excluded other who represents the potential danger gays and lesbians pose to American society if they are refused marriage protection, an issue I explore in chapter 6.

Many members of Marriage Rights Now feel that marriage is important to the "gay and lesbian community" as a form of protection from dangers associated with social stigma. The reality of the fear of gay bashing, and the hope for marriage to offer gays and lesbians protection from violence, poignantly came to the forefront of members' minds on an MRN trip to a rural community, "Pine Haven," in the eastern part of the state.

I tagged along on the trip with Dana and Marsha Fitzpatrick, who had been together for five years and were legally married in Massachusetts. Dana and Marsha fit the common demographic of MRN chapter leaders: white, middle-class, and in a committed same-sex relationship. Dana and Marsha often introduce themselves to a public audience as a couple who have been "married to each other more than once in the past five years." They used their savings to travel around the United States, "collecting several marriage licenses," one of which had recently been revoked.

While their toddler sat with me in the backseat of their SUV describing her love for peanut butter crackers, Marsha signaled our entrance to Pine

Haven County: "Wow, did you see that sign?" Marsha was referring to a posted poaching warning; "We have definitely entered the country." Dana seemed to voice Marsha's unarticulated assumption: "Yes, we have now entered a scary place." Once we reached the town of Pine Haven, we were greeted by a banner hanging from an overpass that, for Dana and Marsha, immediately defined this small community's stance on marriage equality: "Homosexuality Is a Sin." With a population of 150, Pine Haven was the type of community MRN city folks found reminiscent of a "close-minded" place like Laramie, Wyoming.[14]

Pine Haven was on MRN's target list of towns in a county that did not yet have an MRN chapter. The MRN leadership council found a contact in the town named Margaret, a white business owner who recently celebrated her sixtieth birthday and who might be willing to create some support for the organization. Dana, Marsha, and I arrived at Margaret's family-owned hotel and bar as she was introducing herself to fellow MRN activists Jense and Derek Miller.

I had met Jense and Derek three months prior to our visit to Pine Haven as MRN chapter leaders willing to participate in a face-to-face interview. Typical of MRN leadership, the Millers are an affluent, married, white male couple in their early fifties. Jense and Derek's enthusiasm for marriage equality paralleled their struggle to become a legally married couple. As Derek remembered, when the state began to reconsider the legality of his marriage license, "we were spurred to activism, and we kind of got a taste, a taste of what equality was. It made us both decide, 'OK, it's time to take a stand.'" Since their recent ascension within the MRN ranks, Derek and Jense have utilized their social network of upper-middle-class professionals to organize successful fund-raisers for marriage equality. The visit to Pine Haven was their first experience in promoting new branches of MRN.

After offering us a cocktail, Margaret warned of the "antigay fanaticism in Pine Haven." Just last week, she said, a truck full of young men with shotguns drove by yelling, "Fuck faggots!" One of them actually put a bullet in the entry door of the old hotel. Margaret sarcastically called it a "country drive-by" and casually suggested that we keep a low profile. Jense, who seemed particularly moved by Margaret's "country drive-by" story, suggested that her experience was precisely why marriage is so important for gays and lesbians. He argued that it would eventually establish more social acceptance so that people "like them" would not have to be afraid just because they were "living their lives as who they are." Dana continued with this reasoning by suggesting that Margaret start a Pine Haven chapter of MRN in order to address some of the "hate and bigotry" she experiences on a day-to-day basis.

Stories like the "country drive-by," ones that posit marriage as the solution to the fear of living as a socially stigmatized population, are frequently retold in MRN meetings and informal conversations. These stories serve to remind marriage equality activists that their fight for marriage is not a selfish one; it is made on behalf of a "community of gays and lesbians." MRN activists often act as unelected representatives of folks like Margaret who, in her own words, must "keep a low profile" in order to "avoid being a target of antigay fanaticism in Pine Haven." In this formulation, marriage is important precisely because it is not just a lifestyle choice—it is an institution with the productive, regulatory power to create normative acceptance of gays and lesbians as full citizens. Thus, risk-based political rationalities not only help individualize responsibility for those who willingly advocate self-governance of population-level problems; they also generalize the power of marriage to assuage the fear even in the absence of explicit consent to the marriage contract.

MRN members are not alone in their belief that denying same-sex couples the right to marry generates social stigma. The American Psychological Association, in its amicus brief in support of the plaintiffs in *Li v. Oregon*, argued that by refusing to legitimate same-sex marriages, the state perpetuates the social stigma against gays and lesbians: "By denying same-sex couples the right to marry and thereby devaluing and delegitimizing the relationships that are at the very core of a homosexual orientation, the State compounds and perpetuates the stigma historically attached to homosexuality. This stigma affects not only the members of same-sex couples who seek to be married, but all homosexual persons, regardless of their relationship status or desire to marry."[15] In this statement, the APA testifies that marriage is important for "all homosexual persons" because marriage is a means by which individuals become valued members of American society. As Patrick said in the opening of this chapter, marriage could cure and maybe even prevent the "discrimination disease" by placing a state seal of approval on same-sex monogamy.

According to many proponents of same-sex marriage, state legitimization would not only prevent acts of violence against gays and lesbians, but it would also alleviate the fear and anxiety that comes from being a stigmatized population. Mitzi Henderson, the national president of Parents, Families and Friends of Lesbians and Gays (PFLAG), in her testimony before the U.S. Judiciary Committee considering the constitutionality of DOMA in 1996, drew from personal experience to express the fear she feels because her son is a target of violence against gays and lesbians. "As a parent of a gay son, I face particular challenges. I am forced to worry about my gay son in a way that I do not worry about my other children. Some parents have lost their child to suicide, or to gay bashing. . . . And so I fear for Jamie—not because of who he is, but because I know the price of intolerance. In 1994 more than 4,000 people were physically assaulted in nine cities because they are gay or lesbian. I live with that fear."[16] Henderson asked the Judiciary Committee to understand her and her son's *fear* and lack of *security* as a political grievance that the state ought to consider.

Many other proponents of same-sex marriage whom I met discuss problems of social stigma and see marriage as a historically proven way to legitimate and protect populations. Sue, whom I introduced earlier, relates gay stigma to racial stigma and argues that once gay marriage is legal, then Americans will learn to accept gay couples just as they learned to accept interracial couples. Although they cite no evidence to suggest that Americans have actually accepted interracial couples, same-sex marriage advocates feel that they have some precedent to suggest that marriage does in fact reduce risk factors associated with being a stigmatized population.

Proponents of same-sex marriage also argue that stigma can make all gays and lesbians more susceptible to self-hatred. Many same-sex marriage activists believe that social stigma not only perpetuates external acts of violence from those hostile to gays and lesbians; stigma can also be internalized, making gays and lesbians question their own self-worth.

Before we traveled to Pine Haven, Jense Miller explained this argument to me when I asked him in an interview why he thought marriage was so important for same-sex couples. Sitting next to his husband, Derek, who explained his motivation for marriage as securing the "same rights as heterosexual couples," Jense distanced himself from his husband's explanation and instead remarked:

> To me, marriage is important for a more fundamental reason than just tax benefits and inheritance rights. It has to do more with the whole stigma put on the gay population that being gay is essentially, whether people admit it or not, is essentially wrong. . . . Kids feel pressured to hide their sexuality. This is also why gay teen suicide rates are so high; they are afraid to admit that they are gay.

> This also ties into the gay-bashing thing. . . . I think that marriage is important
> because it is just one other way to lift the stigma on being gay.

In this heartfelt explanation, Jense sees the financial gains from lower taxes
as a fringe benefit rather than a primary motivation to fight for marriage
equality. Thus, Jense's passion about marriage cannot simply be described
as an effort to secure class privilege as an upper-middle-class professional.
In fact, he and Derek see their class status and age as a fortunate advantage
that allows them to sacrifice personal assets of time and money for all gays
and lesbians. Derek clarifies: "It takes the people that are older and . . .
willing to donate time and financial resources to the cause." Similarly,
Jense does not see his role in MRN as a way to secure the smooth operation of neo-liberal governance; instead, Jense gets fired up about marriage
when he thinks about the physical risks that living without marriage poses
for gays and lesbians who feel compelled to "hide their sexuality."

Jense reflects upon his first marriage, to a woman, and the silence and
shame it represented as it relates to what he sees as risks endemic to gays
and lesbians in general:

> I felt pressure to get married and to do everything that my church and society
> expected of me, and the, the pain of the breakup that my wife and family ex-
> perienced could have been avoided had I seen that there were other possibili-
> ties. And a lot of people think, "Well, now things are so much different." They
> are much better than when I was growing up, but there are still plenty of kids,
> people that feel pressured to hide their sexuality. They are afraid to admit they
> are gay. . . . You have kids who are afraid to admit that they are gay, and they are
> still going to get married, and they are still going to find that this just really isn't
> working for them either, and you will continue to have broken families. So, and
> gay bashing, the whole thing, and it all ties together.

For Jense, marriage is a form of liberation from stigma because it would
allow gays to be able to tell the truth about "who they are" and address
the self-hatred and fear that come from internalizing one's classification as
a stigmatized member of society. In this sense, managing the risk factors
that contribute to teen suicide and gay bashing would also heal gay and
lesbian shame.

The "country drive-by" that Margaret warned of can be viewed as an
externalized effect of stigma; on the other hand, the teen suicide rates
Jense points to are even more insidious because internalized social stigma

results in a form of self-destructiveness to which every member of the gay population may be exposed. Same-sex marriage activists claim a political grievance on behalf of an abstract collectivity of current and future gay and lesbian teens who, by virtue of their stigmatized status, experience higher rates of suicide.

Jense's fears are backed up by the same American Psychological Association amicus brief that charged the state with perpetuating social stigma by denying same sex couples the right to marry:

> Like heterosexuals, gay people can be adversely affected by high levels of stress. The link between experiencing stress and manifesting symptoms of psychological or physical illness is well established in human beings and other species. To the extent that the portion of the population with a homosexual orientation is subjected to additional stress beyond what is normally experienced by the heterosexual population, it may, as a group, manifest somewhat higher levels of illness or psychological distress. Differences in stress between the heterosexual population and the homosexual population can be attributed largely to the societal stigma directed at the latter.[17]

The APA expresses stigma as a factor that increases stress levels and thus raises levels of illness in the "homosexual population." This argument finds voice in a risk-based perspective concerned with managing *rates* of illness across a population. In concluding its brief, the APA argues that allowing same-sex marriage will help heal the social stigma attached to gays in general and lower the extent to which the entire gay population is at risk.

Some proponents of same-sex marriage emphasize an additional way that marriage will protect gays and lesbians from social stigma: it will reduce sexual risk taking on the part of gay males. This argument has more conservative and less conservative aspects. According to a more conservative point of view, expressed by many Log Cabin Republicans, sexual risk taking is a direct consequence of sexual promiscuity. According to the less conservative articulation of this argument, sexual risk taking comes from a "culture of subterfuge" in which stigma against gay sex leads gay men to make risky sexual decisions in order to conceal their sexual orientation. For both ends of the spectrum, marriage would prevent gay men from destroying themselves by making dangerous sexual choices.

The more conservative side of this argument articulates Jonathan Rauch's (2004) view that same-sex marriage will "civilize" gay men and help them reduce the risks of promiscuous, public, and anonymous sex.

The claims for a political remedy are based on a vaguely defined sense of a "male homosexual community" whose collectivity is more "at risk" than the "heterosexual community." From this perspective, the collectivity of gay males is at risk in part because they have been denied access to marriage, an institution that Rauch characterizes as the "great domesticator" (2004, 20).

Craig Shilling, a former chapter leader for the Waterford Log Cabin Republicans, expressed the most conservative iteration of this argument—at least in comparison to the members of MRN and affiliated groups with whom I spoke. Craig's ten-month tenure with the Waterford chapter had won him access to a position of leadership within the national organization. Craig shares many of the social characteristics of the MRN leadership: he is a white upper-middle-class professional between the ages of thirty-five and fifty. However, unlike many MRN members, he expressed no interest in national health insurance or economic equality. Craig also distanced his approach from that of MRN in terms of the intended audience. Craig describes his main activity as educating the Republican Party, rather than the American public in general, about the importance of marriage.

When I asked Craig why he felt passionate about advocating for marriage, he responded with the equal rights discourse commonly used by members of MRN: "It goes back to the basic doctrine that there is no such thing as separate but equal. Marriage is a legalized way that same-sex couples can have the privileges of heterosexual couples. They can have property rights, the ability to care for their spouse and their kids, and all of the things that heterosexuals take for granted. . . . It promotes stability within families." When I prompted Craig to say more about how marriage promotes stability, he echoed Rauch's sentiments about the promise of marriage to tame gay male sexuality:

> The gay culture is promiscuous, and part of that, like I said, is because there is no defined progression to the point of marriage. I believe this 100 percent. . . . I haven't studied the gay and lesbian movement. It is just my impression that they want to do what they want. Since there isn't marriage, it is not part of their lives. You know, straight couples start in junior high school. You know, they start holding hands, and it is a progression to get married and have kids. There is nothing like this in the gay community.

For Craig, marriage would provide a clear way for gay males to live more structured lives. Instead of having anonymous sex in bathhouses and parks, the expectation of marriage would house gay sex in the sanctity of the marital bed. By this logic, sexual promiscuity and "wanton" male behavior (Rauch 2004, 77) are naturalized, as if men are inherently more insatiable than women. For Craig, one does not need scientific proof to believe that gay men are more likely to engage in "risky sex." From his perspective, society sees promiscuity on the part of gay males just by tuning in to *Queer Eye for the Straight Guy* or footage from Gay Pride parades that to him signal a lack of sexual restraint.

However, according to more liberal proponents of same-sex marriage, gay males may not be particularly promiscuous or rogue, but social stigma forces gay men to create what Patrick, a registered Democrat, calls a "culture of subterfuge where people sneak around and have sex on the side and are not honest about it. . . . If you just look at HIV, for example, you know the damage that is done because people cannot be honest about who they are." From Patrick's perspective, risky sex is a problem for gay males, not because they are promiscuous but because they live in a society that does not allow them to be honest about themselves. Patrick reasons that marriage would help address this sexual risk taking by providing gay males with enough social legitimacy that they would no longer feel the need to "sneak" around.

Jorge Caberro, a member of a small group affiliated with MRN, describes himself as an open-minded person concerned about a number of social justice issues, including marriage. Motivated by his parents' experience emigrating from Latin America to the United States, Jorge volunteers for a local immigrant rights group assisting with citizenship applications. Like Patrick, Jorge mentions risk and protection associated with HIV/AIDS to explain the importance of marriage for gay men. Jorge contrasts the "gay community's desire for sexual freedom in the 1970s" with the unfortunate consequences of AIDS, which had the unintended impact of "showing us that the gay community is about compassion, not just sex." Jorge connects the importance of the marriage debate to the lack of government protection and recognition during the AIDS crisis: "Marriage provides legal protections, and it would allow gays to take their rightful place, to be recognized for their humanity."

Proponents of same-sex marriage also draw from more probabilistic models to argue that marriage would in fact reduce sexual risk taking among gay men. In a policy brief prepared on behalf of the National Bureau of Economic Research, Thomas Dee compares European countries that have adopted some form of marriage for same-sex couples and those that have not in terms of the rates of syphilis, gonorrhea, and AIDS among self-identified gays.[18] Dee argues that there is a statistically significant relationship between same-sex marriage laws and reduced levels of syphilis. He concludes that "the empirical evidence presented here is consistent with the view that gay marriage reduces risky sexual behavior."[19]

From each perspective on gay males' "risky sexual behaviors," marriage is viewed as a viable form of insurance to reduce the public health risk factors for disease in the gay male population. Thus, the freedom to marry, according to this logic, is more about restricting "potentially dangerous" forms of behavior rather than increasing personal choice and sexual autonomy for same-sex couples. As Pat O'Malley and Mariana Valverde (2004) argue, in risk-based rationalities, pleasure is defined by the carefully regulated pursuit of happiness that aids the governmental strategy of governing at a distance. O'Malley and Valverde (2004) use the example of early 1900s discussions of alcohol use among the American working class. They found that reform discourse aimed at managing the "disorder" and "chaos" caused by working-class men defined the overconsumption of alcohol as a way to make up for the loss of pleasure. From a risk-based perspective, pleasure and freedom do not come from a complete lack of control or full expression of unbridled passions; instead, true pleasure can come only when one carefully regulates her- or himself by restricting unbridled passions.

*   *   *

According to proponents of same-sex marriage, the government prevents them from managing potential dangers in their lives the way straight couples can. Their immediate families and the collectivity of gays and lesbians as a whole are vulnerable, unprotected from potential economic hardships and the insecurity that comes from living as a stigmatized population. While most of the same-sex marriage activists involved in groups like MRN think this risk comes from being denied the same protections as straight couples, other more conservative arguments for same-sex marriage see the risks that marriage can manage as inherent in gay male culture or the physiology of males in general. In each case, marriage would bring equality to gays and lesbians by transforming moments of ill fortune and crisis into manageable and predictable accidents.

Proponents of same-sex marriage actively work to construct gay subjectivities as ones capable of self-regulation. This is a prerequisite to government efficiency because the state must be able to count on those subjects who are given the "privilege" of regulating themselves. The arguments proponents use often include specific statements about the worthiness of the gay population to control itself and the demonstration that they have been inculcated with risk-based knowledge that helps them make life decisions to reduce their chances of succumbing to dangers. The inability to legally marry becomes a political grievance because it prevents gay subjects from regulating themselves according to a risk-based rationality.

By understanding how same-sex marriage activists articulate marriage as a form of insurance, sociologists can shed new light on why same-sex couples would work so hard to gain access to an institution constructed in opposition to ideals of sexual freedom once central to the gay rights movement and how it makes sense to conflate same-sex couples who want marriage with the so-called homosexual population as a whole. From proponents' perspective, why would gays and lesbians waste time advocating sexual freedom in a world full of risk factors stemming from anonymous sex? What harm would it do to conceptualize a "homosexual population" and conflate it with same-sex couples when it only makes sense that people would form stable couple dyads in a country devoid of any other mainstream model of social care? Understanding marriage as a form of insurance allows sociologists to see how marriage itself is an expression of neo-liberal mentalities of governing populations.

CHAPTER FOUR

The Bribe

Free Choice and Privacy

Judy Marshal found herself at the center of same-sex marriage activism in the spring of 2003. She had volunteered with several gay, lesbian, and transgender rights groups for years, speaking at public events and organizing community awareness campaigns. When Hamilton City Hall began issuing marriage licenses to same-sex couples, Judy started to educate herself about the kinds of protections that the state routinely denies same-sex couples because they cannot marry. While not ready to marry at the time, Judy felt a passion for "marriage equality" because it appealed to her own "sense of justice" and seemed to provide an avenue for addressing the social stigma she blamed for gay teenagers' high risk of suicide.

For Judy, the risk of teen suicide is the justification for marriage equality that "is closest to her heart." Her teenage brother Charles tried to kill himself a few weeks after he came out to his sister. According to Judy, Charles felt a great deal of internalized shame over being gay in a world where some treat gay people as freaks. Like others I spoke with, Judy felt as if broadening marriage to include same-sex couples would begin to dissolve social hatred of gays and lesbians and give gay youths "more self-respect and more of a sense of being normal, and not being a freak."

Although Judy clearly expressed the power of marriage to validate "gay people," she felt confident enough about her own sexuality to reject the need for the validation that marriage could offer her:

> It is not really that I want society to tell me that I'm OK. It is not like I need approval from society. I know I am OK. I don't think that I am a sinner or anything. I don't think that there is anything wrong with me. It's not that I need

validation. It is just that I want my rights. Everyone can have whatever beliefs they want, but they can't take away my civil rights just because they don't like me. I am not on some kind of a quest for legitimacy. I know I am legitimate. Just give me my damn rights and leave me alone!

Judy's personal motivations to fight for marriage equality cannot be explained by the normalization or assimilation model; rather, the campaign for same-sex marriage rights appeals to Judy's sense of justice. Marriage provides rights to privacy and free choice to which she believes gays and lesbians are entitled. From her perspective, justice for gays and lesbians means the right to choose marriage so that they can regulate themselves without the state invading their private lives.

On what basis does it make sense for proponents of same-sex marriage to avidly support this neo-liberal logic of governance that comes with marriage? When marriage is constructed as a personal lifestyle choice, the shift of governing responsibility seems to be an expression of freedom rather than a burden. Marriage appeals to marriage equality activists because it offers a zone of privacy without sacrificing state protection. In sum, the "right to marry" and the "right to privacy" effectively equate a state-constructed realm of governance with a freely chosen lifestyle. Proponents of marriage equality juxtapose the fear and anxiety of living without marriage protections from life's risks with the rewards of privacy offered to subjects who enhance rather than threaten the terms of neo-liberal self-governance. Similar to Janet Halley's (1993) concept of the heterosexual bribe in the context of equal protection, marriage operates as a neo-liberal bribe by offering its subjects distance from direct state regulation of intimacy. In exchange for the protection of privacy that marriage affords, activists serve as agents of state classification by constructing "homosexuals" as a responsible and self-regulating class worthy of self-governance.

Rewards of Self-Governance: Democracy and the Promise of Privacy

As I argued in chapter 2, when addressing critiques from the Left, proponents use the language of "lifestyle choice" to distinguish their advocacy of marriage from support for universal care structures, which they see as a separate, yet compatible political goal. However, marriage equality activists also use the language of choice to frame marriage as a family structure that uniquely embodies the values of democratic governance, including the right to "privacy" from direct state surveillance.

Underlying MRN's language constructing the right to marry as a personal choice is a parallel discourse about the importance of responsible choices in democratic forms of governance. Hazel Butler, for example, explained how she has difficulty understanding why people cannot just marry whomever they choose: "Why shouldn't you have the right to marry whoever you are attracted to, and not the person that society has arranged? You know it is like society is creating an arranged marriage for you [those who would like to marry someone of the same sex]. That's not what this country is about, so we should have this right." With this statement, Hazel calls to mind the same set of representations historian Nancy Cott (2000) describes: early theorists of democratic governance understood consensual, monogamous marriage as a foundation for citizens who could handle the responsibility of choosing their state representatives. The right to vote for political representatives was held analogous to the right to choose one's marital partner. "An arranged marriage represented coercion" (Cott 2000, 151), whereas romantic-love marriage represented democratic ideals of freely choosing one's government. Arranged marriages = coercion = undemocratic, whereas freely chosen marriages = consent = democratic. The symbolic effect of this equation is to associate the free choice of one's marriage partner with the freedom of living under a system of democratic self-governance.

Moreover, by juxtaposing arranged with "freely chosen" marriage, Hazel appeals not only to democratic values but also to neo-liberal ones. The fact that marriage since the second half of the twentieth century operates according to the logic of democratic free choice does not imply the absence of legal or normative regulation. Instead, marriage has shifted in accordance with the terrain of neo-liberal governance, which requires subjects to freely choose self-regulation (Rose 1999). Hazel articulates the freedom of choice with, rather than against, the grain of neo-liberal governing strategies whose appeal is constructed in opposition to "arranged," hierarchical, or coercive technologies of governance.

Feminists who study the historical construction of domestic/family life provide a framework for understanding how proponents of same-sex marriage could view an explicit government contract as freedom from government intrusion. According to Jane Collier and her colleagues, in modern Western societies, the family operates as an ideology, a symbolic system, and a private "moral unit" defined in opposition to the so-called public and impersonal spheres of the state and the market (1997, 76). Even though the market and the state clearly shape the form and function of the family, the family operates as an ideology because it conceals the public construction of domestic life. On the ideological level, the family is "sacralized in our minds as the last stronghold against The State, as the symbolic refuge from the intrusions of the public domain that constantly threatens our sense of privacy and self-determination" (Collier, Rosaldo, and Yanagisako 1997, 78). Not only does family ideology mask the interdependent relationship among the state, the economy, and domestic life, but it does so in the name of preserving individuals' freedom from government intervention.

Feminist theorists argue that the ideology of family and the "zone of privacy" effectively mask multiple forms of domination, including patriarchy, racism, and classism. For example, from this perspective, systems of patriarchy naturalize sex difference by associating men with the public world of work and women with the private, unpaid world of the home (Ortner 1974). According to Nancy Fraser (1998), for example, the public/private dichotomy does not accurately describe social space; instead, it operates as an ideology to justify women's subordination. Drawing from this line of inquiry, Lauren Berlant (1998) argues that the public/private dichotomy masks not only the power of patriarchy but also the power of the state to legitimize and protect some intimacies above all others.[1]

While these theorizations can explain how privacy masks domination, they cannot account for how governance does not require that individuals "sacralize" the family as a "stronghold against the state." In what follows, I explore how proponents of marriage equality understand the relationship between the family, privacy, and the state. I find that privacy does not operate primarily as an ideology that *masks* the power of the state to shape intimate life but as a political goal that *reveals* the irony of the state's being the ultimate source of protection from its own surveillance technologies. In other words, the power to govern through marriage does not require that subjects buy into the illusion that the public world of the state is in opposition to the private world of the family. Rather than expose the ideological function of this public/private distinction, as is characteristic of many feminist analyses of discourse, law, and patriarchy, I analyze the way privacy works to sustain a "subjective commitment from citizens" (Rose 1987, 68) in the form of a neo-liberal bribe. In short, I explore how marriage offers subjects the rewards of privacy and protection in exchange for regulating risks associated with poverty and illness.

Marriage equality activists argue that current state marriage law violates same-sex couples' right to privacy promised under the due process clause of the Constitution's Fourteenth Amendment. While many of the same-sex marriage cases ruled on by state courts have focused on equal protection arguments, the issue of privacy also forms part of the legal debate. For example, in New York's *Hernandez* case, supporters of same-sex marriage asked the court to rule current law that limits marriage to a man and a woman unconstitutional because it violates same-sex couples' right to privacy. In written statements, the plaintiffs argued that current marriage laws expose same-sex couples to "unjustified government interference" in their family lives.[2]

In its 2003 decision in *Lawrence v. Texas*, the United States Supreme Court expanded the "zone of privacy" to include acts of same-sex sodomy. In this decision, the court took an explicit turn away from *Griswold* and subsequent decisions that interpreted marriage as the proper boundary for privacy rights.[3] Justice Anthony Kennedy makes this explicit in the majority opinion: "After *Griswold* it was established that the right to make certain decisions regarding sexual conduct extends beyond the marital relationship." Given this enlarged scope of the right to privacy, in official testimony, proponents of same-sex marriage find it difficult to argue that exclusion from marriage leaves their intimate sexual lives vulnerable to state intrusion.

At the level of everyday activism, on the other hand, many MRN adherents see privacy and marriage in a pre-*Lawrence* context. Dana Fitzpatrick, for example, was very adamant about this point, insisting that if she were to write a book about same-sex marriage, she would suggest that the marriage equality movement distance itself from the issue of "gayness" altogether. For her, access to marriage allowed same-sex couples to have relationships defined by "partnership" and "commitment" rather than "the kind of sex you are having." Dana dedicated her weekends to the quest for marriage equality because she believed that only marriage would publicly proclaim that "it is none of the government's business who gays and lesbians have sex with." Regardless of protections offered by the Fourteenth Amendment, Dana believed that marriage would give gay and lesbian couples access to a common language and set of labels that publicly recognize mutual dependency while also privatizing sexuality.

Dana and Marsha also view marriage as an institution that would free them from state intrusion into their lives as parents. In public forums, while she moves down the list of the forms of discrimination that she and

Marsha face by being denied access to marriage, Dana emphasizes the process of obtaining legal parenthood. Even though Marsha and Dana were a couple when their only child was born, and Marsha is a stay-at-home mother, nearly four years later, Marsha still struggles to obtain legal parental rights.

We know the extent of state surveillance involved in the process from written affidavits to state supreme courts considering the constitutionality of denying marriage to same-sex couples. In one particularly articulate account, Lauren Abrams testified to the New York Supreme Court about difficulties she and her partner, Donna, encountered when trying to fulfill their desires to become parents. Their statement poignantly illustrates how the birth of their child, Elijah, was a joint endeavor: they even took measures to select a sperm donor who physically resembled Donna. Lauren also told the court that Donna continues to be a full parent in Elijah's life: "Elijah insists that Donna, whom he calls 'Mama Ba,' tuck him into bed at night after I give him his bath. She often sings to him before he falls asleep."[4] Lauren contrasts this intimate experience of parenthood with the state process of second-parent adoption necessary to make Donna a full, "legal" parent. "For Donna's rights as a parent to be recognized, we had to have friends write letters on our behalf to the State indicating that she would make a good parent: we had to be finger-printed; and we had to have a New York State probation officer come into our home. . . . I felt that this experience was very intrusive and extremely unjust, since married couples can obtain full parental rights automatically when they have a child."[5] Lauren's statement brilliantly expresses why same-sex couples, particularly those who want to be legal parents, would find themselves committed to fighting for access to the institution of marriage. Lauren and Donna articulate two sides of governance: hierarchical forms of state intervention that come with direct surveillance as opposed to forms of self-governance (embodied in marriage) in which the state operates at a distance by "protecting" privacy. Thus, the rewards of privacy are also bribes whose underlying threats include subjection to more authoritarian technologies of governance.

Rather than viewing marriage as a form of government surveillance that records and regulates intimate relationships, many proponents of same-sex marriage see the marriage license as a way to protect themselves from unwarranted intervention from state officials such as those who intruded into Lauren and Donna's home. Same-sex marriage activists, thus, do not view privacy as the opposite of state intervention; instead, privacy comes from the kinds of "legal protections" that state-issued marriage licenses afford. Court cases considering the constitutionality of same-sex marriage currently limit the right to privacy to "protect" personal, consensual expressions of intimacy that occur in one's own home, but same-sex marriage activists also want the courts to protect same-sex couples' right to raise children without state surveillance. By demanding the right to privacy that comes with marriage, in a post-*Lawrence* context, same-sex marriage activists are essentially asking the state to trust that same-sex couples can responsibly fulfill the governing functions of marriage—namely, to care for their own children so they do not become a financial burden for the state.

The ability to be free from direct government intervention also has more symbolic rewards. It may seem logical that if one were considered "good enough" to warrant distance from direct government intervention, then the state must, at least on some level, recognize one's worth as a responsible citizen.[6] In light of the Supreme Court's decision in *Lawrence*, the lack of privacy may indicate a suspicion about the sound character and quality of the subjects in question, but the right to privacy does not imply explicit government recognition: "The present case . . . does not involve whether the government must give formal recognition to any relationship that homosexual persons seek to enter. The case does involve two adults who, with full and mutual consent from each other, engaged in sexual practices common to a homosexual lifestyle. The petitioners are entitled to respect for their private lives."[7] Cases such as Lauren and Donna's show that there is a fine line between government recognition and government respect for privacy. The state may respect Lauren and Donna's right to legally engage in sexual acts, but the state clearly does not respect their right to parent without government intrusion. Why would there be a difference? The difference between intimate sexual acts and parenting may reside in the governing function of marriage. In a neo-liberal context in which marriage operates to economize the function of the state, privacy becomes a problem only when its costs outweigh its benefits. From this perspective, it makes sense that the state would care more about how children will be independently reared than what kind of sex people might be engaging in.

Lauren and Donna's case reveals why advocates of same-sex marriage would want privacy protection from invasive state procedures such as fingerprinting and direct surveillance from parole officers. For individuals like Donna and Lauren, marriage seems to come with a set of protections against forms of state intervention. On the other hand, proponents of same-sex marriage also see limits to the benefits of privacy. If the state did not intervene in marriage at all, many activists fear that their interests would not be protected in the event of a divorce.

The activists with whom I spoke expressed a range of views about the point at which the state's involvement in intimate relationships should be limited and appeared unsure what they really thought. The differences of opinion range from people who believed that the state has a role in regulating intimate relationships but should not be involved in individuals' intimate sexual lives to others who believed that the state should play no role in private relationships. While this last position may seem like a contradiction coming from individuals asking for a marriage license, it makes sense given a particular set of assumptions.

Kim Chow and Roni Plumb understand government involvement in intimate life as a prerequisite for protection against discrimination. Kim and Roni personally committed to each other at the age of nineteen, one year before I met them in the summer of 2005. They felt a bit anxious about the newness of their relationship, but Roni accepted Kim's marriage proposal, worried they might miss the opportunity. Roni's fears were realized when days later the court ordered the city to stop issuing marriage licenses to same-sex couples. In a matter of weeks, several national cable news programs and general-interest magazines showcased Roni and Kim's story.

At the time of our interview, both Kim and Roni were full-time undergraduate students passionate about LGBT youth. Roni described the brief and unexpected same-sex marriages as the event that redirected her and Kim's energies from LGBT youth to "steady involvement" with the marriage equality movement. Roni explains her priorities: "I definitely think marriage is the most important issue. . . . I think that if that was conquered [marriage for same-sex couples], that would really eliminate a lot of the hate crimes and things like that, because it would be accepted by the majority. I think that it would be a lot like interracial marriages." Being in an interracial relationship themselves, Kim and Roni explained marriage equality as an obvious civil rights issue.

When I asked Roni what she felt would be the ideal relationship between the state and individuals' intimate lives, she shifted her weight around in the dining room chair and thought about how the state can sometimes protect intimacies and at other times make intimacies illegal. She responded to my question as if thinking out loud: "Well, what about protection from discrimination? There are sodomy laws, too, but I want protection that I can sleep with anybody I want to. I want protection . . . antidiscrimination protection." For Roni, the state should be involved with the personal, private lives of individuals to the extent that it guards them against discrimination. For proponents of same-sex marriage who agree with Roni, the state or public is not in a mutually exclusive relationship with privacy. Roni is not operating from a belief in the ideology of the public/private division. For her, the state, as a public entity, does in fact create zones of privacy that are meant to protect people from discrimination. Thus, privacy acts more as a subjective reward, offering a sense of safety and well-being, rather than an ideology that masks other hierarchies. In other words, Roni, like Judy, argues that the state needs to give her privacy so that her relationship can be protected from scrutiny.

Other proponents of same-sex marriage argue a similar point in a slightly different way. The state does involve itself in Americans' intimate lives regardless of marital status. Caitlin McCleary explained how she came to this conclusion as a result of talking with close friends who wondered why she would advocate for marriage when it essentially invites the government into one's personal relationship. She remarked:

> When stuff happens, and especially like divorced partners disagree or somebody dies and a child needs to have somebody get custody of them, or there is property that needs to go somewhere, the state is going to come in. You can either have a system where your relationship is recognized or you can have a system where you have no protections. It may be feasible, especially when you are younger, to say, "We have our relationship, Big Brother. Stay out of it," but I think that you need to recognize that down the line, the state does come down and make decisions.

Caitlin, and other activists who share this perspective, believe that one never really has privacy from the state: regardless of whether one has an official marriage license, the state will at some point determine the distribution of property and settle disputes over child custody. The subjective reward of marriage, as Roni also articulated, is the peace of mind, or the comfort and security that come from believing that the legal recognition of marriage will protect individuals in the case of a marital dispute.

Many of the activists I interviewed described themselves as "fence-sitters," not exactly convinced the state should have any role in intimate life at all, but not sure enough to abandon the fight for marriage. For example, in my interview with couple Jennifer Dowdy and Cathy McMahon,

Cathy's uncertainty about whether she believed that the government should have a role in people's intimate life came as a shock to Jennifer.

JENNIFER: I imagine there are a lot of left queer people who don't want marriage in their own lives because they want as little intrusion by the government as possible. This is the case for our straight friends that don't want to get married but have been together forever. They don't want the government to be involved. They want to stay off of the grid.

CATHY: I think that I would have to be a fence-rider. So, on a scale with the queer community on the left, I would probably say, whatever, that's OK.

JENNIFER, *looking to Cathy*: You don't want to marry me? [*With a grin and a giggle, Jennifer abandons her serious expression.*] Bitch, you are going to hear about that. But, really, seriously, do you think that?

CATHY: Well, marriage is not something that I am dying to have.

At the time of this interview, Cathy and Jennifer had been together for over fifteen years and participated in same-sex marriage activism for at least three years. Jennifer was clearly shocked to hear of Cathy's affinity with what she called a queer left desire to "remain off of the grid." In contrast to Roni and Caitlin, Cathy was ambivalent about marriage because to her it signaled a violation of personal distance from the state; at the same time, however, she worried about the lack of security for her family, particularly their daughter, Opal, because she was not in a legally recognized relationship.

For those who are on the side of the fence more opposed to the state's involvement in intimate life but who nonetheless advocate for same-sex marriage, the ultimate goal of political action should be to reduce the state's power over intimate life as much as possible. This view was epitomized by the official line of the 1996 Libertarian Party platform, which endorsed same-sex marriage as a way for gays and lesbians to be treated as equal citizens.[8] As Rick Tompkins (1996 Libertarian Party presidential candidate) candidly stated, "As a Libertarian, it's my hope that someday such government sanction of marriages will be less and less important. . . . One step at a time, Libertarians hope to prune away all the government interventions into our private lives which supposedly 'necessitate' the state keeping track of who's married to whom, in the first place. . . . But today, in the world as we find it, real people are suffering if the state refuses to record their marriages."[9] Tompkins argues that the state has no business issuing marriage licenses at all, but since it does, it ought to issue them for same-sex couples as well. The official line from MRN would never hint at the desire to eventually ease the government out of marriage, as such a move would feed into arguments made by the religious Right that same-sex marriage activists hope to destroy the institution of marriage once they gain access to it.

Regardless of the political viability of the Libertarian perspective on marriage, it is clear in all these statements about privacy and the state that proponents of same-sex marriage are not under the illusion that there is a public/private dichotomy in social life. Thus, it would be inaccurate to understand these points of view as an expression of the ideology of privacy that masks other power arrangements, such as patriarchy. This is why perspectives on the public/private dichotomy do not explain why same-sex marriage activists find themselves invested in marriage. Proponents are not invested in marriage because they believe it to be a private world free from the state; instead, they find an affinity with marriage precisely because it provides official state protection.

According to some MRN members, the state not only acts as the "new man" (W. Brown 1995), protecting same-sex couples from its own technologies of authoritarian governance, but state-mandated privacy also protects the secular world of democratic society from the encroaching threat of theocracy. Thus, MRN activists such as Hazel do not like the idea that the state has the power to recognize some consensual intimacies as legitimate and declare others illegitimate; however, in their opinion, that is far superior to leaving those decisions to religious authorities. When I asked Hazel, for example, what she believed would be the ideal role of the state in intimate life, she replied:

> I don't really think that we can even have a choice at this point, because I think that it already exists. It's kind of like, it's already there. There [are] already [more than] 1,130 federal rights that come with marriage, and it grows; it is constantly growing. . . . The government is already in our relationships; it is just there, you know? Ideally, government would give the same rights and benefits to same-sex couples as it does to heterosexual couples. I think that it is unrealistic to think that we could get government out of our relationships. I think that the distinction we need to make in this country is getting religion and government separate. That is a really big problem. That is a much larger problem than the government in our relationships. In other countries, there is a much clearer distinction, like it doesn't matter which religious person you go to, you're not married until you go to the state. In this country, religious people can

marry you, and so that's part of the complication that people have. Like, "Oh, marriage is a religious thing." No, it's not. The ceremony is a religious thing, if it is done by a religious person. A marriage license and a marriage is actually a government thing. It is a legal contract between people, and you can't separate that out at this point.

Like many MRN members, Hazel legitimates the role of marriage as a form of governance that will protect same-sex couples from what she sees as capricious religious doctrine. Hazel does not believe that the private world of the home is separate from the public world of the state. She recognizes and even accepts the democratic state's jurisdiction over marriage, and, given that she sees religious authorization as the only realistic alternative, she does so without regret or hesitation. Most same-sex marriage activists recognize that the state plays a large part in deciding which intimacies, individuals, and spaces get to enjoy the privileges of privacy and see this power as a good thing. From the libertarian perspective, on the other hand, they also recognize the power of the state to define the meaning of "privacy," but they view this as an illegitimate exercise of state power. In both cases, privacy is not acting as an ideology that masks some other kind of hierarchy; instead, it more closely resembles an explicit and visible bribe in the sense that Halley (1993) describes. In exchange for practicing the monogamization of care, participants receive peace of mind that the state will protect them not only from "life's inevitable ups and downs" but also from the state's own technologies of direct surveillance.

Prerequisites for Self-Governance: The Cost of Privacy and the Limits of Free Choice

Unlike welfare clients explicitly bribed to marry by the federal government's "healthy marriage initiative" (Moon and Whitehead 2006), marriage equality activists are asking the state to offer its nuptial deal to same-sex couples. In the process of arguing that same-sex couples meet the prerequisites required for effective self-governance, MRN activists produce, rather than simply describe, a "gay collectivity" defined by its desire to privatize sex acts and its inability to choose the gender of those they sexually desire. Thus, in the context of same-sex couples, the neoliberal marriage bribe, like the heterosexual bribe (Halley 1993), is primarily built upon practices of constructing identity categories. However, rather than focusing on the diacritical construction of hetero- and homosexuality as Halley does, I discuss how marriage equality activists construct a default "gay collectivity"—*a new homonormativity* (Duggan 2003) set aside for homosexuals who reserve sex acts to the private sphere and the expression of sexual desire to nature.

The rewards of privacy that marriage affords, as Dana Fitzpatrick explained in the previous section, not only provide protection from direct state surveillance but also promise to reclassify gay and lesbian couples. Just as Michael Warner's (1999) critique of same-sex marriage as normalizing project would predict, Dana and other MRN members like the idea that marriage would allow gays and lesbians to be defined as *normal* life partners who share responsibility for managing life's risks rather than sexual *deviants* who reject the purification of sexuality within the private sphere.

As if extending our conversation about desexualizing same-sex couples, in a public discussion held at a local church sympathetic to marriage equality activism, Dana juxtaposed the representation of gays and lesbians in terms of "sexualized stereotypes" with what she called the positive effects of the legal marriages that occurred in the spring of 2004. "One of the important things that happened last year, with the legal weddings, is that people have the option to see real people—not the stereotypes that they are used to. We are real people. We coach soccer. Marsha was a teacher, and now she is a stay-at-home mother with our daughter. She works in the home, and I work outside of the home. We are normal. People trust us with their children" (reconstructed from field notes). Dana is practicing what I heard many MRN leaders explicitly advocate as a political strategy: reject stereotypes that portray gays and lesbians as "free lovers" and emphasize commitment to the family, as if commitment to the family requires monogamous sexual fidelity. In an effort to deemphasize sexuality, Dana goes one step further by also tying her and Marsha's relationship to recognizable patriarchal marriage scripts (breadwinner/caretaker) that presumably make them "real people" who can be trusted to care for children. Not only do Dana and Marsha "circumvent rather than embrace the challenge to heteronormativity" (Bernstein 2001), but they appropriate this discourse in making their personal lives more authentic.

Early on in my fieldwork, I learned that Dana's formulation represents the "party line" of MRN activism in general. When attending one of my first membership meetings with an MRN branch just outside of Hamilton, I noticed chapter leader Muriel Stokely, a white woman in her midfifties, explicitly policing group discourse on these terms. When two new members of MRN continued to use the phrase "same-sex marriage" to refer to the object of their political activism, Muriel finally interrupted by stating with authority, "It's called 'marriage equality,' not 'same-sex marriage.' We really don't want to use those words because it brings the bedroom into it. This is a term that beats us before we actually get started with a conversation" (reconstructed from field notes). As Muriel made clear, using a metaphor characteristic of framing sexuality as an act that occurs in the privacy of one's bedroom, it is actually official MRN policy to avoid "live sex acts" (Berlant 1998) by emphasizing efforts to frame gays and lesbians as the marrying kind.

The way Muriel sees things, the mainstream American public needs to feel some empathy for the gay and lesbian population in order to sway public opinion in favor of same-sex marriage. In fact, Muriel uses the example of her white racial identity to explain how she came to be involved in marriage equality activism as a "straight ally": "People always tell you, you know, 'If you are a white person in America, you really don't understand what it is like to not be white, because people treat you differently and you don't realize that you're getting the perks.' I think it is the same thing about being heterosexual. When I got married, . . . it didn't occur to me to think about the difference between that and anyone else who would want to go in and get married but they just happened to be LGBT." Muriel's micromanagement of group discourse emanates from her genuine attempt to forge a successful marriage equality strategy.

In an interview I conducted earlier that year, Muriel described how she thinks resistance to marriage equality comes from constructing gays and lesbians as a community defined by *deviant* sex acts:

> I guess, especially from the gay community, it is all about sex. It is all about new relationships. It is all about the drama and transitory relationship of it. I don't think that is true of the lesbian relationships out there. I think there is a feeling [from those who resist marriage equality] of, "We are not sure that these people [gays and lesbians] know what they are talking about in terms of asking for marriage." [People who resist marriage equality see gays and lesbians as] teenagers. "Oh, they're in love, but they don't really understand it." It is not really going to be a long-lasting commitment on their part, but they want all of that.

Muriel explained how advocating for marriage yields a new collective identity for gays and lesbians, defined by responsible adult citizenship rather than the "risky sex acts" that marriage allegedly insures against:

And I think that . . . those people [same-sex couples] lined up [at Hamilton City Hall to marry] was one of the best things to overcome that stereotype. Some of those people were not teenagers, and they didn't just do it on the spur of the moment. You know maybe they had already done a commitment ceremony. . . . That was something that the world saw that they had not seen before—that these are established families. It is not just the hedonism aspect of it. It is not the bars and the bathhouses. After all of the—some of it deservedly—bad press about how the so-called gay lifestyle got its name in the early days of the AIDS epidemic. You know, there were a lot of people who were living that lifestyle without any care in the world about being promiscuous. So we have the flip side, and now for everybody that was out there living it up having anonymous sex, whatever, that you have all of these people who had found somebody and settled down, and essentially had sowed their wild oats and were able to be mo- nogamous to the point of being able to become normal suburban parents. . . . Some people are just going to reject that and say, "I don't think that happened too much," but there are other people that are going to say, "If there are so many people showing up, then how many people are there out there that are like that?"

Muriel articulates what many other MRN activists assume—that the pri- vacy of the marriage relationship symbolized by the suburban home actu- ally constructs what she sees as a new and improved image of gays and lesbians in general. Muriel appropriates a set of symbolic associations— monogamous, private/suburban, safe sex = legally married; anonymous, public/bathhouse, risky sex = homosexual lifestyle. She hypothetically speaks for those who reevaluate their resistance to marriage equality, hop- ing they reflect on same-sex marriages by asking, "How many people [gays and lesbians] are there out there like that [settled down]?"

The promise of privacy to protect same-sex couples from "life's risks" and direct state surveillance requires the construction of a neo-liberal "gay collectivity" whose ability to achieve self-regulation rests upon purifying and taming sexual desire within the marital bed. When Dana asks the American public to see her and Martha as "real people" rather than "stereotypes" by invoking the image of the breadwinner and stay-at- home mother, she is crafting a gay collectivity defined by responsible self- governance rather than explicit sex acts. When Muriel speaks as the voice of marriage equality, she articulates the promise of legal marriage to create a gay collectivity defined as "normal suburban parents," in contrast to "hedonistic" and "promiscuous" sexual subjects who risk death by re- fusing the protections that privacy affords.

The gay collectivity that marriage equality activists construct is not just defined in terms of controlling sex by locating it within the protected zone of privacy; it is also reinforced by aspects of sexual desire that one cannot choose or change. Same-sex marriage activists argue that marrying someone of the same sex is a responsible and moral choice for those who "naturally" desire same-sex intimacy. In this way, proponents often base the morality of the choice to marry someone of the same sex on the assumption that same-sex desire is not an option but rather a natural expression of one's inherent identity. Marriage equality activists use the "born-gay" discourse to reject the state's effort to exclude them from self-governance by refuting the assumption that same-sex couples are not responsible subjects capable of self-rule.

From small membership meetings to larger town-hall gatherings, proponents often articulated an ardent belief that same-sex desire is an innate characteristic of gays and lesbians as a group. Born-gay discourses often surfaced in direct reference to conservative opponents' efforts to depict homosexuality as a "lifestyle choice" inimical to the marriage norm. Rather than arguing that same-sex sexuality ought to be a valued choice (similar to the choice to marry), marriage equality activists ceded this ground by tacitly accepting—or at least not refuting—that only identities beyond one's control deserve state protection. When I asked Muriel what she believed was the strongest argument put forward by the conservative opposition, she replied without hesitation:

> Probably the one time I went out to a protest outside the [Waterford] City Hall, . . . there were a number of people coming in and out, and some of them stopped to talk to me for a little bit. They started telling me about this guy who was in the navy and a part of the church group. He had been a part of that [she makes quotation marks with her fingers] "lifestyle."
>
> They said he had come back to the fold of the church, and he knew that he didn't have to do that anymore. And I was thinking, "Oh, this poor guy" [laughter]. I wonder how long he will be able to take that before he has to get out of there. I think that the most difficult thing to deal with is the people who have been raised to believe, like people who were raised at one point to believe that blacks are almost like another species, believing that there is an abnormality or that being gay is something that you can overcome by willpower.

Muriel attributed opponents' belief that homosexuality is a lifestyle choice to a type of conservative socialization in which people learn to regard natural variations as "abnormalities" that individuals can reform if they try hard enough. Muriel continued her explanation by highlighting the importance of understanding normality according to scientific knowledge rather than commonly accepted beliefs:

> [Homosexuality] is not normal, in the sense that not everyone has it. But they are talking about abnormal in the pejorative, not in scientific terms, which most of these people don't use. In scientific terms, yes, technically it is not a mainstream, normality kind of thing. Most people are born heterosexual; therefore, people who are not can be seen as abnormal. On the other hand, that does not necessarily make them bad. It is not a situation where you have to go in and change things immediately, unlike the Siamese twins or something that need to be separated. This is not something where you need to take steps immediately to change things. On the other hand, no one is going to look at those twins and say that they are immoral either. The moment you take away the choice issue and say, OK, people didn't choose to be born this way, you can focus on how to make their lives as good as possible.

According to this widely agreed upon logic, the free choice to marry is predicated on constructing gays and lesbians as a natural classification rather than a social group.

The belief that same-sex attraction is "natural" does not require scientific narratives; Christian marriage equality activists also see same-sex sexuality as an innate characteristic. Patrick Singleton, whom you met in the previous chapter, is a leader in the United Methodist Church who spends his time gathering support for marriage equality from multiple "faith communities." Patrick often finds himself debating the extent to which same-sex sexuality is a part of God's plan for humanity. He describes fundamental disagreements with some church leaders who refuse to accept that "God created each one of us exactly the way we are—complete and whole and deserving of the rights anyone else has." For Patrick, because gay sexuality is a part of God's design, marriage equality is a "civil right."

> I work with a lot of pastors from the historic black churches, and there is always this constant debate that goes on about whether the gay rights movement should not be compared to the civil rights movement. It is a conversation that I find myself being engaged in a lot. Some of the articulate and prophetic black pastors I know, especially the ones that marched with Dr. King and had been involved from the very beginning, are very clear that there is no difference, if we

are talking about discrimination and about the way people are treated based on a characteristic that is beyond their control. There can be no difference between the gay rights movement and the civil rights movement.

Patrick finds support from historic black churches when they discover an agreed-upon foundation for civil rights. Marriage equality activists have gained the most success in contexts in which people can agree that gay and lesbian sexuality is defined by compulsion (from God or nature) rather than choice.

This way of understanding personal choice, as it flows from the natural desires inherent in personhood, allows proponents of same-sex marriage to argue that excluding gays and lesbians from marriage robs them of their own identity. Thus, rather than considering the burden of governance that one agrees to take on with the marriage contract, same-sex marriage activists focus on how access to marriage would finally allow society to appreciate gays and lesbians as natural persons. The born-gay discourse is flexible and mutable, because it is not inextricably linked with one particular strategy. In the case of same-sex marriage, the born-gay discourse operates in the service of a strategy of governance that shifts the responsibility for population-level problems from the state to individuals through legal marriage by calling on couples to manage life's risks by making responsible choices.[10]

The born-gay discourse is not specific to the MRN activists with whom I spoke; it is central to the national marriage equality discourse in the United States. It is so prevalent in arguments in favor of same-sex marriage that psychologists Richard S. Colman, Rodica N. Meyer, and Lorah Sebastian wrote an amicus brief dedicated to proving to the Oregon court in the *Kennedy* case that sexual orientation is an immutable characteristic. While they do not argue that homosexuality is a genetic condition, they cite psychological studies that suggest homosexuality is an "alternative form of biopsychosocial development and not a mental disorder."[11] According to this perspective, homosexuality is a "deeply-ingrained and identity-forming characteristic" essential to one's identity because it is formed at an early age.[12] The authors base this conclusion on evidence that suggests individuals express same-sex desire before reaching the age of sexual maturity, thus assuming that if same-sex desires come before same-sex sexual activity, then sexual orientation must come before sexual experience: "That homosexuality is established at such a young age, before any sexual activity, indicates that it is an immutable characteristic."[13] While the logic of this argument is shaky, it expresses the lengths to which proponents of same-sex marriage will go in order to find some scientific support for the contention that homosexuality is a natural condition, beyond personal choice.

The born-gay discourse shields gays and lesbians from conservative claims that homosexuality is a risky, sinful, and "dangerous lifestyle choice." The ACLU's official advice for same-sex marriage activists, for example, encourages activists working at the grassroots level to make sure the public understands that young children cannot be "converted" to homosexuality, because "people cannot be persuaded to be gay or straight. It is just a part of who they are."[14] The naturalized sexual orientation argument acts as a retort to conservative arguments that the legalization of same-sex marriage will actually produce more nonheterosexual intimacies.[15] For proponents of same-sex marriage, the state's official sanctioning of same-sex intimacy will not produce more gays and lesbians; it will just grant those who were born gay access to institutions that allow couples to manage life's risks.

In my time with MRN, I never heard anyone argue that increasing the intimate choices of future generations would actually be a moral and responsible thing to do. As Dawne Moon found in her study of progay Protestant congregations, the born-gay argument "linguistically forecloses the possibility of sexual fluidity. If people are born gay, then it must follow in this language that they cannot and should not change" (2005, 567). Proponents of same-sex marriage argue that it is immoral not only for individuals but also for the state to discourage people from living their lives according to the (presumably) immutable identity with which they were born. Thus, proponents of same-sex marriage advocate increasing individuals' options to marry the person of their choice, but many proponents deny the possibility that individuals can actually choose the gender to which they are attracted. It seems that this limit on what individuals should or should not choose is partly based on what arguments same-sex marriage activists believe will elicit the least opposition from conservative opponents.

An additional political danger to conceding that one's sexual desires may be chosen only makes sense when we understand it in the context of the political rationality of risk and insurance. Representative Ed Fallon expressed this sentiment in his address to the Iowa House of Representatives in opposition to a state bill that would prevent the recognition of same-sex marriages:

> The message we're sending today [by passing the state bill against same-sex marriage] is that it's OK to discriminate against people of a different sexual

orientation, even though, for the most part, that's the way they were born and
there's nothing they can do to change it. And for those who would argue that
homosexuality is a choice, I ask you: do you really believe that anyone in their
right mind would voluntarily choose to be in a class of people who are constantly made fun of, despised, beaten up and even killed, discriminated against,
fired from their jobs, denied housing, and prevented from marrying?[16]

From this perspective, anyone who might choose to be homosexual would
not be of sound mind, because such individuals would be exposing themselves to a host of social risks and excluding themselves from insuring
against these risks with marriage. For those who believe homosexuality
is a sinful choice, those who choose it are not actually in their right mind
(Moon 2005). However, for proponents of same-sex marriage, the born-
gay argument maintains that it is inherently self-destructive to the point of
suicide not to live one's life according to one's natural sexual orientation
(ibid.). In this case, why would individuals such as Judy Marshal's brother
willingly decide to hate themselves to the point that they wanted to die?
Why would people like Margaret choose to have her hotel shot at or put
herself at risk of gay bashing by loving someone of the same sex?

Proponents argue that same-sex marriage is a responsible choice precisely because same-sex intimacy is not a conscious decision but a desire
that is natural for some. This discourse posits irrationality as a product
of individuals who may choose homosexuality rather than a product of
this society's condemnation of same-sex desire. In the risk model, people
choose to minimize risk and maximize opportunities to protect themselves with some form of insurance. For proponents of same-sex marriage,
given the social risks that being born gay brings, marriage is a responsible choice, because it helps gays and lesbians reduce risks. The born-gay
argument is a way to reconceptualize gay individuals as responsible citizens who deserve access to self-governance rather than being restricted
to authoritarian technologies aimed at those deemed "risky subjects."
The born-gay discourse provides a narrative format that allows same-sex
couples to interpret the burden of governance as a path toward freedom;
it also provides a justification for their demand to be seen as insurable
subjects—responsible citizens who can govern themselves.

*   *   *

Proponents of same-sex marriage find an affinity with this neo-liberal logic
because of the promise of privacy and free choice that comes from having

access to technologies of self-governance. Unlike the direct state surveillance that same-sex couples face—when trying to establish legal parenthood, for example—marriage embodies distant governance that provides
couples privacy. For proponents of same-sex marriage, the state is essentially asking them to govern themselves without offering them access to
technologies that make self-governance effective and pleasant. The legal
protections offered those deemed fit for self-governance would provide
same-sex couples access to avenues for managing their own risks. Marriage would allow Amber access to Hazel's health insurance. Marriage
would legally protect and sanction the sacrifices that Mark makes to take
care of Dennis's father. Marriage would officially acknowledge Curtis's
status as the family's breadwinner and give Daniel grounds for seeking
economic support in the event of a divorce or Curtis's death. Marriage
would give same-sex couples access to state-consecrated zones of privacy
that allow individuals to experience freedom without fearing they lack
state protection. From the perspective of many same-sex marriage activists, marriage not only promises privacy but also allows same-sex couples
to freely choose partnerships that reflect their "natural" desires.

In the process, marriage equality activists construct a default gay collectivity defined by its desire to embody the code of Victorian sexual morality
that reserves "good" sex to the private sphere (Rubin 1993). As Michael
Warner (1999) predicted early in the same-sex marriage debate, the official marriage equality line intentionally forecloses discussions of sexuality
and intimacy for fear that bringing sex into public discourse in this way
will diminish claims that gays and lesbians represent "real" people rather
than hedonistic sexual deviants. In tandem, same-sex marriage activists'
insistence that marriage is a personal choice is grounded on relinquishing the possibility that sexual orientation itself ought to be considered
a choice left to citizens of democratic nations. In fact, as Ed Fallon's ad-
monishment claims, one would have to be literally insane (read: incapable
of responsible self-regulation that both democracy and neo-liberalism require) to voluntarily choose to experience sexuality outside of the bounds
of heterosexuality.

CHAPTER FIVE

The "Gold Standard"

Belonging and Recognition

Steve Kemp "had a feeling about that day." He leaned back in his black leather executive chair, pushed his paperwork to the side, and wondered "if today was going to be *the* day." Steve started to daydream, reminiscing about the first time he met Jack in the fall of 1987. Jack recalled feeling that he knew he wanted to spend the rest of his life with Steve: "I told my best friend from college that I had met my future husband." Steve took a moment to reflect on his relationship. For almost twenty years, Jack and Steve had built a life together in Hamilton. Steve grinned to himself as he thought about how they have always shared a sock drawer and how Jack tries to compromise when Steve begs him to watch the latest serial killer movie. The sound of his office phone ringing abruptly brought Steve back to reality . . . kind of. "When the call came, I mean there was no doubt that this was historic. You know, I just jumped up and ran out of my office, and my coworkers were like, 'What is wrong?'" March 3, 2004, would be Steve and Jack's wedding day.

The prospects of marriage had been so far from Jack and Steve's minds that they had to stop and ask for directions to city hall. As Steve put it, "We realized that we didn't know where to go. This is an institution that had, up until that moment, explicitly excluded us; we never thought we would be able to get married, [and] as a result, we didn't actually know how to get married." A year and a half after the event, Jack remembers what he experienced at the moment he exchanged vows with Steve:

> On a personal level, it felt like this feeling that layers of shame were sort of shedding off of me. It was also an extraordinary window to see how much we

were carrying along these issues that we would never be treated as equal, that we would always be on some level treated as less than, treated as [you] can be here but there is something wrong with you, and there is always going to be something wrong with you. You are never going to be full and equal under the eyes of the society. So, to be in that beautiful old city hall, which is such a symbol of government and community and society, to be hearing those words when we never imagined we would be there, it was the essence, in a sense, of what it means to be gay.

There are thousands of stories like this from same-sex couples who finally received recognition from their government in the form of the statement "By the power vested in me by the state, . . . I now pronounce you spouses for life." For Steve, his wedding day was more powerful than any straight couple could ever imagine, for it was not just a union between him and Jack but a vow by the state to finally treat gay men and lesbians with dignity and respect.

The same-sex marriages that occurred in parts of New Mexico, Oregon, California, and New York in the spring of 2004 gave some same-sex couples a taste of the power of recognition and belonging that comes with marriage. It confirmed what most same-sex marriage activists already believed, that marriage is an institution that could provide the kind of protection unmatched by any other government contract. It could give same-sex couples access to hospital visitation rights and Social Security survivors benefits at the same time that it removed layers of shame and stigma experienced by the "gay community."

The state offers enticements to marry not only through specific legal entitlements that help couples manage life's risks or grant access to the rewards of privacy but also with normative returns that include bestowing a sense of belonging and recognition in family, community, and nation. Marriage furthers goals of economization and profit maximization by producing rather than suppressing emotional connections to the social world. Marriage is rewarding for the state because it promotes its goals of economization, but marriage is the gold standard for proponents of marriage equality because it fulfills emotional desires to belong.

In the United States, marriage does not just connote a specific set of obligations and entitlements between a man and a woman; instead, it implies a supreme form of recognition as an American citizen. Centuries of legal history in the United States define the category of legal monogamy—marriage—as a social status unmatched by any other intimate relationship (Cott 2000). Given this historical legacy, it is no wonder that same-sex marriage activists equate access to marriage with recognition of full citizenship. It is also no surprise that Steve and Jack would feel an incredible sense that their "full humanity was recognized" when the state pronounced them "spouses for life," and a sense of rejection and "extraordinary pain" when the state revoked their marriage license. The historical construction of marriage as a site for national belonging, and subsequent struggles for recognition, reveal why proponents of same-sex marriage could see marriage as an institution worth fighting for. From the perspective of marriage equality activists, marriage is far more than an individualized form of social insurance; it is the only institution that can provide full access to American citizenship and consequent relief from the negative consequences of social stigma.

Feminist and queer theorists have recently developed a line of inquiry focused on how sexuality becomes articulated within the terrain of citizenship claims (Duggan and Hunter 1995; Phelan 2001; Richardson 2000). The sexual citizenship literature provides a starting point to understanding the shift in mainstream gay and lesbian activism from goals of sexual liberation to those of inclusion in dominant institutions (Richardson 2000). By deconstructing citizenship claims made by the mainstream same-sex marriage movement, Lisa Duggan (2003) and Diane Richardson (2005) have convincingly argued that neo-liberal processes of privatization and cultural politics of normalization are often mutually reinforcing. In what follows, I extend this discussion in two primary ways: First, I argue that we must understand these citizenship claims as a recursive process that works from the bottom up as much as from the top down. I use ethnographic methods to show how citizenship is constructed through the *practice* of everyday life rather than primarily authored by political/cultural elites. Second, I borrow the concept of *symbolic power*, a term coined by Pierre Bourdieu (1990a, 1990b, 1991, 1996, 1998, 1999, 2000, 2001; Bourdieu and Wacquant 1992), to describe how these ordinary efforts to make one's relationship socially legible not only explain the prioritization of same-sex marriage but also reinforce the state's power to create social groups.

Symbolic power is a "metacapital" that refers to the degree to which social actors may possess more or less authority to classify and order society, an intrinsic political process that Bourdieu calls "principles of vision and di-vision" (1991; 1998, 53; 2000, 184) or symbolic power. Symbolic power includes processes of cognition (*connaissance*) and recognition (*reconnaissance*). Bourdieu distinguishes between the official act of cognition, or nomination of social categories through the state, and the process by which individuals, by being products of these categories, come to recognize themselves according to prevailing state classifications (1990a, 22). The "symbolic capital of recognition" specifically connotes a struggle for the values of belonging and recognition under the prevailing categories, as opposed to the "symbolic power of cognition," which refers to a struggle over the authority to constitute these categories. Proponents of same-sex marriage do not question the symbolic power of the state to create social groups or categories (*connaissance*); instead, they struggle for the capital of recognition that these categories afford (*reconnaissance*). This capital of recognition is particularly important for proponents of same-sex marriage, because, as the gold standard, marriage provides its potential participants with a sense of "full citizenship" and the safety and security that this designation affords.

Symbolic power describes how the practice of governance includes normative functions, and it does so by positing a model of agency that avoids the assumption that actions of conformity are motivated by either false consciousness or the desire to adhere to the norm. For Bourdieu, marriage, for example, is a strategy, not just a ritual act that symbolizes an objective structure with which it has no recursive relationship. In his anthropological studies of the Kabyle in Algeria, and his study of bachelors and their marriage strategies in his native village of Béarn, France, Bourdieu thoroughly critiques structuralist anthropology's objectification of marriage as a simple ritualization of the norm (1998; 2004). Specifically, marriage operates as a "reproduction strategy" aimed toward maximizing economic and symbolic capital. In the context of the Kabyle and Béarn peasantry, marriage provides a basis for the expansion of wealth as well as a point of honor and recognition for the entire kinship group. Similarly, we only skim the surface of the normative value of marriage by attributing proponents' motives to the desire for conformity or false consciousness.[1] Underlying this tendency toward assimilation is a desire to make one's relationship more legible to bureaucracies, communities, and families in order to facilitate order and enhance meaning at the level of everyday life.

National Recognition: From Second- to First-Class Citizens

Proponents of same-sex marriage use the phrase "second-class citizen" to describe their exclusion from the sense of belonging and recognition that marriage provides. One of the first times I heard this phrase from same-sex marriage activists was when Marriage Rights Now (MRN) sponsored a door-to-door canvass to assess opposition to a proposed state constitutional amendment barring same-sex couples from marrying. To prepare for the canvassing process, participants attended a workshop organized by Buck Crawford, a part-time paid staff member for MRN.

More than a decade before we met, Buck Crawford and his husband, Matt, both white males in their early forties, began training to become "professional activists." Their interest in marriage equality was sparked by a local DOMA initiative designed to prevent their state government from recognizing same-sex marriages performed in other parts of the country. In a later interview, Buck describes the growing pains of the early marriage equality movement:

> We went to [a same-sex marriage activist group], and we said, "We want to get involved. We want to defeat this." We are a couple that had been together for fourteen years, or for whatever it was at this time. We wanted to get out there and talk to people as a couple. "We will do it as a volunteer, or we will do it as paid. Whatever it is, but we want to get out there and do something." They said, "We want your help, but we don't want you out there as a couple. We're not really talking about marriage. This isn't about marriage; this is about how bad the right wing is." And we were like, "Huh? You're not— I mean this is an initiative that is trying to take away marriage rights, and you do not want us to talk about being in a relationship together? You know, caring for each other and protecting our rights?" So, we were, like, "Forget this. If you are not going to use . . . the most valuable aspect of what we have to offer, than we don't want to be a part of that." And I'm glad to say that the LGBT community learned a lesson from that. We don't talk about that kind of strategy anymore. Now we know that we need to focus on the message that our relationships are real and we deserve equality and so on.

Buck joined MRN as a paid staff member because he agreed with the organization's messaging and applauded how it encouraged couples to become organization leaders.

At the canvassing event, Buck maintained his focus on introducing the standard MRN "rating scale" used to rank the level of each registered voter's support. The scale went from high to low support for "marriage equality":

1. Supportive and more—this person might volunteer for the group or at least donate money.
2. Will only give a vote.
3. Undecided.
4. Will vote against us.
5. Unspeakable—will volunteer for or give money to the other side.

While Buck was drawing up the rating scale, one participant raised her hand and asked, "What if they are in support of domestic partnerships and not marriage? Should we give them a 2 or—?" Buck replied before she could finish her question: "No. Actually, these folks are more like a 3. Remember, domestic partnerships are not marriage equality. You need to explain this to them. Marriage is the gold standard. It is the highest expression of commitment. You need to tell them, even beyond the issue of legal benefits and protections, that you are essentially saying that our relationships are not as valued as heterosexual relationships. You are creating second-class citizens, and that is not right" (reconstructed from field notes). Buck argued that regardless of the specific rights and protections that could be offered through domestic partnerships, same-sex couples will not be equal until they receive the recognition that comes with marriage. Thus, many proponents of same-sex marriage agree with the state's logic that there is something special about marriage that promotes safety and belonging, and ask to be recognized accordingly.

Buck elaborated the difference between domestic partnerships and the gold standard in our interview: "Domestic partnerships are great, but it doesn't represent acceptance, because as long as that word *marriage* is kept back, people are saying, 'Hey, there is something that you guys don't get, because you are not in the same category as the rest of us. You don't deserve true equality, and we don't really accept you.' And so, when it is called marriage, it is a whole other thing. It is like saying, 'Yeah, we are all together. We are all a part of the same piece here.'" Here Buck connects his earlier discussion of marriage as a form of citizenship to the status it communicates, not only to the state but to the population as a whole.

At the canvassing workshop, I also had the opportunity to meet, and later that week interview, Joe Franklin, an eighteen-year-old white college student whose mother described him as "the activist of the family." Joe founded a group on his college campus specifically dedicated to the movement for marriage equality. When I asked him why he thought marriage was so important for same-sex couples, he quickly indicated that he was not gay but that denying same-sex couples access to marriage "bothered

[him] at such a fundamental level." When I encouraged him to describe this discomfort, he leaned forward in his chair with a sense of urgency and explained, "If the government doesn't accept the class as equal, how can society? The government has got to come around first. . . . Marriage is the last frontier, the last barrier we have to making gay and lesbian people full citizens. That is really what it is all about for me." Thus, from the viewpoint of many proponents of same-sex marriage, the difference between gays and lesbians being full rather than second-class citizens is access to the social recognition that only the "married" label can provide. More important, Joe believes that social recognition must come from the state: why would Americans in general grant gays and lesbians full recognition that their own government refuses? In the process of advocating for marriage equality, Joe bestows upon the state the power to make classifications that grant social belonging and recognition.

"Second-class citizen" is not just used by the activists whom I had the opportunity to meet. This same phrase appears repeatedly in many court testimonies of same-sex couples asking courts to extend to them the "fundamental right to marry." In July 2006, the New York State Supreme Court heard testimony considering the constitutionality of restricting marriage to opposite-sex couples. In a prepared statement to the court, lead plaintiff Daniel Hernandez testified that "for me, some kind of domestic partnership or other status short of marriage would not be enough. It would not convey the same commitment for one another and respect for our relationship that marriage embodies. Even if it provided us all the same rights, a second-class recognition of my relationship with Nevin would continue to dishonor the life we have built with one another as somehow something less than other couples' shared lives."[2] Marriage is thus a categorical distinction that can define the difference between full citizens, who enjoy all of the rights and benefits the social structure has to offer, and second-class citizens, who have access to some basic democratic rights but are denied the honor of state legitimacy. Like Joe and Buck, Daniel is upholding the state's authority to define legitimate social identities though the language of "citizenship." Daniel believes that his life with Nevin will not be granted the honor and respect it deserves in general society without official state recognition.

Connaissance and the Separation of Church and State

Proponents of marriage equality largely recognize the government, rather than religious institutions, as the primary author of the symbolic power of marriage. Partly in response to arguments from religious conservative opponents, MRN is careful to articulate the desirability of the separation of church and state and assert an alternative narrative that stresses the spiritual and emotional experience of marriage as a direct result of civil rights rather than religious sacrament. In arguing that it is the government rather than the church that makes marriage the gold standard, MRN members look toward the state to bestow feelings of recognition and belonging.

During the course of my fieldwork, I noticed members of MRN routinely meeting religious conservative opposition to marriage with the reassuring message that gays and lesbians are asking for legal rights, not religious acceptance. After meticulous training from Buck, I tagged along with Joe, whose previous experience canvassing won him a demanding assignment in a well-known middle-class, white, conservative neighborhood. Shrugging off any hint of nervousness and appearing eager to accept Buck's challenge, Joe lamented, "It's too bad that most people will not be home, you know. This is a perfect time to go on vacation." Breaking the rhythm of several unanswered doorbells, a man who appeared to be white and in his early sixties slowly opened the front door. With a curious Pomeranian poking through his legs, he asked with suspicion, "How can I help you?" Without looking at his clipboard, Joe initiated the script: "Are you [briefly breaks eye contact to announce the name of the registered voter associated with this home]?" After the man uttered an unenthusiastic "Um-hum," Joe continued: "Hi. My name is Joe, and I am with the volunteer organization Marriage Rights Now. We are a gay and lesbian rights group, and we are going around the state and talking with people about the issue of same-sex marriage. Right now the extreme antigay groups are trying to not only ban same-sex marriage but also the good benefits many gays and lesbians enjoy from domestic partnership legislation. I would just like to know how you stand on this issue" (reconstructed from field notes). The registered voter paused before replying, "Well, this is a Christian household, and we believe that marriage is for a man and a woman. So I would not be in support for same-sex marriage." Joe nodded as if he understood the man's reticence to accept the marriage label. "Do you think that gays and lesbians deserve rights?" The man nodded enthusiastically. "Oh, yeah, I believe that they should have the same rights, but it is against Christianity for them to get married." Joe ended the conversation emphasizing common ground: "Great! Does that mean that we can count on you to oppose efforts that would jeopardize domestic partnerships?" Closing the door while speaking, the voter remained uncommitted and claimed that he would have to read the text carefully, which he "always does." When we had barely reached the end of the voter's driveway, Joe pumped his arm, looked at me, and exclaimed, "Yes! Our first Christian. You see that a lot, where people believe that gays and lesbians should have equal rights but not marriage. It is really hard to get through to them that you have to have marriage for equal rights" (reconstructed from field notes).

Although Joe did not follow through with the entire script in this case, the "Common Questions and Answers" handout distributed to canvassers emphasizes the separation of "civil" from "religious" marriage that Joe implied in his parting concession. Two questions found in the handout are specific to the Christian opposition:

Q5: I don't want to see gay people getting married in my church.

A: Civil marriage and religious marriage are separate institutions. We're talking only about having government treat all couples the same when it issues marriage licenses. No one is even suggesting that any church would ever be forced to marry any couple—gay or straight—who they don't want to.

*   *   *

Q6: Doesn't the Bible say that homosexuality is wrong?

A: You don't have to like gay people to agree that all couples—gay and non-gay— deserve the same basic legal protections via marriage. The Bible has historically been used to justify denying marriage to a variety of people, including mixed-race couples and slaves.

In "question five" MRN attempts to defuse the conservative Christian opposition by distinguishing civil from religious marriage and staking its claim to rights granted by the government rather than official religious recognition or inclusion. Similarly, the scripted answer for "question six" distinguishes symbolic acceptance of and affinity for "gay people" from access to practical "legal protections."

In the context of a canvass, where the group attempts to gain widespread public support, MRN members craft this concession as if civil and religious institutions can share the authority to define marriage: the state provides access to legal rights and responsibilities, and the church performs symbolic and ceremonial functions. During personal interviews, however, all members of MRN were unequivocal in their belief that the federal government ought to have the ultimate authority to define the meaning and boundaries of marriage. Moreover, according to MRN, as you will see throughout this chapter, the state's authority is not limited to legal rights and responsibilities but also includes symbolic functions such as lifting the feeling of stigma and shame—an intangible benefit that Jack describes after being legally married to Steve.

In describing the state's authority to define the meaning and boundaries of marriage, Caitlin, an MRN leader introduced in chapter 2, distinguishes the United States from Europe:

> In Europe, there is more of that. Like you go to the government office and you get your piece of paper and that gives you all of the state rights and responsibilities, and if you want to get a religious marriage, you go to the priest or the preacher or whatever and they conduct a ceremony. . . . I think that it goes back to the separation of church and state. People [in the United States] want to project their religious values onto other institutions, but I think that marriage is a contract provided by the state that guarantees all of these rights and responsibilities. I think that the people that enter into that contract have an agreement with each other.

Patrick, the minister of a liberal Christian congregation in Waterford, backs up this argument with a historical narrative explaining why Americans might be confused about the role of religion in marriage:

> The church has always blessed marriages or had marriage ceremonies, but it never had anything to do with civil contracts. That was something that was done through the secular government. . . . But because there were not enough resources for the secular government to solemnize marriage, they passed that legal ability on to the church, to the Episcopal Church. So we got into a situation in this country where clergy can marry people. I think that the whole thing might be much simpler if we never had that—if marriage was just a civil contract between two people or whomever. The church, depending on what tradition they are, could choose whether they wanted to bless that union or not. You know they would be two separate things.

Several MRN members feel that the religious Right is responsible for the general public's confusion about marriage as a civil contract. Patricia Bloom is a social worker who describes herself as a "straight ally" who grew up in a conservative community and credits college with opening her eyes to the issue of marriage equality, which she now sees as one of the most important social issues of our time. In our interview, Patricia spoke at great length about the audacity and power of the religious Right:

> The Christian right-wingers are very strong politically, and this is a frightening group to me. . . . I was not married in a church; I don't look at my union with my husband as a religious issue. I do not tend to walk a Republican line in general, but a lot of it is based on "This is how it has always been, so this is how it has to be." Well, yeah, we used to do a lot of things, but as we move on, we find out there are better ways to do things. . . . This infusion of religion in government that seems to be going on is just mind-boggling. I really object to that a lot. My marriage is not a religious thing; it is a legal thing and a symbolic thing for me and my husband. I really have a problem with that infusion of religion in politics.

MRN's separation of church and state counterargument parallels members' sincere feelings that the symbolic importance of marriage as the gold standard stems from this historical authority of the state rather than the church. While Kim, whom you met in chapter 4, is not as versed as Patrick in the history of religion and marriage in the United States, she implicitly connects the state's historical authority to define marriage with the state's symbolic power to create belonging and legibility. When I asked Kim how she responds to those who argue that marriage is a religious institution, she replied as if she were currently having a debate:

> No, it is not. Marriage was not even started in the church. So don't think that it was. It has been documented that they [religious authorities] were very late to get on that. I think that is the biggest problem. . . . [Marriage] has nothing to do with religion. The ceremony is religion. But when it comes down to the rights, if they just got married in a church but did not sign anything, it would not be legal. . . . I do hear people say that what if domestic partnership and marriage were completely equal, would that be OK? No! Why does there need to be that separation of the word? Separation causes people to feel inferior or superior. So it is all or nothing. It has to be equal.

According to this logic, which is shared by the overwhelming majority of MRN members I met, even if domestic partnerships provided all the federal and legal rights found in marriage, true equality would come only when the symbolic status of the marriage label is available for same-sex couples.

Caitlin makes the connection between civil marriage and symbolic power more explicit as she explains the importance of the separation of church and state:

> As long as we don't have access to marriage protection, the government is making a statement that our relationships are second-class. So when we have full access to the same protections, then that will be making a statement that our relationships are equal, and I think that's incredibly important. And I think that it is an important matter in terms of separating church and state—that we're going to make public policy based on equal rights for all citizens, not based on, you know, a small group's religious beliefs.

Caitlin's point of view represents an assumption broadly accepted by MRN members: second-class citizenship is not just about formal legal exclusion; it is also about social stigma that the state has the authority and responsibility to remedy.

Contrary to what Joe would lead the man of the "Christian household" to believe, MRN members argue for marriage (as opposed to federal domestic partnerships or civil unions) precisely because of the symbolic benefits of the marriage label that have the potential to make same-sex couples feel more accepted. Christian conservatives opposed to same-sex marriage may not "have to like gay people to agree that all couples—gay and non-gay—deserve the same basic legal protections via marriage," but several MRN members have a personal investment in marriage precisely because they have experienced the symbolic power of state recognition. As Jack put it in the opening section of this chapter, legal marriage immediately dispelled layers of shame and social stigma—the feeling that "we would never be treated as equal, that we would always be on some level treated as less than, treated as [you] can be here but there is something wrong with you, and there is always going to be something wrong with you."

Proponents of same-sex marriage understand that marriage is the gold standard, valued more than any other intimate relationship. Partly in response to the religious Right's insistence that marriage is a Christian institution, proponents reinforce rather than challenge the state's prerogative to create classifications that connect intimate relationships with rewards of social recognition (*connaissance*). MRN activists are asking to be included as the marrying kind: potential bearers of symbolic capital deserving of the protection that comes from official recognition (*reconnaissance*).

Community Recognition: Welcome to the Club

Recognition as a "full citizen" is important for MRN activists precisely because it has social ramifications beyond their specific relationship to the state. The legal marriages that occurred in some cities in the spring of 2004 only reinforced proponents' belief in the power of a state license to provide social legibility in their communities.

Sue and Ann Jacman witnessed the power of everyday acts of recognition in their own small community. Sue and Ann were together for thirty years before they had the opportunity to legally marry at Hamilton City Hall. While motivated by the exclusion they had felt when they rushed to their seriously injured daughter's side at the hospital, Sue and Ann experienced a sense of belonging and recognition upon getting married that they had never expected. Ann explained:

> We had a civil union in Vermont, and we told people, and it felt nice. We got married in Hamilton, and we called our neighbor, and we called the newspaper. By the time we got home, we had flowers at our front door. And I said [to the neighbor], "That is the most marriagey thing that I could think of." She said, "Good, that's what I wanted it to be." Marriage is something that people totally get. They understand what it means. They know that it means commitment and love. It is just part of the world that everybody else lives in. Everybody just opened up their arms to us, and it was like, "Welcome to the club. We are all together in this."

Sue echoed Ann's sentiment by explaining the sense of belonging they felt after they were married: "When we got married, that whole wall over there [she points to the wall of her house facing the entryway] was full of cards from mostly straight people. They were thrilled with our marriage. It was, like, welcome to the thing." A week or so after their marriage in Hamilton, they were shopping at the local farmers' market when a woman recognized their picture from the local paper's front-page news story about their wedding. Approaching Sue as if they had known each other for years, this woman said, "Congratulations! Can I hug you now?"

All of the couples with whom I spoke who were married in Hamilton experienced this sense of belonging to the marriage "club." Jack and Steve's neighbor decorated their apartment door like a "just-married wedding limo." Hazel and Amber Butler can remember a distinct feeling of love and acceptance in the Hamilton community as a whole when the city began issuing marriage licenses to same-sex couples. As Amber put it, "It was awesome. It was like the whole city erupted with this altruistic love for one another. It was like a lovefest. People would just walk around smiling. . . . You would just see couples beaming down, holding hands through the streets, and people would just start honking and waving." Amber also remembered her coworkers commenting on her wedding ring, which she had actually worn to work every day for eight years, but they had never noticed it before she was legally married.

Jense and Derek Miller remember feeling shocked by a newfound sense of acceptance when they took their dogs to the groomer, and he said, "Well, I guess congratulations are in order." Derek and Jense had never been close with their dog groomer, so his spontaneous interest in their intimate life caught them by surprise. Others, at the very least, were given cakes and gifts in celebration of their marriages. Although the same-sex marriage licenses issued in Hamilton were out of the ordinary, the giving of gifts, congratulations, and other forms of welcoming newlyweds to the institution of marriage are a regular occurrence. People create registries for gifts at their favorite stores. Families have weddings and receptions as a way of saying, "Welcome to the club."

These feelings of belonging that come with legal marriage are a sharp contrast to the experiences of stigma discussed in chapter 3. Marriage seemed to lift these couples out of the abject category of "homosexual lifestyle" to the celebrated classification of "spouses." Instead of feeling the fear that comes from knowing that you are part of a detested social group, these couples were able to revel in the feeling that they finally had a more complete sense of belonging in their communities. As Hazel explained to me, "It irks me the way that we [gays and lesbians] are treated like second-class citizens. You know, there is such a feeling out there that we have to do everything twice as hard as everybody else and we are still inferior. You know, no matter how good you are at whatever it is, you know you are still gay and there is still something wrong with you. And that, by our relationships being on equal footing, again, it just takes out the discrimination." The flowers, cards, hugs, and words of acknowledgment that come with marriage powerfully speak to the acceptance of being gay or lesbian in general.

The acceptance and recognition felt by same-sex couples who were permitted the status of married for a few weeks can also be contrasted with the kind of illegibility they feel in going about their daily routines. Many individuals with whom I spoke told of the humiliation and degradation they feel when filling out forms that require checking the box "single" or "married" that others may just view as a common bureaucratic nuisance.[3] For Steve Kemp, the symbolic power of being legally authorized to check the "married" box would allow him to finally tell the truth about his relationship.

> We [Jack and I] completed our income taxes, and you go down a third of the way down the 1040 form, and they have that box that says "single" or "married." It just struck through to the heart, that we couldn't check that box. We had to say "single" after having sixteen years together. We were being forced under penalty of perjury. So we were forced to lie about the most important part of our lives and the truth of our family by the federal government. . . . It is a humiliation that comes right into your own body. It is very disturbing.

Steve's feelings when he fills out his tax form exemplify the visceral, symbolic violence people experience when state classifications do not reflect the reality of their own life, highlighting the contradictions in state policies that they must attempt every day to negotiate. For Steve, whenever he fills out forms with "single" or "married" boxes, he feels forced to lie. As he explains, he feels humiliation in his "own body" because what seems to be a real, natural, and sacred relationship is illegible to American bureaucracies.

Steve does not just feel victimized by the state; having internalized the state's mandate to tell the truth on government forms, he also feels frustrated by the state's refusal to allow him that honesty. For Steve, this presents a painful paradox: telling the truth (from a legal standpoint) means he cannot be honest (from a personal standpoint).

While most of those same-sex couples with whom I spoke do not feel as if checking the "single" box is an act of perjury, the majority feel frustrated at constantly being questioned about their lives. Many couples feel as if the routine forms they fill out for their children's schools, hospitals, the Department of Motor Vehicles, and medical appointments open their lives to ceaseless and intrusive scrutiny. One plaintiff, in her testimony to the New Jersey Superior Court considering the legality of the state's marriage statute, described how insulting it felt for her to have to constantly justify her relationship because she could not legally check the "married" box:

> [There are] forms that need to be filled out in our everyday lives: every new form at the doctors' office, for us and our kids, forms for soccer or dance class

or other after-school activities, or forms at the beginning of the school year or at the motor vehicle department, or goodness knows what this week or next. Often times we have to explain our family, either because the form won't work for our family or because the person taking the form thinks we filled out the form wrong. . . . It may seem like a small example, but this need always to explain is a struggle. We are getting the constant message that our family doesn't count, or isn't legitimate, and that is insulting and very demeaning to us . . . as if our family is a fraud.[4]

This burden to explain one's family can feel like a violation because same-sex couples do not have the privilege of existing under the naturalized, commonly understood category of marriage. The sense of humiliation and insult are forms of internalized pain from being excluded from prized categories of existence. It is almost as if these couples have been defined out of existence even though they feel as if they live married lives.

When same-sex couples had the opportunity to marry, their intimate lives became a source of celebration rather than degradation. Marriage gave these couples a sense of belonging in their communities: strangers hugged them, neighbors gave them cards and presents, they were "welcomed to the club." The gifts, hugs, discounts, decorations, and the ability to honestly fill out a form explain why proponents of marriage equality advocate inclusion into a form of governance that privatizes responsibility for managing social problems.

Family Recognition: A House Divided

The lived reality of exclusion from the married category also affects the degree to which same-sex couples feel that they belong in their extended families. Many of the same-sex couples with whom I spoke had some kind of wedding (commitment) ceremony without the official marriage license to communicate to their close friends and families that they intended to, as Amber put it, "make a commitment for life." For some couples, the commitment ceremony itself was enough to signal to friends and family that they were essentially a married couple; for other families, however, there were times of illegibility, with same-sex couples feeling a sense of invisibility and emptiness because they did not have a state-sanctioned relationship that their families could easily understand.

This sense of emptiness was particularly true in cases where extended family members felt that the legal status of marriage conferred a sense of responsibility that a commitment ceremony never could. This is one of the main reasons why Mei Tsui quickly proposed to her partner, Alison Wang, when Hamilton began issuing same-sex marriage licenses. In fact, when I asked Mei to explain how she became interested in marriage equality, she revealed, "Initially—well, a long time ago—I thought, 'Marriage is sort of for straight people. It doesn't really apply to gays.' I didn't really have any strong feelings about it one way or another. But I think when my partner and I got involved, part of the reason for making us want to go through the ceremony and the ritual and the importance of having it recognized institutionally came really from a personal point of view." Mei and Alison both come from "traditional" Asian American families who brought them up to believe that "marriage is an institution that you ought to have respect for." When Alison and Mei announced to their families that they were going to have a child, Mei remembers Alison's parents expressing a lot of questions and controversy: "There were a lot of things like, how are you going to have a child? You are not married. Shouldn't you get married first? It is unacceptable in our culture to have a child out of wedlock. And yet we are constrained from having to say, '. . . Well, I am not going to have this child on my own. I do have a partner, and we consider ourselves married.'" Alison and Mei felt as if their official marriage did make a difference in the eyes of their families, even though their marriage has since been annulled by the state. Marriage, for Mei and Alison, provided a way for them to bridge the space between them and their families.

In her declaration to the California Superior Court, considering the legality of same-sex marriages that occurred in San Francisco, plaintiff Lancy Woo articulated the same sense of rejection from her Chinese family as well as a sense that she and her partner, Cristy, were "invisible . . . [and] not fully adult." She described how she felt reminded of this rejection every Chinese New Year: "[My mother] and some of my other more conservative relatives still give Cristy and me *lycee*—that is, good luck money in red envelopes. Traditionally these envelopes are given to children, until they marry."[5] While Lancy knows that her family means well, it is emotionally difficult for her to deal with this rejection. She feels that official state recognition of her and Cristy's relationship would help her family understand that her relationship is "real and valuable."

But for Mei, the importance of marriage for her family is further complicated by some vocal and prominent Asian Americans who are opposed to same-sex marriage. In fact, Mei directs her efforts toward marriage equality from within the Asian American community, rather than as a member

of MRN, because she sees her family's misrecognition as intimately connected to misrepresentations of Asian Americans as "antigay."

> If you look in [the Asian American press in Hamilton,] . . . [lately there has
> been] a lot of opposition to gay marriage, and they had full-page ads of points
> of view of members of the Asian community all condemning same-sex mar-
> riage. And in many ways, the debate was very virulent; there was a lot of strong
> language that you normally don't see in the English press. You know, we are a
> part of the Asian community, you know, our daughter is going to go to school,
> and she is going to have Asian friends. We didn't want [our daughter] to be
> involved and exposed to such negative, very strongly negative, attitudes. Part of
> what we have done, as far as same-sex marriage goes, is to try to support Asian
> politicians that come out for it . . . to show that the Asian community is not all
> antigay. We know a lot of friends who are gay and who are Asian. And, you
> know, they vote. They are citizens here, and they do form a voting block. And
> it's not just the silent minority that you maybe hear of.

Mei and Alison's efforts to achieve family and community recognition as a
legitimate couple are intrinsically connected to their experiences as Asian
Americans. Even though MRN members rarely discuss how race and
ethnic identity intersect with the struggle for marriage equality, Mei reveals a complex relationship between sexual orientation, racial identity,
and marriage. She explains that there is more at stake for her family, as
she fears intense backlash from her daughter's future Asian classmates
and friends. At the same time as she points to the negative attitudes in the
Asian community, Mei also feels compelled to distinguish her fears from
common racial stereotypes that assume all Asians are antigay. For Mei,
this experience of multiple marginality[6] only strengthens the pull of marriage as an unparalleled form of community belonging.

The sense of belonging "in a family" that comes with marriage also
came up in my conversation with Steve Kemp. Steve expressed how as-
tonished he was to see the impact that his marriage to Jack had on his
brother's perceptions, even though Steve's brother had known Jack for
seventeen years. In the middle of a holiday gathering that immediately fol-
lowed Steve and Jack's official marriage, Steve's brother "jumped up and
said to Jack, 'Oh my God! You are my brother!' and gave him a big hug."
Jack could not help but feel a sense of belonging and acceptance.

Even in cases where families are supportive of same-sex couples' relationships, the inability to use the labels attached to marriage becomes a

source of resentment and anger. For example, in her affidavit to the New Jersey Superior Court, Karen Nicholson-McFadden described the unintentional "cheapening" of her relationship that occurs when her mother and father talk with friends of the family: "They can say their two sons are married with wives, but they cannot say their daughter is married. So much is implied in the word 'marriage' that never gets associated with the word 'partner.' My parents long to talk about their three married children, all with spouses, because they are proud and happy that we are all in committed relationships. . . . [However,] they have to use a different language which discounts and cheapens their family as well as mine."[7] Throughout her affidavit, Karen continually refers to the pain she feels every day because she is excluded from the recognition that comes from the institution of marriage. Legal marriage, for Karen, is an embodied reality, not just some piece of paper issued by the state to make one's relationship official; it allows individuals to feel a sense of pride and honor. Exclusion from this category prevents her from feeling that the people who matter the most to her, including her mother and father, understand her.

Denying same-sex couples access to marriage also allows the divisions of the outside world to enter their homes. Nancy McDonald, the national vice president of Parents, Families, and Friends of Lesbians and Gays (PFLAG), referred to the impact of not recognizing same-sex marriage on her family: "We live in a house divided. My three heterosexual children share in the equal rights and responsibilities of American citizenship. My lesbian daughter does not enjoy these rights."[8] The language that Nancy uses here poignantly captures the relationship between macrolevel state efforts to define legitimate classifications and the immediate reality of being excluded by them. Nancy's statement further resonates because it reminds us of the harmony and unity we expect to feel in the home. From Nancy's perspective, denying her lesbian daughter access to marriage creates unwarranted divisions of worthiness within her own family.

The power of marriage to unite the family also extends to the overall sense of the legitimacy that marriage brings to same-sex couples' perceptions of their own relationships. When I asked Sue and Ann Jacman if they felt as if their relationship had changed at all once they were married, they did not think the legal marriage itself changed too much about the way they felt toward each other, but Sue remarked, "One thing that changed in our relationship, is that, well, when you are married, you feel like you are on a cloud, and we did, too. I mean, it was exciting. Now I realize that we hold hands in public much more. We are more affectionate, you know, nuzzling. I remember waking up every morning and saying, 'We are still married, right?' " The sense of being able to express intimacy in public by holding hands or kissing, for Ann and Sue, came with the symbolic recognition of their legal marriage. When the state pronounced them "partners for life," they felt a new prerogative to show their love for each other in public. That feeling of being "on a cloud" did not come from a wedding ceremony or the love they felt for each other—it came when the state finally legalized their partnership.

While no one I talked to actually said that being married changed the way that they felt about each other, many proponents of same-sex marriage discussed the importance of the extra, legal commitment that comes with an official marriage. Mei described the effect that official marriage had on the commitment she felt with Alison as "the power of the seal, the institutional seal. . . . We made a promise to each other, and it was a public promise. There is a lot of power in that." The American Psychological Association, in its amicus brief in support of same-sex couples petitioning the state of Oregon for the right to marry, argued to the court that social science evidence suggests that state-sanctioned marriage actually does change the quality of commitment between couples: "Marriage also is a source of stability and commitment for the relationship between spouses. Social scientists have long recognized that marital commitment is a function not only of attractive forces . . . but also of external forces that serve as barriers or constraints on dissolving the relationship. . . . The perceived presence of barriers is negatively correlated with divorce, suggesting that barriers contribute to staying together for at least some couples in some circumstances."[9] Here the APA plainly argues that marriage makes couples' relationships more permanent by providing a set of legal and social sanctions for dissolving a partnership.

Marriage helps couples communicate to their families the love they have promised to each other. The marriage label also creates an official moment where two separate families unite. Because marriage brings families together, from the perspective of many proponents of same-sex marriage, barring same-sex couples from marriage makes them invisible, unrecognizable to their families in many ways. Furthermore, marriage makes couples feel a sense of magic, permanence, and resilience in their own relationships.

The legal status of "married" is a matter not just of law or benefits but of a deeply felt sense of recognition as a fully respected member of society. The payoff is the "symbolic profit of normality" (Bourdieu 1998, 69), which includes acquiring peace of mind, security, and the ability to get things done in everyday life without having to constantly explain one's intimate relations. In this sense, marriage has a value that is both mundane and sacred: it gives couples access to a language and structures that operate as a shorthand method of describing their relationship, and it imbues couples' relationships with a sense of permanency and public entitlement.

Members of MRN help establish the sacred value of marriage by expressing their emotional commitment to the institution. In fact, one branch of MRN created a specific program for activists designed to reframe marriage equality discourse from rights-based arguments to more emotion-based narratives. For example, Amber developed a "media know-how" workshop for proponents of same-sex marriage and invited a public relations specialist to talk about how to effectively communicate the group's argument for equal marriage rights. Speaking from over ten years of experience in same-sex marriage activism, Amber drew from poll data to argue that "love resonates more than rights. What really makes a difference is when you show people your pain." The public relations specialist backed up Amber's contention and put it this way:

> You have to be smart. Don't talk from your head, talk from your heart. . . . One of our advantages is that there is no humanity behind the conservative position, but you also must create an essential message. It is not enough to say that you are denied 1,138 federal rights. You must put a face on it. You could say that you are a loving and committed couple and not having access to marriage breaks my heart. This is powerful, even though I know it is difficult to show this kind of pain. It is their anger [that of conservatives opposed to same-sex marriage] versus our hurt. (reconstructed from field notes)

In the process of showing "humanity," deeply felt emotions about exclusion from marriage also become strategic moments to craft heartfelt political messages. The fact that pain can be used as a strategy does not mean that it is feigned (Hochschild 1983; Moon 2004); it does, however, indicate that by "putting a face" on the movement, marriage equality activists are crafting their life stories in ways that help evoke the magical feeling of belonging and recognition that gives marriage its symbolic power.

In addition to advocating political strategies that help convey the symbolic power of marriage, leaders of MRN have also been charged with censoring narratives from MRN activists who do not sentimentalize marriage in the same way. For example, one former local MRN leader, Tami James, told me that the organization's leaders would not let her tell her story at public events. What was so controversial about Tami's narrative? Tami, an African American woman in her late fifties, had been with her female partner for twelve years but officially married to her husband for twenty years. Tami maintained an official marriage with her husband in order to gain access to his pension and medical insurance. Tami resented MRN leaders who, from her perspective, did not want her story told because it made it seem as if same-sex couples are more concerned with legal entitlements and social advantage than the intimate pledges of commitment and love that give marriage its sacred status. Tami continued her activism, even keeping MRN picket signs and simply covering MRN's name with a piece of duct tape. While holding one that said "Honk for Marriage Equality," Tami confessed to me that the legalization of same-sex marriage would probably make her life more complicated but that she would most likely stay married to her current husband because she had been diagnosed with cancer the previous year and would have a difficult time gaining access to good health insurance with a preexisting condition.[10]

Tami lacks the unacknowledged economic and racial privilege that undergirds MRN discourses of self-sufficiency highlighted in chapter 2. Her story reveals the role of privilege as a down payment for the nuptial deal that affluent MRN activists can take for granted. After all, if a person does not possess the prerequisite economic, cultural, or social capital, how can he or she back up vows to love and care in sickness and in health? If Steve Kemp used Tami rather than "rich gay men" as his reference group, he might have an alternative view of the compatibility of public care structures and the marriage model that leaves Tami with little choice but to stay married in order to receive health benefits.

Tami's story also illustrates spaces of illegibility that MRN activists help reinforce by strategically highlighting narratives that make the marriage package of love and governance seem solvent and natural. Tami's situation complicates what appears to be a seamless connection between strategies of neo-liberal governance and normative processes of social recognition, but this does not mean that she questions marriage as a political goal. Tami continues to fight for the right to marry for the same reasons she left MRN: in her words, "I don't like people telling me that I can't do something." With these words, Tami highlights the defiant "Just give me my damn rights and leave me alone!" perspective articulated by Judy in the previous chapter. In both cases, part of what gives marriage its seemingly universal appeal as the gold standard is its ability to exist as both a practical legal structure and a sacred form of social recognition.

MRN activists are not falsely conscious of the state's ability to conse-
crate forms of social belonging, nor are they under the illusion that sexual
intimacy is irrelevant to the conferral of full citizenship. Proponents of
marriage equality are not just passive receptors of the thoughts of the
state: even though they diminish their own social power, it is through their
activism and attempts to make life more rewarding that they help make
state classifications lived realities. While the United States court system
and legislative bodies clearly have a monopoly over defining the prevailing categories of recognition, symbolic power is also essentially a recursive
process: these classifications are a lived, felt reality for people in their everyday lives that provides a seemingly natural basis for the symbolic power
of the state. The classification of marriage moves from a "nominal fiction"
to a "real group" through practical acts of social interaction that help produce a feeling that marriage is and has always been a sacred institution
(Bourdieu 1998, 68). In Bourdieu's words, the "labour of categorization,
of making things explicit and classifying them, is continually being performed, at every moment of ordinary existence" (1991, 236). At the level
of ordinary existence, people's understandings and emotions align with
judicial and legislative definitions of marriage; in daily life, people take for
granted that marriage provides a sense of safety and stability not associated with other social classifications, such as single, dating, cohabitating,
or promiscuous.

Connaissance: State Supreme Courts and the Gold Standard

As the juridical definition and scope of marriage are up for debate in state
supreme courts, so, too, is the extent to which the state explicitly ties its
interest in marriage law to the benefits of social recognition that it bestows. Marriage equality activists may clearly recognize the state's role
in creating the terms for belonging in community, family, and nation, but
how does the state understand its own symbolic power? Like MRN activists, state supreme courts tend to disavow their own power to confer social
recognition. Recent state court decisions concerning same-sex marriage
reveal the power of the state to construct official collectivities at the same
time that it renounces its own authority to define, and in effect create,
"stable" families.

In Vermont, New Jersey, California, and Massachusetts, supreme courts
concluded that their state constitutions guarantee same-sex couples the
"rights, benefits and protections" that come with marriage. The Vermont

and New Jersey courts left room for a "parallel licensing scheme," but the California and Massachusetts courts mandated same-sex couples' access to the gold standard. On the surface, it would seem logical to assume that the California and Massachusetts courts, unlike those of New Jersey and Vermont, explicitly recognized the state's role in creating the terms of social recognition though legal statutes. However, in all four cases, the state supreme courts saw their role only as "recognizing" what society or nature had already constructed as socially meaningful relationships.

In *Baker v. State of Vermont* (1999), the Vermont Supreme Court based its decision on the specific legal benefits of marriage, whereas the Massachusetts Supreme Court, in *Goodridge v. Department of Public Health* (2003), found that denying same-sex couples the symbolic benefits of marriage was unconstitutional.

The Vermont court did not call for the legislature to enact a specific remedy; instead, it left room for a "parallel licensing or registration scheme."[11] Essentially, the court refused to address the symbolic importance of the marital relation and considered only the legal statutes that entitle married couples to particular benefits.[12] "While many have noted the symbolic or spiritual significance of the marital relation, it is plaintiffs' claim to the secular benefits and protections of a singularly human relationship that, in our view, characterizes this case. The State's interest in extending official recognition and legal protection to the professed commitment of two individuals to a lasting relationship of mutual affection is predicated on the belief that legal support of a couple's commitment provides stability for the individuals, their family and the broader community."[13] From the Vermont court's perspective, the state is concerned only with the "legal recognition and protections" that come with marriage rather than the "symbolic or spiritual significance." The court thus acts as if the law itself were not a source of symbolic significance. As Bourdieu's theory of symbolic power predicts, the court performs an act of *connaissance* (constructing a new category of official recognition with the concept of the parallel licensing scheme) at the same time it disavows the symbolic value of these labels to construct individuals' sense of belonging.

In oral arguments, Beth Robinson, lead council for Baker et al., made this symbolic power of the state clear by reminding the court of the unconstitutionality of creating institutions that are separate and thus unequal: "Your Honor, *the status of marriage is in and of itself a value, a benefit. . . .* The state of Vermont can't impose a separate but equal regime in marriage here, any more than the California Supreme Court could have said in

1948 that interracial couples can have all the benefits that accompany marriage, but we're not going to let them call it marriage because it's a mixed race thing" (emphasis mine).[14] By specifically using the phrase "separate but equal," Robinson invokes the United States Supreme Court ruling in *Brown v. Board of Education of Topeka* (1954),[15] which overturned the court's earlier *Plessy v. Ferguson* (1896)[16] decision, making racial segregation unconstitutional. Using the reasoning found in *Brown*, Robinson argues that the very act of creating separate marriage institutions, even though they may have no legal distinctions, exacerbates rather than remedies gays' and lesbians' stigmatized status in American society.

Unlike Vermont, the Massachusetts court, in *Goodridge v. Department of Public Health* (2003), acknowledged this symbolic effect of the label "marriage"—to provide a sense of national recognition and belonging— and thus ruled that excluding same-sex couples from marriage is unconstitutional. The court rationalized that giving same-sex couples access to marriage is the only appropriate remedy: "We construe civil marriage to mean the voluntary union of two persons as spouses, to the exclusion of all others. This reformulation redresses the plaintiffs' constitutional injury and furthers the aim of marriage to promote stable, exclusive relationships."[17] From the viewpoint of the Massachusetts court, this reformulation of marriage not only addresses same-sex couples' exclusion from state-sponsored intimacy; it also serves the state's interest in promoting "stability."

But why can't the state's interest in promoting stability come from a parallel licensing scheme? The Massachusetts court reasons that marriage "fulfils yearnings for security, safe haven, and connection that express our common humanity. . . . Civil marriage is an esteemed institution."[18] In this formulation, it is not just the legal provisions that make marriage a safe haven to protect against life's risks; it is the recognition that the marriage label affords by providing a sense of belonging, or as the court put it, expressing "our common humanity." More important, the court sees its role as simply *recognizing* rather than actually *creating* the categories to which these yearnings are symbolically attached.

Similar to the Massachusetts decision, the high court in California, in its June 2008 ruling in the *California Marriage Cases*, emphasized the symbolic importance of marriage but disavowed its own role in creating this symbolic power. In the majority opinion, Justice Ronald M. George outlined the "right to marry" as a "constitutionally protected civil right" that obligates the state to publicly recognize couples as families: "Although the constitutional right to marry clearly does not obligate the state to afford specific tax or other governmental benefits on the basis of a couple's family relationship, the right to marry does obligate the state to take affirmative action to grant official, public recognition to the couple's relationship as a family."[19] Here Justice George distinguishes the structural from the symbolic benefits of marriage and prioritizes the state's role in "recognizing" marriage as an official family.

The California court purposefully uses the term *recognize* rather than *create* in order to renounce the state's power to define what constitutes an "official" family. The court premises this disavowal on what it posits as the individual's "right to marry": "If civil marriage were an institution whose *only* role was to serve the interests of society, it reasonably could be asserted that the states should have full authority to decide whether to establish or abolish the institution of marriage. . . . The governing California cases establish that this right [the right to marry] embodies fundamental interests of an individual that are protected from abrogation or elimination by the state."[20] Thus, the court not only privileges the symbolic power of marriage to confer official recognition, but it finds the origin of that power in what it posits as the "fundamental interests of an individual" rather than its own act of constitutional interpretation.

Proponents of same-sex marriage recognize that the symbolic power of marriage comes from the state's ability to construct social collectives; however, this does not mean that MRN activists have opened the state's construction of marriage to "expanded reflexivity" (Meeks and Stein 2006). As you will see in the next chapter, in the Vermont, Massachusetts, California, and New Jersey rulings, the courts justify their decision to allow same-sex couples marriage by reminding the reader what essentially defines marriage and how the category remains salient because it continues to prohibit particular intimate arrangements.

*   *   *

Proponents of same-sex marriage look to this revered institution as a way to provide legibility and belonging that they believe no other classification can offer. When leaders of MRN ask members to deemphasize marriage as a practical strategy and "speak from the heart," they help construct, rather than simply confirm, marriage's symbolic power. MRN will censor stories from members like Tami because they threaten to portray same-sex marriage as a practical strategy rather than a prepolitical longing.

The state has the power to decide what counts as an "official" family, but this official definition of the marriage category is also an immediately felt reality. Rather than existing only in the annals of legal discourse, the state's construction of marriage has real consequences for those relegated to the land of exclusion. The symbolic importance of marriage makes this institution difficult to refuse: in exchange for the responsibility of managing social problems as individual risks, the married couple not only gains access to freedoms of choice and privacy but also reaps deeply felt rewards of social recognition.

CHAPTER SIX

Why Exclude the Willing?

Same-Sex Marriage and the Slippery Slope

Given the state's interest in marriage as a way to economize its own function and the persuasive arguments from the marriage equality movement that same-sex couples embody these neo-liberal goals, why is same-sex marriage legal in only two states? I argue that the marriage equality movement's response to the conservative opposition's "slippery slope" prediction reveals the prerequisite terms and trade-offs for key moments of success for the same-sex marriage movement. In cases where marriage equality has been successful, the winning formula required both adhering to the economizing goal of the state and renaturalizing marriage so as to make the state's role in constructing marriage seem to disappear. Thus, the success or failure of marriage equality hinges on not only embodying the state's interest in economization but also acquiescing to the state's desire to mask this interest, and this is precisely why the marriage equality movement discursively forecloses both redistributive politics and a broader vision of social justice for those whose sexual practices are understood by dominant American society as deviant.

I do not intend to provide a representative and comprehensive account of conservatives' opposition to same-sex marriage in the United States; moreover, I do not aim to explain how churches in general have aligned themselves in the marriage equality debates.[1] Instead, I discuss arguments specific to the slippery slope for three primary reasons: First, it drives marriage equality activists' strategy in a way unmatched by other avenues of conservative opposition. Second, the slippery slope framework is a vivid example of the ambivalent relationship between neo-liberal strategies of governance and the religious Right's discourses of naturalization: the slippery slope is a sufficient but not necessary strategy for securing the symbolic power of the state (to make its project of classification appear natural and timeless); however, this ideological function is in tension with the economizing goal of neo-liberal governance to expand the reach of marriage as a care structure.

Finally, my evidence suggests that the current direction of marriage equality activism in the United States is toward *homonormativity* (Duggan 2003) rather than a model of *postqueer politics* (Meeks and Stein 2006). Moments of success for the marriage equality movement have hinged on consenting to the terms of exclusion and silences born from the logic of the slippery slope framework. Rather than questioning the so-called danger at the end of the slippery slope, proponents insist that gays and lesbians are loyal to monogamy as a form of intimacy and type of care structure. Underlying what appears to be a consensus among marriage equality activists, however, are voices from within the movement who silence their own critique of marriage as an exclusionary institution for the sake of political expediency.

Natural Classifications versus Slippery Slopes

The religious Right's slippery slope framework provides an ideological mechanism for naturalizing state-sanctioned serial monogamy by spelling out the negative consequences of defining marriage as a socially constructed institution. Even though the slippery slope has achieved mixed results at the federal and state level, it continues to influence MRN's insistence that it is asking for marriage inclusion, not redefinition. Conservatives opposed to same-sex marriage use the metaphor of the slippery slope to articulate marriage as an institution that reflects God's will, written in nature's intention for human beings, to base civilization upon the unity of "the two opposite sexes." On the surface, this sentiment may appear to be only an old-fashioned fetter to the logic of neo-liberalism in which economization is the ultimate value and purpose of social institutions. However, at least in the context of federal legislative hearings, conservative politicians use the slippery slope argument to explicitly construct heterosexual monogamy (and assumed sex essentialism) as a basic foundation for capitalist economies. Far from being specific to the same-sex marriage debate, the logic of the slippery slope is part of a larger conservative political-economic discourse articulated in Pat Buchanan's declaration of the culture wars and early Evangelical Christians' insistence that the heterosexual, nuclear family is the last line of defense against communism (Fetner 2008).

The slippery slope argument gained currency in marriage equality circles when Congress debated the Defense of Marriage Act (DOMA) in 1996 and conservatives forged a strategy to deal with the implications of the Hawaii decision. Several political leaders, news columnists, and academics—such as former secretary of education William Bennett, *Washington Post* columnist Charles Krauthammer, and political scientist Hadley Arkes—publicly declared that recognizing same-sex marriage would lead to sexual relativism and thereby remove any social prohibition against promiscuity, polygamy, and incest (Sullivan 2004).The slippery slope resurfaced in a series of hearings in 2004 and 2005 before the Committee on the Judiciary of the United States House of Representatives, which was reconsidering the constitutionality of DOMA and the proposed Federal Marriage Amendment.

The slippery slope argument is grounded in the assumption that there is a reason, found in nature, to bind the definition of marriage to the union of one man and one woman, and once we move away from a natural definition to one constructed by society, we will find no firm principles upon which to define marriage. According to this logic, if the government allows same-sex couples to marry, then it will also bring all other aspects of marriage up for debate. In other words, if we change marriage law to allow a woman to marry another woman, on what grounds can we deny a woman the right to marry two women, three men, a thirteen-year-old girl, or even her dog? From this perspective, marriage is civilized society's way of simply reflecting and supporting a biological fact of nature: that men and women are complementary opposites and require each other for the perpetuation of the species.

Thus, the slippery slope argument is inextricably linked with sex-essentialist assumptions, which Arkes explicitly declared in his statement to the House Judiciary Committee's May 1996 hearings on the Defense of Marriage Act, in which he argued that marriage expresses the "natural teleology of the body." Arkes does not explain how bodies can have a teleology; he simply states as fact that "we are all . . . men and women, there are only two people, not three, only a man and a woman can beget a child."[2] In this formulation, which is one primary conservative argument against same-sex marriage, the world can be neatly and naturally divided between men and women. Furthermore, his reasoning suggests we know nature's purpose because it is inscribed in men's and women's differently sexed bodies, which must come together to create life. Thus, Arkes concludes that same-sex marriage is dangerous because it could "detach marriage from that natural teleology of the body . . . [in which case] . . . on what ground would the law say no to people who profess that their love is not confined to a coupling, but woven together in the larger ensemble of three or four?"[3] Thus, the slippery slope argument rests on the assumption that marriage is a reflection of natural law, and if the definition of marriage is expanded to include same-sex couples, there will no longer be any natural basis for defining marriage at all. Arkes implies that the state's authority to sanction monogamy as the only legitimate family form rests on the logic of sex essentialism.

But there is something even more insidious about this slippery slope argument that has little to do with sexual orientation, sexual behavior, or reproduction. As Gayle Rubin maintains, often these kinds of arguments about where to draw the line between legitimate and illegitimate intimate arrangements actually signify what others have referred to as a moral panic, in which anxieties over sexuality signify "personal and social apprehensions to which they have no intrinsic connection" (1993, 25).[4]

In this case, when people express anxieties over the potential of same-sex marriage to erode the firm foundation for defining the boundaries of marriage, they reveal deeper apprehensions about the ability of the family to function as a social safety net in the absence of an effective welfare state. The terms of neo-liberalism are inextricably linked with the cultural and religious politics of sexuality and family life (Duggan 2003). On the surface, the slippery slope argument may appear to have nothing to do with socialism, capitalism, or the decline of the welfare state in America; however, conservative opponents of same-sex marriage use "nature's purpose" to justify the state's privileging marriage not only as a supreme form of heterosexual intimacy but also as a form of governance that offers a set of legal protections against life's risks. Put simply, from the slippery slope perspective, single people should not be able to name whomever they choose to claim their Social Security survivors benefits, because nature did not intend humans to live alone; same-sex couples should not be able to share the automatic legal custody of children that marriage affords, because nature intended children to be raised by one man and one woman. The list goes on, with all exclusions from marital governance justified as the natural order of things.

Consider, for example, the congressional testimony regarding the constitutionality of DOMA and the Federal Marriage Amendment in the spring of 2004. Drawing from Pennsylvania senator Rick Santorum's April 2003 remarks about the Supreme Court's ruling in *Lawrence v. Texas* that homosexuality posed a threat to American society, Senator Steve King of Iowa, in several sessions, made this link explicit: "If . . . marriage can be distorted in its meaning to include between a man and a man or a woman and a woman, then how do you draw the line between group marriage, bigamy, polygamy, and all the living arrangements there are? How do you slow this race toward a pure socialist society where group marriages can be arranged for the purposes of benefits?"[5] In this statement, Senator King sees marriage as a way to prevent socialism and welfare fraud. From his perspective, denaturalizing the definition of marriage would also erode any basis for relying on the family structure as the primary social safety net in the United States.

This connection between the dissolution of marriage and socialism is not just the opinion of one senator; the same kind of argument is made by various political leaders and social researchers who work for right-wing think tanks—such as Stanley Kurtz, Allan Carlson, and Maggie Gallagher—and it remains an unacknowledged subtext to concerns over "social stability." In each of these articulations, a solid or "natural" foundation for the definition of marriage has stakes well beyond prohibiting particular intimacies; they also posit the nuclear, heterosexual family form as a bulwark that protects Americans from the "threat" of socialism. In this way, the bright-line definition of marriage that the religious Right advocates dovetails with the neo-liberal abhorrence for public care structures.

Not surprisingly, Scandinavian nations with strong welfare states that have also liberalized marriage laws have become a prime example of how the slippery slope leads not only to "polygamy" but also to socialism. If you were to read only congressional testimony, court affidavits, and policy briefs authored by opponents of same-sex marriage, you might assume that Sweden, Demark, Norway, Finland, and the Netherlands are the only countries that have legalized same-sex marriage in some form. On the contrary, as of 2002, the list of European countries that are not typically characterized as being on the "social democratic" end of Gøsta Esping-Andersen's typography of welfare states but have some national recognition of same-sex couples includes Hungary, France, Germany, Portugal, Belgium, and Croatia (Merin 2002).

In the same congressional testimony in which Senator King predicted that same-sex marriage could lead to polygamy and socialism, Stanley Kurtz cited the Scandinavian case as evidence that same-sex marriage in the United States will result in the decline of marriage rates, which will increase out-of-wedlock birth rates and finally require the expansion of the welfare state. He writes: "In short, since the adoption of same-sex registered partnerships . . . marriage has declined substantially in both Scandinavia and the Netherlands. . . . A combination of the Scandinavian cultural pattern with America's already high divorce rate would likely mean a radical weakening of marriage—perhaps even the end of marriage itself. . . . And a further decline of marriage and family is sure to bring calls for a major expansion of the welfare state. . . . [Therefore,] steps to block same-sex marriage should be taken."[6] Here, like the marriage equality activists who argue that allowing same-sex couples to marry will reduce welfare caseloads, conservative opponents articulate the slippery slope metaphor in a way that is meant to appeal to the state's logic of economization. Although, as we saw in chapter 2, Lee Badgett may have accurately projected the number of unmarried same-sex couples who would become ineligible for state assistance once married, from the conservative perspective, she does not account for what Kurtz and others project will be a widespread disinvestment that they fear will come when marriage is uncoupled from the naturalized logic of heterosexuality.

By connecting the denaturalization of marriage to the potential expansion of the welfare state, neoconservative arguments do not simply resonate with religious discourse; they are used in an effort to appeal to the economizing sentiment of the state. In other words, the "dangers" at the end of the slippery slope are not just homosexual, bestial, incestuous, and polygamous intimacies; they are also universal, state-sponsored, national care structures. The slippery slope argument vividly depicts what is at stake in the debate over same-sex marriage: a hierarchy of sexual life that places monogamous heterosexuality above all other forms of intimacy, and a system of economic stratification that relies on marriage as a substitute for economic redistribution.

Marriage Equality Proponents' Response to the Slippery Slope

Hypothetically, proponents of marriage equality could refute slippery slope claims by questioning the alleged dangers that lurk at the end of the slippery slope (polygamy, incest, and bestiality as well as socialism and welfare use). However, proponents relinquish this ground and instead insist that same-sex couples pose no threat to the "natural" order that undergirds the state's authority to constitute a national intimacy and an economized care structure. With the help of romantic love narratives, marriage equality activists argue that the natural foundation for marriage is found in monogamy rather than men's and women's differently sexed bodies.

Armed with their own discourse of naturalization, marriage equality activists articulate the "dangers" at the end of the slippery slope as "red herrings" that the religious Right uses to draw attention away from the homophobia that really motivates conservative mobilization against marriage. This argument allows proponents of marriage equality to refute conservatives' hypotheses that same-sex marriage will lead to "polygamy" and socialism, but it does so only by mistakenly portraying marriage as a natural grouping rather than a historically constructed and state-consecrated classification that inherently privileges one form of intimacy and care structure above all others. In responding to the slippery slope metaphor, proponents of same-sex marriage, while attempting to widen the charmed circle[7] of sexuality to include same-sex monogamies, in effect fortify the boundary between normal (monogamous) and deviant (non-monogamous) sexualities. As such, my analysis confirms that the religious Right has directly impacted the marriage equality movement's political strategy (Fetner 2008). On the other hand, as the case of the slippery slope reveals, both marriage equality proponents and the religious Right are responding to a larger call from the state to disguise its symbolic power as a prepolitical longing. Looking at marriage as a form of governance allows us to contextualize the practices of both of these social movements in their shared political-economic climate.

In response to religious conservatives' gloomy predictions that allowing same-sex couples to marry would erode the natural definition of marriage, proponents of same-sex marriage refute the contention that heterosexuality should be valued above same-sex intimacy, but many do so by pointing to the "natural" superiority of monogamy. As Barney Frank, congressman from Massachusetts, testified to the House of Representatives, reflecting on the potential problems with the proposed Federal Marriage Amendment in May 2004, "There will be no serious effort to extend the right to marry to people interested in polygamy, because while some differences are hard to maintain, the difference between two people and three people is a fairly clear-cut one."[8]

What makes the difference between two and three not only clear-cut but justifiable? When I asked proponents of marriage equality what they thought about the argument that marriage discriminates against non-monogamous ways of experiencing intimacy, many, like their conservative opponents, pointed to sexual behavior within the animal kingdom to argue that monogamy is natural. I asked Jense, a co–chapter leader of MRN, what he thought about the argument that marriage inherently discriminates against those who want to form relationships with multiple legal partners. He replied with trepidation but sincerity: "I say it's—and now this is probably going to sound like the religious Right—but, um, I say, um, OK. Humans are higher than animals, but they have a lot of basic animal instincts, and the pairing-up nature is kind of natural, or at least, the possessiveness and jealousy and things like that. . . . It is just basic human nature. Monogamy is something that most people expect and desire." Here Jense argues that "pairing up" is something that animals and thus humans naturally do, and that even if that isn't strictly true, at least the emotions that come with "pairing up," such as jealousy and possessiveness, are natural.[9]

As he acknowledges by saying "this is probably going to sound like the religious Right," Jense, like his conservative opponents, draws from a discourse of naturalization to counter the claim that state-legitimated monogamy privileges some sexualities over others. By replying in this way, Jense reaffirms his conservative opponents' arguments that exclusion does not constitute discrimination when intimacies are deemed unnatural. But Jense also sounds like his conservative opponents in the way he equates "average" with "normal" when describing his view of intimacies that deserve state protection. We could just as easily say that heterosexuality "is something that most people expect and desire"—a logic for objecting to same-sex marriage that Jense routinely rejects.

As a conservative in favor of same-sex marriage, Craig Shilling, former leader of his local Log Cabin Republicans chapter, emphatically explained the hatred behind the religious Right's position on marriage: "If the government rounded up all of the gays and lesbians and put them in a concentration camp, the religious conservatives would praise it. There is nothing in the world that we are going to do that they like, ever. They hate us so much. Their hatred is so pure. We are Satan; we are the Devil. They would say it is God's work. So their arguments, to me, hold no weight. Because, no matter what we say or what we do, they are not going to like us." Whereas Craig has clearly given up on the prospects for dialogue among some of his fellow Republicans, he does share their belief in the importance of marriage as an institution steeped in tradition. When I asked what he thought about the argument from the queer left that marriage is an inherently discriminatory institution, Craig's initially educational tone ended with a visible torrent of fury:

[Marriage] is an institution that is thousands and thousands and thousands of years old. It is one of the main consistent things that we have had over the past two thousand years. Our society has greatly advanced, and I think that [marriage] is part of it. I am not sure what relationships would be more important than one where two people love each other. I am not really sure, but I think that extreme liberalism is a mental disorder. I just don't see it. I don't understand the argument about why it is inherently discriminatory. The problem with the queer left is that they are discriminatory, because if you don't like exactly what they say, then you are nothing. I get more shit from the gay left than I do from the Republican right. They are useful idiots for the Democratic Party.

Here Craig demonstrates how one can reject the slippery slope while at the same time upholding marriage as a timeless institution essential for civilization. Craig's response also demonstrates the limited discursive ground available for rejecting arguments from the religious Right in a way that upholds monogamy and marriage as the foundation for civilization. But Craig's position is more than political strategy; it is such a deep personal belief that he cannot imagine any sane critique of such an enduring social institution.

For other proponents of same-sex marriage with whom I spoke, the natural desire for monogamy is aimed toward finding safety, shelter, and security. The naturalization of monogamy, in this case, is directly linked to political rationalities of risk and the belief that marriage provides the ultimate form of insurance against problems endemic to human populations. Consider Muriel's response when I asked her why she believes that marriage is important for society. She remarked: "I think that it is built into us; probably because originally for the need to do that for mating and security. It is just built into us. . . . It is a natural part of what we do for security and stability. I think that there is a lot to be said about the stability of society as a whole to have a couple of people say that we are going to commit to take care of each other financially, medically, and whatever for a considerable amount of time." For Muriel, marriage is a social institution that reflects humans' natural desire to pair up, and more important, humans have this drive because it is how individuals deal with problems of the population. This line of argumentation is consistent with conservative opponents' belief that the married couple is not only an intimacy but a care structure explicitly juxtaposed to "group" or "socialist" arrangements.

In fact, the connection that Stanley Kurtz makes between the dissolution of marriage and the spread of socialism remains, at least publicly, uncontested by proponents of same-sex marriage. In the *Congressional*

Record, no one rebuts either that the dissolution of marriage has nothing to do with socialism or, more important, that socialism is a great idea and the dissolution of marriage is the first step in the right direction. Rather, proponents of same-sex marriage insist that Kurtz's conclusions are spurious, claiming instead that declining rates of marriage in Scandinavia have more to do with decreased cultural prohibitions on cohabitation.[10]

Similar to the slippery slope arguments, proponents of marriage equality also express discourses about marriage in a way that naturalizes not just monogamous intimacies but monogamized social care as well. In other words, it is natural not only for individuals to "pair" in order to fulfill emotional and sexual needs but also for two people to "take care of each other" by managing risks associated with population-level problems such as illness and poverty—or what Muriel refers to as financial and medical issues. Thus, we have a twofold naturalization that comes with marriage: the naturalization of monogamous intimacies and the naturalization of monogamous governance.

While some proponents of same-sex marriage point to the animal kingdom or the myth that humans have always been paired up to support their claims that monogamy is a natural basis for security and belonging in society, others naturalize monogamy and remove it from political critique by shielding it from intellectual scrutiny. From this perspective, monogamy is natural and thus beyond political dispute because it "just feels right." In this sense, we can see how the unmarried/married categorical division needs no intellectual justification. Many members of Marriage Rights Now had trouble articulating why they believe that monogamy is superior to other types of intimate relationships. Joe Franklin, for example, said that he could not explain how "any system was better than another," but he did not feel that any other kind of relationship made sense in his "heart." Buck Crawford further naturalized monogamy and removed it from the purview of critique by telling me that he and his husband, Matt, "don't see marriage intellectually. We see it emotionally. We see it as two people together loving each other and being recognized by society as equal and good people." This emotional attachment to monogamy shelters marriage from the possibility of critical evaluation, thus making legal classification seem like a natural and inevitable reflection of monogamous desires.

Emotional attachments to monogamy appear natural, rather than socially constructed, in part because in modern times, monogamy is inextricably idealized with the narrative of romantic love (Coontz 2005): the belief that natural bonds of mutual affection between two people exist as a private reality and express themselves as a lifelong commitment to and sexual attraction for each other.[11] The romantic love narrative posits that intimate bonds with others come from a feeling within a person rather than social conditions. The elements of the romantic love narrative are numerous and historically variant, but in general, the narrative includes the following tenets:

1. *Sex-essentialist:* Romantic love describes a feeling that only men can have toward women, and only women can have toward men.
2. *Monogamous:* Romantic love is a zero-sum emotion; it is shared only by two people who vow to love each other to the exclusion of any third party.
3. *Sexual:* Romantic love differs from other forms of love because it involves a sexual relationship.
4. *Irrational:* Romantic love is a feeling that cannot be captured by reason. It often happens "at first sight," without warning or contemplation.

Although the ideology of romantic love has historically been sex-essentialist, and thus heteronormative (Coontz 2005), the same-sex couples with whom I spoke and those who have written affidavits in court cases considering the legality of same-sex marriage express all the other characteristics consistent with the narrative. Many proponents of marriage equality agree with Arkes's contention that love ought to be "confined to coupling." For example, plaintiffs' affidavits in state court cases considering the constitutionality of excluding same-sex couples from marriage often begin with an expression of a lifelong dream to fall in love and marry "the one" or a story about how the couple fell in love. For example, Lauren Abrams, in her affidavit to the New York State Supreme Court, testified about the first time she met her partner at a Christmas tree-trimming party and how they "knew almost immediately that we were right for each other."[12] Lancy Woo, in her affidavit to the California Superior Court, testified about how she met Cristy through a mutual friend and recalled "looking up, seeing her from a distance, and feeling everything around me slipping into slow motion. We started falling in love . . . and have kept falling ever since."[13] Cindy Meneghin, in her affidavit to the New Jersey Superior Court, testified that she and Maureen were "high school sweethearts." She also wanted the court to know that "to this day I can still remember the day when I first saw her on a bleacher in the gymnasium. Now we are growing old together."[14]

These romantic narratives might seem out of place in affidavits, but given the dynamics of symbolic power I propose in the previous chapter, they fit perfectly with the courts' efforts to see themselves as bodies that merely recognize rather than create emotional and symbolic attachments to marriage. This is an image that MRN leaders work hard to maintain by censoring life stories of those who, like Tami, view marriage primarily as a necessary gateway to provisions of social care. By articulating romantic love narratives, proponents of marriage equality offer the courts an alternative to the religious Right's representation of marriage as a prepolitical longing—one that allows the boundaries of marriage to expand to previously excluded neo-liberal subjects without threatening to disenchant and expose the state's political-economic interest in marriage.

This reformulation emerged in the Vermont and Massachusetts cases, where romantic love narratives provided a basis for the courts to conclude that marriage is an "esteemed institution" because it "fulfils yearnings," not because it creates them. The court writes as if the symbolic importance of marriage comes directly from natural human desires—"yearnings"—rather than the state's "power to make groups" (Bourdieu 1990a, 137). In this paradigm, it appears as if love comes before marriage. There is no room for the possibility that the marriage classification process itself can also produce romantic desires that seem private, natural, and inevitable. The Vermont and Massachusetts courts refuse to recognize the historical evidence that suggests that romantic love is a historically constructed ideology that began with industrialization and that marriage became a place to express romantic love only in the modern, industrialized world (Cancian 1987; Coontz 2005).

In addition to the discourse of naturalization and romantic love, MRN members offer an additional alternative narrative that would allow the state to expand marriage to same-sex couples without threatening to erode its symbolic power. Proponents of marriage equality repeatedly characterized arguments from singles or polyamorous communities as "hypothetical," "theoretical," and "intellectual abstractions" that do not affect "real" people. For example, when I asked Joe what he thought about arguments from the queer left that marriage discriminates against alternative forms of intimacy, he replied as follows:

> It is interesting. It is definitely on the fringe. I mean, for me, I am just personally such a strong believer in monogamy that, um, I don't [see it]. I have a hard time seeing it as discrimination. . . . I just don't. It is kind of like, show me the body. I

don't see the discrimination anywhere. I don't see that there are people who are really trying to be polygamous and raise children that way and having a hard time doing it. I mean maybe they exist, and I am just not seeing it.

For Joe, any other form of intimacy besides monogamy really exists only as a theoretical abstraction that the right wing uses to urge the state to maintain the sex essentialism in the current definition of legal marriage. Joe acknowledges that his adherence to monogamy comes from a "strong belief" rather than a transparent logic—a belief that is apparently strong enough to blind him and others to the struggle of many Americans who attempt to forge lives outside of the monogamy/marriage norm.

Similarly, Steve Kemp's partner, Jack, answered the same question by also viewing nonmonogamous intimacies as unreal. He argued that the idea of marriage discriminating against individuals who choose not to live monogamous lives is "a hypothetical abstraction, and what the marriage equality movement is doing is presenting real, live human beings who are directly affected by this discrimination in the law. They are the very people who are affected and have the recognition, protection, rights, and responsibilities denied to them. It is not abstract. It is not hypothetical. And this idea of 'Aren't you denying polyandrous relationships and suborning imperialism?' we have heard these things, and they are just absurd abstractions versus real human beings, people and their lives." Jack, in a tone far more direct and angry than Joe's, refuses to even discuss the possibility of forms of intimacy outside of the marriage norm. In this way, the marriage equality movement has not simply accepted the terms of the religious Right's slippery slope logic, but it has extended the framework by positing alternative intimacies as not just immoral and undesirable but fictional. MRN's construction of nonmarital intimacies as abject distractions makes it really difficult to believe that efforts of marriage equality activism will actually move American law in the direction of recognizing "pure relationships" (Giddens 1991, 1992), as Chet Meeks and Arlene Stein (2006) hope.

The Winning Formula

The United States federal government has weighed in on the same-sex marriage issue only through DOMA and failed attempts at a Federal Marriage Amendment (FMA). In both cases, the debate hinged on the slippery slope argument and issues of states' rights. Even though the FMA did not pass, with the existence of DOMA and the absence of a federal Supreme Court ruling on the marriage question, it is safe to characterize the federal government's position as excluding those willing to take on responsibility for self-governance through marriage. At the state level, however, four supreme courts have decided not to exclude the willing and ruled it unconstitutional to deny same-sex couples the benefits of marriage. As I argue in chapter 2, in all four of these states, the majority opinions concluded that same-sex couples embody the state's interest in economizing governance through marriage. In each decision, marriage equality responses to the slippery slope argument have resonated with the courts, and the courts have redrawn the line between legitimate and illegitimate family forms based on either the implied or specifically stated superiority of monogamy over other "unhealthy" arrangements.

In the state supreme court rulings in favor of allowing same-sex couples at least parallel legal benefits of marriage, the majority opinion acknowledges that the state manages the population by privileging one type of intimate association without questioning whether it should. Instead, the court reconstitutes the definition of legal marriage in a way that allows same-sex couples the benefits and recognition that marriage affords while leaving all others excluded from the entitlements of marriage without recourse. In each case, the courts justify their decisions to allow same-sex couples access to marriage by preempting the slippery slope scenario: marriage remains meaningful not because it is based on the "natural teleology" of differently sexed bodies but because it continues to prohibit certain other "unhealthy" intimate arrangements and care structures.

The Massachusetts court preempted accusations that same-sex couples would undermine marriage by stating plainly, "Here, the plaintiffs seek only to be married, not to undermine the institution of civil marriage. They do not want marriage abolished. They do not attack the binary nature of marriage, the consanguinity provisions, or any other gate-keeping provisions of the marriage licensing law."[15] The court continues by generalizing the plaintiff's desire to same-sex couples in general, whom the majority opinion describes as "willing to embrace marriage's solemn obligations of exclusivity, mutual support, and commitment to one another."[16] Not only is the court convinced that same-sex couples can further the state's interest in marriage—to reduce its expenditures (see chapter 2)—but it also implicitly rejects the slippery slope argument by claiming that same-sex couples' yearning to live married lives is "a testament to the enduring place of marriage in our laws and the human spirit."[17] Thus, rather than recognizing marriage as one of many legitimate intimate relationships and care structures, the winning formula leaves the natural superiority of monogamy unquestioned, and it posits the neo-liberal state's interest in shifting responsibility for managing population-level problems to couples as a natural aspect of the "human spirit."

The Massachusetts court was also quick to respond to any accusations or possibilities that its decision to open marriage to same-sex couples would erase any classification or demarcation between the married and the unmarried. "Nothing in our opinion today should be construed as relaxing or abrogating the consanguinity or polygamy prohibitions of our marriage laws."[18] While same-sex couples can now benefit from the official recognition and insurance that marriage provides, the law still bars some people from these state-conferred privileges. Throughout the decision, the Massachusetts court legitimates the inclusion of same-sex couples on the principles of "individual autonomy" and "equality under the law," but it does not clearly address how marriage law itself can fulfill these values when it prohibits multiple forms of consensual adult intimacies from gaining the legal protection and symbolic profit of normality that come with marriage.

In contrast to the Massachusetts decision, the New Jersey court bought the logic of the Right's slippery slope narrative and rejected plaintiffs' assertions that they pose no threat to the definitional boundaries of marriage. The majority opinion points to what the justices call the plaintiffs' concession that "the State can insist on the binary nature of marriage."[19] Furthermore, in a footnote addressing the limitations of Chief Justice Deborah T. Poritz's dissenting opinion, which accuses the majority of defining the right to marry too narrowly, the court writes:

> The dissent posits that we have defined the right too narrowly and that the fundamental right to marry involves nothing less than the "liberty to choose, as a matter of personal autonomy." . . . That expansively stated formulation, however, would eviscerate any logic behind the State's authority to forbid incestuous and polygamous marriages. For example, under the dissent's approach, the State would have no legitimate interest in preventing a sister and a brother or father and daughter (assuming child bearing is not involved) from exercising their "personal autonomy" and "liberty to choose" to marry.[20]

In this statement, the New Jersey court justifies its boundaries of the "right to marry" not on fundamental principles of consent, liberty, or equality but on an a priori conceptualization of relationships that should never be considered legitimate under marriage law.

In a similar vein, the California court responded to the slippery slope doomsday prediction by arguing that its ruling in no way opens the door to what it calls "incestuous" or "polygamous" marriage, on the grounds that these relationships are "inimical to the mutually supportive and healthy family relationships promoted by the constitutional right to marry."[21] Ignoring multiple examples of "unhealthy" and unstable married relationships, the court made this assertion without feeling the need to cite any kind of social science research required to substantiate the claim that relationships between close family members and relationships involving more than two people are "unhealthy." The court did not demonstrate what exactly makes these relationships unworthy of state legitimization; instead, it justified continued discrimination against these family forms: "Although the historical disparagement of and discrimination against gay individuals and gay couples clearly is no longer constitutionally permissible, the state continues to have a strong and adequate justification for refusing to officially sanction polygamous or incestuous relationships because of their potentially detrimental effect on a sound family environment."[22] Like the New Jersey court, the California court found no need to justify the "disparagement of and discrimination against" relationships that are "polygamous or incestuous" beyond rooting the rejection of "other" family forms in the same legal tradition from which it had rescued same-sex couples.

Not all members of the California court found themselves convinced that the court has a solid constitutional foundation for redrawing the boundaries of marriage in a way that would preserve its "binary" status. In his concurring and dissenting opinion, Justice Marvin R. Baxter argued that the court overstepped its bounds in defining the right to marry in a way that opens the door to permitting official marriage designation for incestuous and polygamous relationships:

> Our society abhors such relationships [polygamous and incestuous]. . . . Yet here, the majority overturns, in abrupt fashion, an initiative statute confirming the equally deep-rooted assumption that marriage is a union of partners of the opposite sex. The majority does so by relying on its own assessment of contemporary community values. . . . This approach creates the opportunity for further judicial extension of this perceived constitutional right into dangerous territory. Who can say that, in ten, fifteen, or twenty years, an activist court might not rely on the majority's analysis to conclude, on the basis of a perceived evolution in

community values, that the laws prohibiting polygamous and incestuous marriages were no longer constitutionally justified?[23]

Baxter goes on to clarify that he does not think same-sex couples are "unhealthy" but that it is the legislature rather than the court's evaluation of community values that should determine the legal status of same-sex unions. Like the New Jersey court, Baxter bases his opinion on restricting other forms of intimacy rather than an ultimate value that intimate relationships or care structures ought to embody. Consequently, he constricts the realm of future possibilities regarding family forms to relationships that were historically "abhorred" according to nineteenth-century Protestant America.

Unlike the Massachusetts, New Jersey, and California cases, in the Vermont decision, there is little effort to actually acknowledge any "other" that would remain barred from the protections that civil marriage affords. From the discourse of the court, it appears as if the last form of exclusion in marriage law has been lifted with the legal recognition of same-sex couples. This view is plainly expressed by the Vermont Supreme Court, which finds: "We hold that the State is constitutionally required to extend to same-sex couples the common benefits and protections that flow from marriage under Vermont law. . . . Whatever system is chosen [as a remedy for the exclusion of same-sex couples from the rights and protections of marriage], however, must conform with the constitutional imperative to afford all Vermonters the common benefit, protection, and security of the law."[24] This statement suggests that once same-sex couples are allowed to marry, "all Vermonters" will be able to enjoy the legal and symbolic benefits of marriage. The court does not recognize a legitimate claim from Vermonters who may want to remain unmarried yet obtain the benefits of passing on their property to whomever they choose without a tax penalty. The majority also write as if there were no legitimate claim of exclusion by Vermonters who, for personal reasons, would like to designate someone with whom they are not romantically involved to be the legal parent of their child without the high cost of second-parent adoption. In other words, the "common benefit, protection, and security of the law" does not appear to apply to the unmarried. The Vermont decision echoes Joe's and Jack's view that nonmarried ways of living are not "real" enough to deserve the court's consideration.

The Vermont court does not address how its constitution's "common benefits clause" is intrinsically violated by the very existence of marriage statues that tie monogamous intimacy to social provisions that allow individuals to manage life's risks. Instead, the court argues that it is "beyond dispute that the State has a legitimate and long-standing interest in promoting a commitment between couples for the security of their children."[25] Here the court preempts the slippery slope scenario by refusing to even consider the empirical evidence that the married family form provides safety and security for children only because of its unique legal status rather than because of the natural superiority of monogamy (Stacey 1990, 1996; Stacey and Biblarz 2001). Rather, the court assumes what Muriel Stokely plainly articulated: the stability of society is predicated on two individuals, regardless of sex, "taking care of each other."

Essentially, the Vermont, Massachusetts, New Jersey, and California courts justify the inclusion of same-sex couples by assuring the reader that the law will continue to exclude certain relationships from the rewards of marriage. Parallel to discourses about autonomy, liberty, equality, and free choice, we find an ill-defined and doxic acceptance that these values may be limited for the sake of preserving the "binary nature" of marriage and prohibiting particular types of intimate relationships from achieving any legal or symbolic support. Thus, marriage equality's winning formula may be "decentering heterosexuality" (Meeks and Stein 2006) but not the power of the court to define access to legal and social protections based on what it posits as socially acceptable and "healthy" relationships.

Beyond the "Party Line"

Not all proponents of marriage equality express beliefs consistent with the "winning formula." Some did not respond to conservatives' slippery slope arguments as Joe, Buck, Jense, and John did: that monogamy is an appropriate, natural place to draw the line between state-sanctioned, legitimate intimacies and "abstract" or theoretical intimacies. Instead, they differentiated their own personal beliefs about marriage from the party line constructed in response to conservatives' slippery slope arguments. However, these proponents kept their personal sentiments hidden from public view for fear that they would undermine the success of the marriage equality movement. Some members claimed that MRN explicitly instructed them to silence their personal opinions, while others regarded their silence on the issue as an act of self-censorship. In both cases, the slippery slope framework provided a discursive context inimical to questioning the superiority of monogamy as an intimate relationship and model of social care.

Several members of Marriage Rights Now do not accept the assumptions central to the winning formula. Albeit avid proponents of marriage equality, these members reject the logic of the slippery slope argument by refusing to recognize a danger in reevaluating the binary logic of marriage or considering deinstitutionalization. For example, when I asked Mei to describe her position on the slippery slope, she drew from her own family background and cross-cultural examples:

> Multiple partners, for example, that is one of the things down the slippery slope. That is the next thing [after same-sex marriage] you are going to have, you know, marriage with multiple partners. And I thought, so what? Really, I mean I come from a culture where multiple wives are commonplace. My great-grandfather had four wives. Muslims today have multiple wives. There are other cultures that have multiple husbands. So what? Does it really matter? I mean this is one where I really do think that the government should get out of it. If people want to move to a colony, OK. Let them. Does it really matter?

Mei sees marriage as a "cultural thing," meaning that it does not have a basis in nature, and its definition and scope change depending on the social context. Because Mei does not naturalize marriage as a "binary" institution, she finds it difficult to justify the state's authority to define marriage at all. For this reason, Mei found herself in agreement with the perception of marriage as discriminatory. "Let's face it—marriage is a discriminatory institution. . . . Marriage, by itself, shouldn't give the rights not there for a nonmarried person. What does it matter whether you are married or single? I don't think that it should matter at all. It should be based on the person that you are. Same thing about having kids, you know? Why should they be given exemptions, because you are creating an incentive to have more kids in the tax code? Should the government even be doing that?" Mei's position on the slippery slope parted from the official MRN argument because she did not personally believe that there was any danger in changing the legal scope of marriage or abolishing it as a legal category. She did not feel that society would be threatened or thrown into chaos if marriage were deinstitutionalized. In turn, she felt no hesitation about telling me her belief that marriage is not a natural or superior relationship but a culturally constructed norm.

Typically, MRN members who share Mei's refusal to assume an imminent danger at the end of the slippery slope purposefully silenced their own opinions for fear of providing ammunition for conservative opponents. Several MRN members felt that nonmonogamous relationships deserve the marriage title or that the government should not legitimate some consensual, adult relationships at the expense of others, but they also feared expressing these arguments openly. One MRN member asked me not to include her remarks about polygamous and polyamorous relationships in any final publication. Others explicitly distanced their own personal opinions from MRN's party line. For example, when I asked Patrick what he thought about arguments from the queer left that point to marriage as an institution that inherently privileges monogamy over any other form of intimacy, he replied hesitantly:

> I actually think that there are a lot of good points to that argument. . . . There are just so many ways where marriage results in benefits that other people don't get. . . . I don't really have any sense that monogamous marriage is morally or physiologically or emotionally better than being single or cohabitating or having multiple partners. . . . When you asked me this question, it was going through my mind, you know, "Should I say this?" I remember seeing all of those signs about "I want to marry my dog," you know? What happens when I say this is that other people start saying "Aha. . . . There *is* a slippery slope. So you think [that] every relationship is OK, or that polygamy is OK," or something like that.

Patrick ultimately shared his opinion with me, but he routinely silences his own views concerning the slippery slope in public discourse. Given the winning formula discussed in the previous section, Patrick's hesitancy is well founded. The dominance of the slippery slope framework makes proponents' work toward inclusion counterproductive to efforts aimed at subjecting marriage to reflexivity: if members point to the institution's flexibility and ask for plurality, they essentially align themselves with, as Justice Baxter put it, relationships that society "abhors," thus dramatically reducing the possibility of inclusion.

Judy made this predicament explicit by clearly distinguishing her opinion from the official MRN position. When I asked her what kinds of relationships she felt should be considered eligible for marriage, Judy responded carefully:

> I can tell you the MRN line, and I can tell you mine. I'm not speaking for MRN. I know that MRN would say that we're not asking for new rights; . . . you know

there [are] already rules against siblings getting married . . . , there are rules against parents and children, rules against more than one partner. You know, more than two altogether. We're not saying that we want something new. We're just saying that we want the same right to get married to one person that is not your family member. Personally, I'm not really sure why the line has to be there at all—again, I mean from a civil point of view. I mean churches can have whatever kinds of rules that they want, but from a civil point of view, there is really no reason to say that siblings can't get married. I mean, the research shows that there really isn't a greater risk of birth defects. Um, . . . I mean I'm not a psychologist, so I don't know if there is some like weird germinant damage caused by incestuous relationships or whatever. . . . When people are like "Oh, it's going to lead to polygamy and incest," I'm like "So?" But I'm not allowed to say that as an MRN member.

Unlike Patrick and Mei, Judy felt the Marriage Rights Now organization directly censored her personal opinions. Judy continued her explanation of why MRN would impose this censorship: "Nobody wants to, it's very un, it's not politic to go on record saying that incest is not automatically a bad thing." In practice, she mechanically recites the MRN party line in public venues even though she does not personally agree with the discursive ground it surrenders.

Judy did not simply assume that "other" intimacies and forms of care are innocent. Instead, she felt that they should be considered as such unless proved guilty. From her point of view, the state should rationally draw the line between legitimate and illegitimate relationships based on scientific evidence rather than tradition, religious doctrine, or political viability.

Again, if there isn't an actual social reason, . . . if they could prove that, you know, it would actually harm people, I could see having an injunction against it, but just, like, that is why we are not allowed to marry four-year-old kids. It's not OK; they could get hurt. . . . So if there is some way that they could prove that something like that is causing harm, then I would be willing to believe that. My point is just that mature—forget mature, consenting—adults, you know, let them live their lives as long as nobody is getting hurt. Let them live their lives. You know, don't single people out and say that your relationships are better and your relationships are inferior. Um, so I guess that the adult thing would be me drawing the line and if there were studies that showed harm.

Judy makes a distinction between civil and religious marriage in order to differentiate the logic that ought to be applied to matters of governance.

Rather than judging law on faith, tradition, or "common sense," Judy asks the state to make its determinations based on research and evidence.

MRN members who did not think it morally right or necessary to limit marriage to couples continued to fight for marriage equality and publicly adhere to MRN's official response to the slippery slope argument. Some reconciled this tension by pointing to political expediency: marriage rights are a winnable battle, and arguing for marriage does not preclude extending marriage rights to other arrangements in the future. Others applied a teleological view of history that recognized a future in which people could think beyond the "binary" logic of marriage.

For example, Kim Chow and Roni Plumb debated the potential for the MRN response to the slippery slope argument to foreclose the possibility of abolishing marriage or extending marriage rights to more than couples.

KIM: I don't think that the United States is ready for extreme radical change. You need to take it one step at a time. We have to gain this right first to be able to say, because now we are talking from a position where we don't have those rights in the first place. This is a radical idea for most people. . . . I think that would definitely hurt the LGBT community, because it sounds like anarchy, probably, to a lot of people.

RONI: Yeah, I definitely think that you have to have this step before you can get to the next step. Just so that you are on equal ground, so that you can say, "OK, now that we have this, we can say this." You can then say, "Now that we can allow this kind of relationship, why not allow this kind?" You know, and what is the big deal?

JAYE CEE: The slippery slope argument the right wing has is kind of correct, then?

KIM: OK, well, thirty years ago they were saying, "Oh no, the next step is gay marriage," so maybe in thirty years, it is not going to sound like such a big deal. That is how I look at it. Yeah, right now it sounds kind of radical, but the things that they were doing in the fifties, we are looking back at that and saying, "My God, I can't believe that they did that." We would never even think of that going on, so in thirty years, they might think like that. They might wonder, why [is] gay marriage such a big deal? Why is polygamy such a big deal? You know, we evolve and things change, and we have to just go with it.

Even though they publicly espouse the MRN party line regarding the slippery slope, like Patrick and Judy, Kim and Roni personally think that marriage should not necessarily have to be limited to couples. They reconcile the difference between MRN's official position and their own beliefs by seeing marriage equality as an incremental, teleological process of historical progression that does not end with the legal recognition of same-sex couples. Unlike the official MRN argument, Kim and Roni do not see reform or elimination of marriage on the bottom of a downward slope toward immorality; instead, they feel as if giving same-sex couples access to marriage is one step up toward what future generations may consider worthy of full equality.

Positions counter to the marriage equality party line are important for two reasons. First, they indicate that the current course of marriage equality activism requires silencing queer critiques of marriage as an institution that restricts multiple forms of consensual intimacy and alternative models of care. In addition, the fact that individuals can ideologically oppose an institution they ardently fight for speaks to a more insidious model of domination at work. Mei, Patrick, Judy, Kim, and Roni are under no illusion that marriage is a reflection of the laws of nature; they are not "falsely conscious" of the social construction of marriage. Nor do they believe that there is an inevitable connection between ways of organizing care and appropriate avenues for experiencing sexual pleasure. Instead, they silence their own opinions and reiterate the party line because they believe that marriage equality is politically expedient and more practical than efforts toward deinstitutionalization.

* * *

In the debate over marriage equality, all parties seem to agree that marriage is a superior family form and care structure particularly suited for reducing state expenditures. What is up for debate, however, is the potential for same-sex coupling to denaturalize marriage and expose its socially constructed boundaries. The threat implied by the prospects of same-sex marriage, however, is not simply its potential to denaturalize marriage as the only legitimate *intimacy*; denaturalization threatens to expose the inequity of marriage as a *care structure* as well. Thus, there is more than one "danger" at the bottom of the slippery slope: the figure of the polygamous family symbolically representing denaturalized intimacy is joined by the communist society representing state-supported care. The reason why willing same-sex couples are allowed to marry in only two states has as much to do with justifying the exclusion of "other" intimacies and models of care as it does restricting same-sex couples in particular. Even those who argue that same-sex couples probably deserve to marry are worried that "redefining" the "traditional" parameters of marriage risks opening the floodgates to all kinds of intimate arrangements and care structures that are presently denied access to the material and symbolic rewards that come with official state legitimization.

At first glance, it may appear that MRN is pressured to formulate its party line because of the political force of the religious Right. There is, in fact, plenty of evidence to suggest that the religious Right has shaped the direction, scope, and structure of gay and lesbian politics since the late 1970s (Fetner 2008). However, the religious Right's arguments and the marriage equality movement's subsequent retorts are both part of the same effort toward *reconnaissance* without threatening to reveal the state's arbitrary power of *connaissance*. The religious Right's slippery slope narrative reminds state officials that making the definition of marriage more consistent with neo-liberal self-governance has consequences: the short-term financial benefits of increased wedding tourism, a decline in welfare eligibility, and so forth are weighed against the prospect of "group marriage" and the overall erosion of the couple as the enchanted unit of social care. After all, without the presupposed assumptions of heteronormativity and the "natural teleology of the body" it implies, how can the state abrogate its own symbolic power to define normative intimate relationships and privatize population-level risks? Like their conservative opponents, the marriage equality movement insists that there is a firm and sacred foundation for marriage that exists outside of the state's own performative power. Even though the marriage equality movement has had mixed success in its efforts to renaturalize marriage boundaries, its successes in state supreme courts have required this reformulation. Those successes have hinged on articulating a type of heteronormativity that does not require sex essentialism. The *new homonormativity* (Duggan 2003) rests on the marriage equality movement's successfully convincing the state that same-sex couples pose no threat to the privatization of care and the naturalization of monogamy.

With the tools of ethnographic research, we can also see how individuals can ideologically oppose homonormativity at the same time that they continue to speak its language. Marriage equality activists whose thoughts differ from the party line attempt to resolve this ambivalence by ultimately basing their actions on values of political expediency rather than equality or freedom.

Conclusion

Marriage as a Technology of Governance

Throughout this book, we have considered marriage from the viewpoint of those who are unwillingly excluded from a pervasive public institution and its concomitant, and almost ineffable, private feelings and intimate experiences. By performatively citing gays and lesbians in general as subjects worthy of the marriage label, proponents of marriage equality provide a window for understanding this specific type of state license as a regulatory ideal rather than a lifestyle choice—a technology of self-governance reinforced by the symbolic power of the state to produce and restrict citizens' options for belonging in their nation, community, and family.

In this final chapter, I identify my contributions in terms of the three main objectives introduced in chapter 1: to explain the contemporary resonance of the marriage equality message in mainstream gay and lesbian national politics, to improve sociologists of the family's understandings of marriage as a site for governing populations, and to contribute to social theorists' perspectives concerning how practices of governance become misrecognized as lifestyle choices. I conclude by summarizing the political implications of my findings.

Why Marriage?

If viewed only with evidence from the official party line, the marriage equality movement may appear to be motivated by the desire to secure the economic and social privilege of the most advantaged LGBTQ political organizations and gay and lesbian individuals, to the detriment of economically disadvantaged and socially disenfranchised queers (Duggan 2003; Ettelbrick 2004). After all, policy briefs from proponents of same-sex marriage point to the number of Americans who, if married, would become ineligible for state and federal assistance; in addition, statements from MRN members such as Amber, who wants access to marriage so "the state doesn't have to" care for her and Hazel, make marriage seem advantageous only for those who have the luxury of assets that could be inherited without undue taxation, health insurance that would cover spouses, or unemployment benefits that would sufficiently brace a legal family in a time of crisis.

On the other hand, it is also true that attention to stories beyond the party line from MRN members such as Cathy, Jennifer, Tami, and other working-class same-sex couples who desire marriage (Hull 2006) shows how the most economically disadvantaged can continue to advocate for inclusion even if it would erode their already limited access to public financial assistance. Members of MRN see marriage as a form of indemnification, a smart lifestyle choice that is similar to an insurance policy in that it provides an unparalleled sense of emotional security by transforming potential disasters into manageable accidents. Ann and Sue, for example, see marriage as the most sensible and available avenue for reducing their risk of being left to suffer or even die in a hospital room without comfort and affection from the person they love the most.

The overwhelming majority of MRN members, however, do not see their political motivations as a selfish pursuit. As the incident in Pine Haven and Patrick's discussion of the "discrimination disease" suggest, MRN members cite marriage as a regulatory ideal, hoping to produce normative acceptance capable of healing gay stigma and thus protecting all gays and lesbians regardless of their desire to marry.

As the logic of neo-liberalism would predict, proponents of same-sex marriage reveal how one could become invested in, rather than falsely conscious of, the economization of the state: technologies of self-governance, unlike authoritarian ones, come with a zone of privacy that offers state protection without direct surveillance. As Roni Plumb asserts, when the state provides privacy, it offers "antidiscrimination protection." As evidenced by statements such as Lauren Abrams's official testimony, proponents also explicitly juxtapose the threat of being exposed to life's risks without marriage with the rewards of privacy offered by the marriage bribe.

However, as I demonstrate in chapter 5, proponents of marriage equality also express an immediate emotional affinity with marriage, seeing it as providing a sense of public legibility, belonging, and recognition. The rewards of belonging within the marriage classification include official recognition by the state as well as an everyday sense of belonging as a member of the community, church, family, and intimate partnership that comes with gestures of acceptance, from greeting cards to being able to mark the "married" box on official documents.

Protection, privacy, and recognition are motivations for same-sex marriage documented in the LGBTQ studies literature; however, my work accounts for the political and social ramifications of the discourses and silences that undergird them. My findings imply that neo-liberalism's relevance to the same-sex marriage debate extends beyond the influence and structure of professionalized (Richardson 2005) and commercialized organizations (Duggan 2003). Proponents of marriage equality reveal how the ethic of self-governance and practical efficiency critical to neo-liberalism bleeds into individuals' most fundamental understandings of equality, choice, and even love. On the other hand, drawing attention to marriage as a technology of governance only magnifies our understanding of the politics of normalization (Meeks and Stein 2006; Warner 1999) by emphasizing the symbolic power of state classifications to ennoble particular care structures as well as intimate relationships.

The silences and ambivalences of MRN activism also speak to the possibility that marriage equality will eventually lead to more equitable care structures, increase family diversity, and widen sexual freedom. My evidence suggests that regardless of their intentions, these historically valued, yet also contested, goals of gay and lesbian politics are neither an inevitable nor even probable outcome of same-sex couples gaining access to the institution of marriage. As Mary Bernstein (2001) argues, this revolutionary potential rests on the discourses that same-sex marriage activists use to frame the debate. In court documents, policy briefs, public forums, and even group meetings, MRN members weave narratives that substantiate the unique importance of monogamy and self-governance and silence potential reticence toward accepting marriage as an appropriate way to define access to care or protect sexual liberty.

First, marriage equality has the potential to denaturalize marriage by exposing it as a "social practice . . . dependent on the recognition of the state" (Meeks and Stein 2006, 138); in practice, however, proponents renaturalize the institution in order to assuage the specter of the polygamous family or socialist political economy. Members of MRN not only acknowledge, but also help construct, marriage as the gold standard, unmatched by parallel licensing schemes, when they privilege personal testimony that seamlessly equates a state license with personal longings. In fact, it is proponents' ability to convince the state of same-sex couples' specific commitment to marriage as a prepolitical longing that offers the promise for legalizing same-sex marriage in the United States.

Second, some proponents justify the marriage exclusions when they speak the language of efficiency and political expediency characteristic of a neo-liberal ethic that values economization over citizen well-being. From this idiom, exclusions inherent to marriage are justified not because they are natural but because they are rational. Remember, Caitlin and Judy think it is wrong for the state to route access to health insurance through marriage, but they continue to advocate for marriage equality because they see it as a practical solution that the state has rationally produced as the best and most realistic way to organize care.

Finally, proponents' narratives of risk, privacy, and the gold standard have the potential to uphold the state's interest in marriage precisely because they construct a normative "gay and lesbian community." Even when MRN members do not personally see marriage as a threat to intimate or family diversity, they articulate narratives inimical to a broad range of chosen intimate arrangements when they base the deservedness of marriage protections on the claim that homosexuality is a natural compulsion with inherent or socially constructed risks that require state protection. Following this logic, proponents also speak as unelected representatives of the "homosexual" population discursively constructed as a collective defined by a desire to tame sexuality and embrace serial monogamy. Those who refuse to tame sexuality in the same way are understood as "abstract distractions" that are literally invisible (as Joe's request to "show me the body" indicates), whereas Marsha and Dana hope to demonstrate their worthiness to marry by revealing how they are "real people" because their lives resonate with cultural marriage scripts.

Arguments for intimate diversity or unhooking health insurance from marriage are avoided or explicitly excluded from official MRN discourse, not because the organization's leaders have a flawed strategy but because they know such arguments would undermine their claims for inclusion as the marrying kind. Thus, my evidence suggests that a successful marriage equality strategy requires ennobling marriage as a superior form of governance and unparalleled lifestyle choice.

Implications for the Sociology of Marriage

In the United States, the current debate over same-sex marriage offers a unique opportunity to reevaluate the function and significance of marriage, and more specifically, how and why marriage is implicit in the project of neo-liberal governance. As Peter Berger pointed out in 1963, a "sociological consciousness" of institutions and meanings that are normally taken for granted is "likely to arise when the commonly accepted or authoritatively stated interpretations of society become shaky" (42). In the United States today, marriage is on shaky ground. On the one hand, panic about the fragility of marriage appears to emerge in response to ongoing uncertainties about its definition and resilience. At the same time that Americans debate the fragility of marriage, many also passionately hope that marriage can solve numerous social problems by thriving as the essential foundation for American self-governance.

Marriage appears to be a technology particularly suited for managing poverty and illness through an ethic and logic of neo-liberal governance. While there are several potential avenues for managing poverty and illness in the United States, marriage emerges as a favored solution because it is consistent with the development of the social welfare state along liberal rather than universal principles that stigmatize collective dependencies and valorize individual responsibility. Policies from the Bill Clinton and George W. Bush administrations that call on marriage as a solution to illness and poverty, for example, prioritize the state's desire to reduce costs over the actual effectiveness of marriage as a comprehensive and inclusive social safety net. These policies clearly show how population-level problems of poverty and illness are being constructed as individual dilemmas (Mills 1959). My evidence suggests that these issues are not only individualized but monogamized: the marriage license rests on the perceived dependency between spouses, not the complete autonomy of individuals.

The public arguments, personal motivations, and silenced opposition from within MRN speak to a set of important questions about the relationship between neo-liberalism, intimacy, and governance that ought to be a central concern for sociologists of marriage and family. In my analysis of arguments for same-sex marriage, I hope to encourage an avenue of research attuned to understanding how and why this institution is evoked as a commonsense method for managing social problems. This perspective allows sociologists of marriage and family to explain why marriage would be associated with health, financial well-being, safety, and security by theorizing its role in managing the problems of the population. Along with employment, marriage is one of the only ways for Americans to gain access to affordable mechanisms of social insurance. This being the case, the benefits that result from marital status are not explained by the characteristics of marriage itself but by its elevated importance as a mechanism to manage life's risks. This means that an adequate explanation of why marriage is associated with all these advantages requires attention to the operation of neo-liberal governance.

My examination of arguments in favor of same-sex marriage provides only one of many potential angles to explain the importance of marriage as a project of neo-liberal governance. Additional directions might include an examination of how and why some segments of the unmarried population in the United States refuse to struggle for the symbolic power of recognition that marriage provides. This approach would allow us to examine whether divestment from marriage is related to a rejection of neo-liberalism. Do some individuals who reject marriage also refuse the terms of neo-liberalism? Are there marriage resisters who tacitly accept neo-liberalism, such as libertarians, but feel that marriage cannot fulfill goals of distant governance and economic efficiency?

A comparative approach between Scandinavian countries with more universal social safety nets and the more classical liberal models found in the United States would also provide an avenue to explain under which contexts safety, health, and wealth are associated with marriage. For example, in those countries that provide national health insurance based on citizenship rather than marital status, is marriage a primary predictor of health and well-being? One could also study whether marriage is even understood as a form of insurance against health risks in countries that actually provide universal health insurance.

By contextualizing family patterns according to the relative demands of particular political rationalities, it becomes clear that pressures on family life are inseparable from the governing functions that the state demands that families fulfill. Additionally, starting with the model I have proposed, sociologists of marriage and family can imagine new ways of asking questions that can account for the interconnection between intimate life and the management of the population without ignoring or trivializing the importance of love, belonging, and care.

Implications for Theories of Governmentality

The day-to-day efforts of advocates of marriage equality speak to the re-lationship between subjection and political resistance; specifically, they address how social actors can bring life to forms of neo-liberal gover-nance even when they remain ideologically opposed to the economization of social life. Even though theorists of governmentality do not explain how love, belonging, and the desire for recognition can become elements essential to the management of population-level risks, by drawing from Pierre Bourdieu's work, we gain a deeper understanding of why individuals might ardently struggle for the symbolic capital of recognition regardless of its potential to solidify and justify exclusionary categories. Theorizing marriage as a technology of governance, as I argue in chapter 5, does not erase the values of marriage as a source of care, belonging, recognition, romance, and love. Instead, it allows us to see the negative consequences that come from restricting these values to the marital form.

Very few accounts of neo-liberal governance from the governmentality perspective utilize research methods that allow one to see how political ra-tionalities, worked out in codified texts, become a part of individuals' feel-ings and thoughts. By watching and listening to how individuals imagine their own desires and goals by drawing from these macrolevel rationali-ties, one can understand how and why social agents may ardently struggle for the "right" to be governed. While theorists of governmentality point to subjective rewards contained within political rationalities—such as pri-vacy and the freedom of choice offered to subjects imagined by neo-liberal political rationalities—without interviews and participant observation, one cannot empirically determine the degree to which individuals actually internalize the terms of particular rationalities.

Perhaps because he utilized ethnographic methods, Pierre Bourdieu provides a model for understanding how and why agents may imagine their own desires, emotions, and thoughts according to state-consecrated categories that may be at direct odds with their material interests. For theorists of governmentality, Bourdieu's framework indicates how politi-cal rationalities actually become a commonsense and naturalized basis for individuals' perceptions and how individuals can become invested in particular political rationalities without explicitly accepting them. Agents' investment in social categories does not require any cognitive acceptance of the terms of a political rationality but rather prereflexive strategies and investments in the practices of everyday life that are crafted according to the terms of particular political rationalities. In this sense, individuals can imagine their feelings and thoughts in line with the terms of a political rationality without accepting the domination they imply or the tantalizing prospects for privacy and autonomy that they promise. Many proponents of same-sex marriage, for example, do not simply consent to marriage as a form of governance; instead, they *believe* in marriage as the gold standard, a natural category that would acknowledge rather than create the legitimacy of their relationships and subsequently provide protection from social stigma. This symbolic violence is particularly insidious not only because it excludes agents from acquiring social recognition and rewards but also because it crafts agents who are invested in the categories that oppress them (Bourdieu 1990a, 1991, 2000).

Bourdieu's theorization of symbolic power and habitus (1984, 1986, 1993, 1999) can help explain how individuals may misrecognize marriage as a natural, commonsense category, but it cannot account for how individuals may explicitly recognize marriage as a social fabrication and yet continue to believe in its symbolic power. For Bourdieu, naturalization is a necessary condition for symbolic power. To the contrary, my evidence suggests that within a neo-liberal political rationality, individuals can see marriage as a social fabrication with inherent inequalities and still believe in it to the extent that it optimizes practical efficiency—which is highly valued according to the logic of economization.

This study also provides an important revision to the contention that neo-liberal political rationalities operate primarily by individualizing responsibility. By viewing marriage as one technology for managing the problems of the population, it becomes clear that neo-liberal rationalities can also work through technologies that offer couples, not individuals, access to legally sanctioned avenues for protecting themselves as much as possible from the harmful effects of poverty and illness. As I argue in chapter 2, the responsibility for managing unemployment and health problems in the United States often falls on couples who have vowed to take care of each other "for richer or poorer, in sickness and in health." By making access to health insurance contingent on not just employment but also marital status, the United States actually provides incentives for individuals to manage risk as couples.

Uncoupling Intimacy and Governance

The debate over same-sex marriage provides a moment to reevaluate the package deal that gives marriage its Sphinx-like qualities (Cott 2000): it is as much a rite of passage as it is a legal contract; a symbol of love and commitment and a personal pledge of sexual fidelity; a mutual obligation to care as well as an agreement to share assets and liabilities; a spiritual covenant and fundamental unit that defines lineage. There are a number of ways to group and deconstruct various parts of marriage to expose some of its secrets: scholars and activists alike have pointed to marriage's public versus private dimensions. In addition, many members of MRN hope to distinguish religious from civil marriage. In the pages that remain, I argue that untangling marriage as an intimate arrangement (associated with sexual desire, love, and companionship) from marriage as a technology of governance (a specific mechanism for managing population-level social risks) provides a way of imagining alternatives with the potential to offer fairer and more effective care structures and to destigmatize consensual sexual relationships. This differentiation would allow the American public to judge mechanisms for the regulation of care separately from provisions pertaining to consensual intimate relationships and sexual practices.

When evaluating the efficacy and fairness of marriage as a form of governance, it makes sense to use criteria that we would apply to other political-economic interventions. Does marriage embody democratic values of equality and inclusion? Can marriage be constructed in a way that allows equal participation and representation for all Americans? Is it fair to connect access to structures that help manage life's risks with one particular way of organizing intimacy? Is it just or effective for the state to ask couples to individually manage population-level social problems—does this approach actually promote "social stability"?

Without divorcing intimacy from governance, it is difficult to ask these questions. Individuals may find meaning and pleasure from love tied to the monogamous form, but as a discourse, romantic love tends to obscure marriage as a practice of governance. After all, marriage is like no other government-issued license; its sacred cultural status is written into the document itself, forged in calligraphy and sometimes elegantly garnished with stenciled roses. If the technology of risk management that marriage offers were separated from the personal experiences of love and sexual fulfillment, MRN activists like Buck could see marriage "intellectually." We could ask difficult questions about the model of governance

marriage implies without scrutinizing the multiple, consensual, and sometimes creative ways that individuals experience love, romance, and sexual
pleasure.

My evidence supports arguments for disestablishing marriage and constructing methods for managing life's risks that acknowledge caretaking
as a collective responsibility rather than a burden placed on individual
families, many of whom lack the material resources to accept responsibility for care (Fineman 1995, 2004; Metz 2007, 2009; Polikoff 2008; Tronto
1993, 2001, 2004). In fact, it is inappropriate for the management of
population-level risks to be subsumed under the family at all. In addition to securing national territory, the role of the state is precisely to act
as the voice of the public in managing social phenomena that individuals
themselves cannot adequately deal with in an advanced industrial society,
such as ensuring access to jobs that offer a living wage, affordable housing,
and medical technology and expertise. As it operates now, marriage is an
increasingly imprecise proxy for caregiving: not all married couples care
for dependents (Fineman 2004). As the number of children, elderly adults,
the chronically ill, and unemployed who are cared for in structures other
than the married relationship increases, it makes sense to restructure the
state's relationship to care in a way that more directly supports and benefits caretakers (Tronto 1993, 2001, 2004).

Avoiding the conflation of intimacy and governance inherent in the
marriage model makes the state's interest in managing intimate life more
transparent—yet not irrelevant to politics, as MRN activists claim when
they order newcomers to "keep the bedroom out of the conversation." I
agree with Mary Shanley (2004) and others that the state does have a positive role in assuring equality and safety in personal relationships; however,
the marital form is neither an accurate nor a fair proxy for intimate equality. Patrick voiced this stance from outside the MRN party line when he
confessed that he had no reason to believe that marriage was any more
"healthy" or "equal" than other relationships. In fact, Patrick emphasized
the degree of domestic violence (shielded from state regulation by protection of privacy) in marital relationships that poses a far greater risk to
intimate life than polyamorous relationships.

The state's role in preserving negative liberty in intimate life must come
with a reconsideration and potential deconstruction of the zone of privacy
already set in place with the *Lawrence v. Texas* (2003) decision. Marsha
and Dana's attempts to secure full parenting rights are met with strict state
surveillance precisely because they are not granted the same presump-

tion of "fitness" applied to biological parents—yet genetic similarity itself is a problematic indicator of parenting skills. Moreover, what Roni calls the "antidiscrimination protection" that privacy provides comes with the repudiation of a livable cultural existence for public sexualities that have the potential to multiply experiences of pleasure and trust (Berlant and Warner 2000). Instead of "leaving the bedroom out of it," we need to have an explicit politics of sexuality that is not clouded by questions of social stability. By uncoupling intimacy and governance, we can imagine how multiple forms of adult sexual relationships can be valued, not because of the "stability" they may or may not provide to society but because they bring meaning, pleasure, and happiness.

The marital package also yields a conflation of negative rights to intimate privacy with the value of autonomy that tends to mask the multiple dependencies required for the operation of self-governance. As I demonstrate in chapter 4, many MRN members see through the eyes of the state when they interpret the responsibility for managing population-level risks as a necessary trade-off for the rewards of privacy. From the perspective of the government, marriage operates as a site for dependency in which the state can offer the promise of privacy in exchange for relinquishing its care obligations (Donzelot 1979; Fineman 2004). This sleight of hand is built upon what Martha Fineman calls "the autonomy myth," which masks how the state and the economy are dependent on "the caretaking labor that reproduces society and populates its institutions" (2004, xxvii). Uncoupling intimacy from governance offers a way to deautonomize caretaking without threatening privacy.

Furthermore, by acknowledging how all Americans are dependent on the aggregate work of caregivers, risks associated with illness and poverty become deindividualized as problems endemic to populations rather than specific to individuals or couples. Untangling the marriage knot does not imply that individuals need to change the way they organize intimacy or establish care; change needs to happen at the level of governance to provide structural support for caretaking and avoid prohibiting consensual sexual relationships. Many proponents of MRN described alternatives to marriage as "utopian" or "impractical," but sound and technically feasible legal avenues for institutionalizing such a distinction already exist. Martha Fineman (2004), Tamara Metz (2007), and Nancy Polikoff (2008), for example, offer specific proposals for uncoupling sexual and romantic relationships from legal avenues for supporting multiple care arrangements.

State-supported care structures, just by acknowledging dependency, do not necessarily yield a loss of privacy nor a growth in state intervention that exceeds what already exists under marriage laws. Instead, with Fineman's (2004) suggestion of shifting marriage advantages to the caregivers, state intervention would qualitatively shift, from a system based on privileging some forms of sexual and intimate relationships above all others to one based on giving material support to those who actually do provide much-needed, yet unpaid care services. As the slippery slope metaphor predicts, abolishing marriage as a legal category provides an opportunity to reevaluate dependency and care as public responsibilities.

The marriage model not only obscures the nature of caregiving dependency as an autonomous act shielded from scrutiny by legal protections of privacy but also masks the dependencies inherent in risk-based insurance technologies. In part because it fuses a model of governance with an intimate arrangement, the pleasures individuals experience within marriage can be easily confused with the effectiveness of marriage as a way to insure risks. If we disentangle the multiple functions marriage allegedly performs and sort them according to intimate versus governing purposes, we can imagine alternative, more equitable technologies for insuring life's risks.

Risk-based discourses used in the service of neo-liberal governing technologies seem to have little or no potential to govern according to more equitable standards, but the language of the risk-insurance model provides a means of reconceptualizing community in a way that valorizes rather than demonizes dependency. In other words, the political rationality of risk may offer a language that would make policy suggestions for disestablishing marriage more palatable for the American public. Essentially, as Foucault often argued, this means that the revolutionary potential for imagining alternatives to marriage comes not from attempting to work outside of the discourse that gives it meaning and legitimacy but from finding fissures in the discourse that would suggest possibilities for alternative arrangements.

Theorists of risk rightly point out how insurance technologies of risk management are necessarily collective; I argue that risk technologies also require multiple relationships of dependency. This makes the individualization of responsibility (Rose and Miller 1992; Rose 1999) associated with risk technologies particularly paradoxical; while risk management strategies, at least in capitalist, market-dominated societies like the United States, essentially call for individuals to regulate danger by making responsible choices, risk technologies (such as insurance) work only when risk is distributed across a population (Ewald 1991). By being a part of an insurance collectivity, individuals tacitly agree to make their potential exposure to and compensation for danger dependent upon all members of the collectivity. Insurance requires collective responsibility and acknowledges financial interdependence.

Within the risk-insurance model, there is a great deal of potential for publicly recognizing relationships of dependency and mutual commitment to care that are usually subsumed by the logic of American individualism. For example, Deborah Stone's work suggests that individuals' decision to enter an insurance pool is a "moral choice: To participate in a risk-pooling scheme is to agree to tax yourself not only for your own benefit should you incur a loss, but also for the benefit of others who might suffer from loss when you do not" (1999, 26). From her perspective, insurance provides an important "moral opportunity" for individual cooperation, altruism, community involvement, and civic responsibility. Insurance allows individuals to imagine how social justice and economic progress are not achieved through autonomy and self-determination but through cooperation and mutual aid. In this sense, while insurance models clearly have the potential to lend themselves to neo-liberal values of profit maximization and the individualization of responsibility, they also have the potential to acknowledge the kinds of underlying dependency that Fineman (2004) points to in her analysis of caregiving.

Given these diverging potentials of insurance technologies, it might seem sensible to conclude that the form insurance takes will depend on whether it is controlled by private economic elites or the state. On the contrary, Stone (1999) argues that even privatized insurance schemes controlled by business elites broaden the ethics of mutual care: the expansion of the private insurance industry promotes values of dependency and social responsibility by enlarging the market under the rubric of mutual aid rather than self-sufficiency.

While I admire Stone's optimism, regardless of the ethics used, private insurance schemes whose goal is to maximize profits will continue to prioritize economization over citizen well-being. On the other hand, shifting the control of insurance technologies to the state will not necessarily solve this problem either, particularly if the logic of the economy continues to dictate the ethics of governance. In this sense, the revolutionary potential of insurance technologies may depend on a larger battle to fight the very terms of neo-liberalism that account for the diffusion of economic logic into multiple spheres of social life.

It seems that some, from a neo-liberal perspective, are in fact questioning the efficiency of the marriage model and alternatively suggesting the "privatization of marriage." Colin Jones, an American lawyer and professor of law at Doshisha University in Kyoto, Japan, for example, suggests replacing outdated state marriage licenses with "marital corporations (MCs)" voluntarily formed by multiple couples who would act as shareholders who agree on basic common values of marriage.[1] For Jones, MCs would remove marriage from the purview of the state and place intimate contracts in the economic field, where individuals would allegedly have more choice. He argues that privatizing marriage would have economic advantages. MCs would increase the wedding industry by creating a demand for personalized wedding ceremonies tailored to the desires of individual MCs. Jones also envisions the creation of exclusive MCs with entrance fees that would boost profits by making marriage a symbol of economic achievement.

It is not difficult to imagine how this form of privatized marriage insurance would exacerbate the already growing economic inequality in the United States. But Jones's proposal also illuminates how marriage reform must not be pursued only under the mantle of increasing individual choice or the individualization of responsibility. This language tends to obscure the economic inequalities and relationships of dependency that underlie economic structures. This conceptual leap necessitates a public ethic of care that acknowledges relationships of dependency that exist as much between janitors and professors as between husband and wife.

As logical and fair as legal provisions for deinstitutionalizing marriage are, they are unlikely to achieve popular support without developing a rhetorical strategy for supporting public care and intimate diversity. Unfortunately, my evidence suggests that this support for intimate diversity and public care is neither a priority nor a likely outcome of the current iteration of the marriage equality position in the United States. However, excluded voices from within MRN ranks and a close examination of potential gaps within risk discourse reveal fertile ground for narratives that leave room for legal strategies beyond marriage. By tapping into the moralization and realization of interconnectedness that insurance structures yield, a place for dependency and care can be imagined as a quality that can appropriately characterize public, rather than just intimate, structures. The answer to the increasing economization of social life is not to reinforce the importance and unique significance of marriage but to enlarge our sense of family and community in a way that recognizes the dependencies and care that governance requires without stigmatizing nonmarital intimacies.

Appendix A

*Punk, Friend, or Scholar: Navigating
Embodiment and Distance in the Field*

"Children Deserve a Mother and a Father," "Sodom," and "Homosexuality Is a Sin You Can Recover From" were the slogans carefully stenciled on homemade plywood boxes extending as a canopy that framed the
beds of two American-made, full-sized trucks. The words offered a framework for interpreting the accompanying life-sized, cropped image of two
young white men kissing, eyes closed and mouths open. One of the thirty
or forty protesters outside the Corvallis City Hall, Nancy, must have interpreted our shocked reactions as a sign that we were not locals. She pointed
at the mobile display and explained, "That's Dan and his son Donny." She
continued, "They do this every year at our antihate rally." Marsha took
this as an opportunity to introduce herself as a chapter leader of MRN and
explain her intention to find a "leader in the LGBT community" to begin a
chapter in Corvallis. Before Nancy had the opportunity to respond, three
teens approached Marsha and asked for a roll of her stickers that read,
"Marriage Rights Now," and included the MRN logo.

My attention immediately drifted from Marsha and Nancy's conversation to one of the three teens dressed in camos patched with pictures of
the Ramones and colorful streaks of pink and purple accenting her black
hair. Armed with an entire roll of MRN stickers, she divvied up the loot
among herself and the two other teens. As Dan and Donny circled back
around to city hall and slowed down, the three teens bravely spent their
roll of stickers plastering the plywood boxes with the marriage equality
message. Without critical reflection, and no doubt expressing my deeply

ingrained streak of social deviance, I immediately responded to the punks' impromptu protest with a few solid claps and a full-face smile.

Throughout my twenty months with MRN, I often felt an affinity with what I assumed was the motivation of the small gang of young punks in Corvallis. Like the teenage Ramones fan and her gang (who I learned later that day do not "believe in marriage" and instead see it as "about a bunch of paperwork"), and despite my serious reservations about marriage as an institution of social care, I felt willing to drop my scholarly posture and abolitionist attitude toward marriage, and grab any tools available to voice my opposition to conservative messages against same-sex marriage. This moment represents my multiple and at times conflicting social dispositions as a rebel, scholar, and friend of MRN, whose mental, emotional, and physical reactions were largely dependent on the particular social context. Moreover, it speaks to the analytical leverage produced precisely when the habitus of the scholar and those she studies sit uncomfortably in the same social space.

The relative ease with which my various position-takings aligned largely depended on the social context of MRN activities. For example, during public protests where conservatives against same-sex marriage were present, I found myself torn from my role as a neutral scholar and pushed toward my embodiment as the punk rebel and loosely allied friend of MRN. At these moments, it took a great deal of strength not to grab a roll of stickers, wave an MRN sign, or voice a popular MRN slogan. I usually redirected my disdain by rolling my eyes or shaking my head. There were a handful of cases when I turned to a member of MRN and muttered some sarcastic comment about the conservative opposition. Even though these reactions were genuine "slips" rather than well-crafted research strategies, I suspect they did help me gain rapport and establish trust with MRN members. My visceral reaction was to latch onto the MRN message, but that feeling did not accurately reflect my own intellectual suspicions about marriage as a social institution.

In small-group meetings and even public gatherings where the conservative opposition was not invited, I found my objective approach much easier to maintain, and my scholarly disposition (Bourdieu 2000) easily activated. During regularly scheduled MRN group meetings, I usually wrote field notes and did not participate in the conversation unless called upon. Occasionally during these meetings participants would call on me to confirm their recollections of events. For example, after the protest in Corvallis, Marsha asked, "Hey, Jaye Cee, didn't that truck in Corvallis include an advertisement for a website?" In a few cases, my role as an outside observer was breached by chapter leaders who would momentarily see me as a "member" rather than a researcher to make the group seem larger or more vibrant. Chapter leaders in Waterford often included me in their count of total members and asked me to be the group "representative" for regional programs. Because the representative's role was simply to show up and describe the event to the larger group, I did not object. Although MRN members often hailed me as a fellow member, I regularly found my more immediate suspicion about marriage harder to assuage in contexts where members expressed a strong consensus. I maintained my role as a relatively distant observer and immediately afterward would unleash all my reactions as I converted my jottings into field notes.

At public gatherings that did not include members of the conservative opposition, I privileged my social position as a friend of MRN. I found it easier and more appropriate to mentally marginalize my own political opinions and set aside my scholarly reflections in order to experience the events on their own terms. In these cases, I took a more active role because I genuinely wanted to be polite and help out in order to show my appreciation for MRN's hospitality. I would set up chairs and fetch items left in the car. I could also be found distributing props and flyers at public gatherings. Depending on the season, I would hand out plastic Easter eggs containing MRN stickers and advertisements for local businesses, holiday messages for equality, and valentines featuring a same-sex couple's love story. MRN members seemed to appreciate these efforts and embraced my role as the group's gofer.

I could have approached this project as more of an active participant observer in every social context, but I chose to restrict my involvement in spreading the MRN message largely because I did not want to act as a "poser." Although any scholar who enters the field comes for reasons other than simply participating in that social world, I entered the field ambivalent about same-sex marriage as a worthwhile political goal: my personal rejection of marriage as a cultural norm and social institution also came with the belief that the institution of marriage may be transformed for the better by including same-sex couples. Overall, however, I did not feel it would be appropriate or even advantageous to carry on as if I were in full support of marriage equality.

Regardless of the particular context, I adopted Arlene Stein's (2001) "neutral approach" by not announcing my personal, political, or scholarly beliefs about marriage during any of my interviews or observations.

Like Stein, I was prepared to answer questions about my position on marriage, but I was surprised when no one asked. When I solicited activists' responses to queer critiques of marriage, I began my questions with the phrase "Just to play the devil's advocate" or "I have heard some on the left say." I gave activists time to ask me questions at the conclusion of the interviews, but they never asked about my own position on marriage. Instead, most respondents appeared to view me primarily in my role as a scholar. The most common questions activists asked during my observations or after interviews were how long I would be doing my research and what I hoped to do with my results when I completed the project.

I suspect that many of the activists assumed that I agreed with their views, or at least supported their right to have access to the rights and responsibilities of marriage. I often felt that I had a default insider status due to my educational background and personal life. Because I was a PhD candidate at the University of California at Berkeley, activists often assumed I was progressive, thus supportive of marriage equality. I also found that MRN activists saw scholars as political allies uniquely positioned to offer data to back up their assertions about the importance of marriage equality or the negative consequences associated with living as an excluded population. Unlike my previous work (J. Whitehead 2007) with activists fighting for the rights of women prisoners who viewed intellectuals as generally ungrounded and often unnecessarily idealistic, members of MRN greeted me without suspicion and seemed to have a positive outlook on academia.

I believe my default insider status also came as a result of activists' viewing me as a part of what they often problematically referred to as "the LGBT community." As I became more familiar with members of MRN, they would ask about my life outside of academia, and I would not hesitate to tell stories about my girlfriend or commiserate about unfair car insurance policies that give the married an extra discount. My relationship status was yet another indication that I must be on their side of the debate, and I think it enabled me to gain MRN members' trust. I also felt ambivalent about this acceptance; on one hand, I did benefit from this insider status in terms of feeling a sense of belonging as well as gaining access to a research site. On the other hand, I felt as if my belonging was predicated on a form of identity politics that I critique in chapters 3 and 4.

The "neutral observer" strategy proved its worth as many activists felt comfortable speaking to me "beyond the party line" or in some cases expressing their disagreements with MRN leaders. Over time, I felt many activists open up to me in a way that I do not think they would have had I been an active participant in MRN activities or closely allied with its leadership. On several occasions, I heard members express discontent about how the organization ignored transgender issues or tended to sideline members, like Tami, whose lives did not neatly match the narrative that MRN was trying to tell. I also believe that my efforts toward neutrality allowed respondents to be more forthcoming about their views of marriage as a discriminatory institution or monogamy as only one of many ethical ways of organizing intimacy. By appearing as a researcher rather than an activist, I could capture voices within the movement that are often repressed or concealed due to political expediency. My activities could not be confused with those of a regular member of MRN, as I was known to be a researcher immersed in the field as a friend or "tagalong."

At the same time as I collected frequently self-censored narratives, I maintained enough distance in the field to also question problematic assumptions that go unnoticed when one has a practical relationship to the social world (Bourdieu 1990b). As Paul Lichterman (2002) also notes, wearing the "researcher" as opposed to the "activist" hat allows one the distance necessary to critically reflect on the taken-for-granted reality of activists. When one puts on the MRN hat, she essentially must suspend any disbelief, as the social milieu is constructed around the shared assumption that marriage is an institution worth defending.

Without reflexive embodiment in the field, however, my own orientation toward MRN activity as a subject of scholarly debate threatens to simply echo my distant social positioning as a scholar and parallel disposition to "construe the world as a *spectacle*" (Bourdieu and Wacquant 1992). Regardless of my efforts at an embodied understanding, I approached marriage equality as a scholar whose primary stake in MRN activism required detaching it from the taken-for- granted world that is its defining feature. Because I was aware of this dilemma beforehand, my approach was to enter the field reflexive of my social position as a scholar and constantly force myself to make my claims and observations accountable to the lived reality of my participants. I was particularly aware of this danger, as my methods did not include attempts at complete immersion in the role of the activist. While my investments are in the field of scholastic production, as a queer woman, I came to the field with practical stakes in the marriage question. Regardless of my own personal views about the marriage equality movement, I share the practical experiences of exclusion that motivate MRN activists. In the final analysis, I took "Bourdieu's wager" (Wacquant

2002b), knowing that I would not resolve the gap between the logic of practice and science but could speak from that gap.

By the time I completed my fieldwork, my skepticism about MRN strategies had intensified, as had my respect for the kind of personal conflicts and ambivalence that many MRN members regularly confronted. Thinking of the teen punks in Corvallis who used available tools to combat the heteronormative and exclusionary ethos of conservatives opposed to marriage, I often questioned my more radical and purist tendencies by pushing myself to think reflexively about my distant social positioning as a scholar and how my work could be more grounded and practical.

Appendix B

Interview Participants

Individuals who participated in an interview are listed below by pseudonym, group membership, racial/ethnic identity, occupation type, and relationship status. Participants' relationship status is based on how they understand themselves rather than official legal standing. To protect the confidentiality of my participants, I do not include specific occupations, and I indicate panethnic, panracial identities instead of specific ethnic affiliation. Any identifiable information found in the text has been altered to protect my informants' confidentiality without misrepresenting the data. While the details in the text have been altered, they provide a more specific contextualization of occupation, class, race, and relationship status than can be found in this appendix.

*   *   *

Patricia Bloom, group affiliated with MRN, white, middle-class professional, married (straight)

Hazel Butler, MRN, white, upper-middle-class professional, married to Amber

Jorge Caberro, group affiliated with MRN, Hispanic, middle-class professional, unknown

Kim Chow, group affiliated with MRN, Asian American, student, married to Roni

Buck Crawford, MRN, white, middle-class, married (gay)

Jennifer Dowdy, MRN, white, working-class, partner is Cathy

Dana Fitzpatrick, MRN, white, middle-class professional, married to Marsha

Marsha Fitzpatrick, MRN, white, stay-at-home mother, married to Dana

Joe Franklin, group affiliated with MRN, white, student, single (straight)

Ann Jacman, MRN, white, retired, married to Sue

Sue Jacman, MRN, white, retired, married to Ann

Jack Kemp, MRN, white, middle-class professional, married to Steve

Steve Kemp, MRN, white and Asian American, middle-class professional, married to Jack

Judy Marshal, MRN, white, lower-middle-class service industry, single (lesbian)

Caitlin McCleary, MRN, white, graduate student, married (lesbian)

Amber McDaniel, MRN, white, middle-class professional, married to Hazel

Cathy McMahon, MRN, white, working-class, partner is Jennifer

Derek Miller, MRN, white, unemployed, married to Jense

Jense Miller, MRN, white, upper-class professional, married to Derek

Roni Plumb, group affiliated with MRN, white, student, married to Kim

Craig Shilling, Log Cabin Republicans, white, middle-class professional, gay (single)

Patrick Singleton, group affiliated with MRN, white, middle-class professional, married to Bryce

Muriel Stokely, MRN, white, middle-class professional, divorced (straight)

Mei Tsui, group affiliated with MRN, Asian American, graduate student, married (lesbian)

Notes

Chapter One

1. The names of my participants and identifying details have been altered to protect their confidentiality. All names and locations specific to my observations and interviews are pseudonyms. I only use real names and locations when referring to data collected from my content analysis. Please see appendix B for additional information.

2. I am referring to *illegibility* in the sense in which James Scott (1998) uses the term, as a way of describing the feeling of being unreadable, invisible, and misunderstood without the standardizing social practices that come with modern state recognition.

3. Theorists of governmentality are a multidisciplinary group of academics who draw from Michel Foucault's 1978 "Governmentality" lectures (1991) to study governance as a set of "technologies" and "rationalities" that quite often exist outside the explicit purview of state control but nonetheless are directed toward the management of the population.

4. This name derives from the riots at the Stonewall Bar in New York City on June 28, 1969.

5. The homophile movement refers to gay and lesbian rights organizations with a liberal-reformist philosophy formed in the 1950s, the most prominent of which were the Daughters of Bilitis, ONE Inc., and the Mattachine Society.

6. In the academic world, "culture wars" is a tagline coined by James Hunter in his 1991 book *Culture Wars: The Struggle to Define America*, which attempts to explain the political typography of the United States since the 1960s. According to Hunter, the American cultural-political landscape shifted from divisions based on theological differences to new ones based on fundamental ideals about foundations for moral authority that cut across denominational boundaries. Hunter defines two basic divisions in the new cultural-political context: orthodoxy—the belief that moral authority rests on "an external, definable, and transcendent authority" (44),

and progressivism—the belief that moral authority rests on the specific demands and "assumptions of contemporary life" (ibid.). Hunter argues that these classifications (orthodoxy and progressivism) explain differences on contentious political issues more than religious affiliation, class, gender, or race.

7. See Walder 2009 for a comprehensive and insightful critique of the shift in social movements literature from foundational concerns about broader social structures to a "narrow" focus on mobilization and framing that tends to neglect important questions about underlying structural and ideological circumstances.

8. "Culture of poverty" refers to Oscar Lewis's (1959) theory that poverty includes a distinct set of customs, behaviors, and attitudes characteristic of people who live below subsistence levels. From this perspective, families become structures by which the culture of poverty is transmitted through generations.

9. See, for example, Wilson 1996 and Wacquant 2001, 2002a, and 2007.

10. Although marriage promotion existed in the 1996 PRWORA legislation, most state programs focused on the new work requirements. Anna Korteweg argues that the emphasis on work over marriage programs may reflect the state program leaders' "own experience with welfare-reliant women . . . that intimate relations were the cause of, rather than a solution to, women's poverty" (2003, 470).

11. Health and Human Services, "The Personal Responsibility and Work Opportunity Reconciliation Act of 1996," accessed January 20, 2007, http://aspe.hhs .gov/HSP/abbrev/prwora96.htm 6.htm.

12. Deficit Reduction Act of 2005, 109th Cong. (February 8, 2006), accessed January 26, 2011, http://thomas.loc.gov/cgi-bin/bdquery/z?d109:s.01932.

13. National Father Initiative, Institute for Marriage and Public Policy, and Institute for American Values, "Can Government Strengthen Marriages? Evidence from the Social Sciences," 2004: 6, accessed January 20, 2007, http://www .marriagedebate.com/pdf/Can%20Government%20Strengthen%20Marriage.pdf.

14. See Stacey 2004 for a lucid analysis of how neo-liberal media nourish conservative family values discourse and frame it as the objective truth despite widespread critique of their methods and conclusions.

15. See Polikoff 2008 for a lucid legal history of the deinstitutionalization of marriage in the United States.

16. See also Allison Pugh's (2005) work on the commodification of parenting practices and Susan Thistle's (2006) historical explanation of women's shift to paid labor.

17. Nikolas Rose (1999), for example, argues that since the mid-nineteenth century, truth claims and projects of governance have been increasingly articulated in less formalized contexts. From this perspective, the primary locus of governance occurs not in formalized texts but in the microlevel attempts to make governance work.

18. I am using the term *discourse* as Michel Foucault (1994a, 1994b, 1995) defines it. For Foucault, power operates through historically constructed "discourses"

that constitute systems of thoughts, beliefs, and practices that produce knowledge, hierarchies, and exclusions by constructing and limiting social actors and interactions to said discursive boundaries. With both genealogy and archaeology, Foucault provides a distinct method for understanding how discourses are historically constructed and craft objects, practices, beliefs, categories, and individuals in their image.

19. I focus on proponents because my primary aim is to understand how discourse aimed at reform and inclusion can operate in the service of governing technologies. I am not attempting to give a balanced account of arguments for and against same-sex marriage.

20. I use pseudonyms for the cities and do not disclose the state in an effort to protect the confidentiality of my participants.

21. In order to ensure my subjects' confidentiality, and because ethnic diversity within Hispanic and Asian panethnic categories was minimal, I have remained vague when referring to the specific ethnicity of my participants.

22. See Sullivan 1989, Liebman 1992, and Bawer 1993.

23. "The 2004 State of the Union Address: Complete Transcript of President Bush's Speech to Congress and the Nation," White House Office of the Press Secretary, January 20, 2004, accessed January 26, 2011, http://whitehouse.georgewbush .org/news/2004/012004-SOTU.asp.

24. "Mayor Defends Same-Sex Marriages," CNN.com, February 22, 2004.

25. "Gay Couples Marry in New Mexico," CNN.com, February 20, 2004.

26. Kenneth Sherrill, "Same-Sex Marriage, Civil Unions and the 2004 Presidential Election," 2004, accessed January 26, 2011, http://thetaskforceactionfund .org/studies_analyses/2004electionandmarriage.pdf.

Chapter Two

1. The police powers reserved for states make it constitutional to create categories that inherently disadvantage some classifications over others. Since the 1950s, however, these police powers can be restricted when the Supreme Court determines that they do not protect the citizenry (Korematzu v. United States, 584 F. Supp. 1406 [1984]; Brown v. Board of Education of Topeka 347 U.S. 483 [1954], 74 S. Ct. 686, 98 L.Ed. 873; Romer v. Evans, 517 U.S. 620 [1996], 116 S. Ct. 1620, 134 L. Ed. 2d 855, 1996 U.S. LEXIS 3245). Thus, the court developed a set of tests to determine the level at which the police powers of the state will be scrutinized. The court draws a basic distinction between legally constructed categories under the police powers, based on the degree to which they are "suspect"—meaning the extent to which the classifications have been historically associated with political disenfranchisement and a history of minority status. If a classification is determined suspect, then the court must use the "strict scrutiny" standard to test the legitimacy

of the classification in terms of whether it embodies a compelling state interest and whether the contained categorical distinctions are central to achieving this state interest. If a classification is not determined suspect, then the court uses the "rational basis" test, which only requires the state to show a legitimate state interest, and the presumption of innocence resides with the state. The California Supreme Court (2008) was the first court considering the constitutionality of same-sex marriage to deem sexual orientation a suspect classification.

2. Marriage Cases, S1479999, 43 Cal. 4th 757 (76 Cal.Rptr.3d 683 P.3d 384), p. 11 (2008).

3. Ibid., 58.

4. Bruce C. Hafen, "The Constitutional Status of Marriage, Kinship, and Sexual Privacy: Balancing the Individual and Social Interests," *Michigan Law Review* 81, no. 3 (January 1983): 485.

5. Ibid., 57n36.

6. Concern over the cost of illegitimate children is not unique to twentieth-century neo-liberal thought. Illegitimacy provided a key impetus to the modern state's creation of civil marriage (Donzelot 1979). Although Jacques Donzelot bases his conclusion on data from France in the eighteenth century, one can see the same concerns for the burden of illegitimate children in US debates about same-sex marriage.

7. Baker v. State of Vermont, 170 Vt. 194 (1999), 744 A.2d 864, LEXIS 406 ¶31. It is unclear from the Vermont court's decision if it is talking about legitimacy in a broad sense of the term, as the American Psychological Association (APA) refers to legitimacy as a feeling of rightful belonging (see chapter 3), or in a more narrow sense of legitimacy as a child with two legally and financially bound parents.

8. Goodridge v. Department of Public Health, 440 Mass. 309, 789 N.E. 2d 941 (2003), LEXIS 814 ¶70.

9. Lee Badgett, Institute for Gay and Lesbian Strategic Studies, "The Fiscal Impact on the State of Vermont of Allowing Same-Sex Couples to Marry," October 1998, 5, accessed September 21, 2005, http://www.buddybuddy.com/iglss-2 .html.

10. Ibid., 4.

11. Congressional Budget Office, *The Potential Budgetary Impact of Recognizing Same-Sex Marriage*, June 21, 2004, 6–7.

12. As of May 2006, the Williams Institute reported similar benefits for the states of New Hampshire, Alaska, California, Connecticut, New Jersey, and Vermont.

13. Lee Badgett, Bradley Sears, Steven K. Homer, Patrice Curtis, and Elizabeth Kukur, "The Impact on New Mexico's Budget of Allowing Same-Sex Couples to Marry," The Williams Project on Sexual Orientation Law and Public Policy, UCLA School of Law, March 23, 2006, 2, accessed August 23, 2006, http://www.law.ucla .edu/williamsinstitute/publications/new%20mexico%20econ%20study.pdf.

14. Bradley Sears and Lee Badgett, *The Impact of Extending Marriage to Same-Sex Couples on the California State Budget*, The Williams Project on Sexual

Orientation Law and Public Policy, UCLA School of Law, June 2008, accessed July 3, 2008, http://www.law.ucla.edu/williamsinstitute/publications/EconImpact CAMarriage.pdf.

15. Kevin Yamamura, "Schwarzenegger Says Gay Could Be Good for the Economy," *Sacramento Bee*, May 21, 2008, accessed July 3, 2008, http://www.sacbee.com/111/story/954781.html.

16. Daniel Clement, "Same Sex Marriage Stimulates Economy," accessed July 3, 2008, http://divorce.clementlaw.com/2008/06/articles/marriage/same-sex-marriage-stimulates-economy/.

17. Alliance for Same-Sex Marriage, *Facts on Marriage*, accessed January 20, 2007, http://www.allianceforsamesexmarriage.org/facts.htm.

18. Kathleen Hull (2006) found similar perspectives among working-class, same-sex couples who are not marriage equality activists.

19. Lisa Bennett and Gary Gates, *The Cost of Marriage Inequality to Children and Their Same-Sex Parents*, Human Rights Campaign Foundation report, April 13, 2004, 9–10, accessed January 20, 2007, http://www.hrc.org/Template.cfm?Section=Get_Involved1&Template=/ContentManagement/ContentDisplay.cfm&ContentID=18078.

20. Affidavit of Dennis Winslow, Lewis v. Harris, N.J. Super. LEXIS 186 ¶5 (2005).

21. Bradley Sears, Gary Gates, and William Rubenstein, "Same-Sex Couples and Same-Sex Couples Raising Children in the United States," The Williams Project on Sexual Orientation Law and Public Policy, UCLA School of Law, September 2005, 8, accessed October 3, 2005, www.law.ucla.edu/williamsinstitute/publications/Policy-Census-index.html.

22. Affidavit of Curtis Woolbright, Hernandez v. Robles, N.Y. Ct. App. LEXIS 1836 ¶9–10 (2006).

23. Evan Wolfson, "Crossing the Threshold: Equal Marriage Rights for Lesbians and Gay Men and the Intra-community Critique," *New York University Review of Law and Social Change* 21, no. 567 (1993–95): 608.

24. American Civil Liberties Union, "ACLU Message Points on Marriage for Same-Sex Couples and the Federal Marriage Amendment," November 2003, 1, accessed January 20, 2007, http://www.aclu.org/getequal/ffm/section1/1a2points.pdf.

Chapter Three

1. Beck calls the age of the risk society "reflexive modernity" because the modernist project to transform and make use of nature is "becoming its own theme." In other words, from Beck's perspective, modernity addresses the dangers that it continues to produce through industrialization. It does so not by reforming industry but by

providing individuals with a sense of security by creating risk calculations that make it seem as if managing the probability of danger is enough to avoid catastrophes.

2. I draw from Nikolas Rose and Peter Miller's (1992) definition of political rationalities to point sociologists' attention to logics of governance that are not reducible to the state. Political rationalities refer to ways of conceptualizing the proper aims and limits of governance, and to governmental technologies, everyday procedures and programs that embody these conceptualizations.

3. From content analysis of affidavits from same-sex couples in the following cases: Andersen v. King County, WA LEXIS 598 (2006); Hernandez v. Robles, N.Y. Ct. App. LEXIS 1836 (2006); City and County of San Francisco v. State of California, Cal. App. 4th LEXIS 669 (2005); Li and Kennedy v. State of Oregon, LEXIS 144 (2005); Lewis v. Harris, N.J. Super. LEXIS 186 (2005).

4. Lambda Legal, "Why Marriage, Why Now?," accessed January 11, 2005, http://www.lambdalegal.org/binary-data/LAMBDA_PDF/pdf/244.pdf.

5. *Defense of Marriage Act*, 108th Cong., 2nd Judicial Subcommittee Sess., 70, 22 (March 30, 2004) (testimony of Vincent P. McCarthy).

6. *Gay Marriage and the Courts*, 108th Cong., 2nd Judicial Subcommittee Sess., 717, 1 (March 3, 2004) (testimony of Maggie Gallagher), accessed May 4, 2005, http://judiciary.senate.gov/hearings/testimony.cfm?id=1072&wit_id=3077.

7. Ibid., 1–2.

8. Ibid., 2.

9. Equality California, "12 Days of Equality," September 2005, accessed September 26, 2005, http://www.eqca.org/site/apps/nl/content2.asp?c=9oINKWMCF&b=}40337&ct=1459165.

10. T. Simmons and M. O'Connell, *Married-Couple and Unmarried-Partner Households:* 2000, Census 2000 Special Report, United States Census Bureau, February 2003.

11. Brief of Juvenile Rights Project, National Association of Social Workers, Open Adoption and Family Services, the Oregon Psychiatric Association, and the Oregon Psychological Association as Amici Curiae in Support of Plaintiffs-Respondents and Cross-Appellants, 9–10, Li and Kennedy v. State of Oregon, LEXIS 144 (2005).

12. *Legal Threats to Traditional Marriage: Implications for Public Policy*, 108th Cong., 2nd Judicial Subcommittee Sess., 76, 146 (April 22, 2004) (article by the American Academy of Pediatrics).

13. Brief of the American Psychological Association as Amicus Curiae in Support of Plaintiffs-Respondents and Cross-Appellants, 34, Li and Kennedy v. State of Oregon, LEXIS 144 (2005).

14. Members were referencing the brutal murder of Matthew Shepard.

15. Brief of American Psychological Association as Amicus Curiae in Support of Plaintiffs-Respondents and Cross-Appellants, Li and Kennedy v. State of Oregon, LEXIS 144, 22 (2005).

16. *Defense of Marriage Act*, 104th Cong., 2nd Judicial Subcommittee (July 11, 1996) (testimony from Mitzi Henderson).

17. Brief of American Psychological Association as Amicus Curiae in Support of Plaintiffs-Respondents and Cross-Appellants, 9, Li and Kennedy v. State of Oregon, LEXIS 144 (2005).

18. Thomas S. Dee, "Forsaking All Others? The Effects of 'Gay Marriage' on Risky Sex," National Bureau of Economic Research, May 2005, accessed August 23, 2006, http://www.nber.org/papers/w11327.

19. Ibid., 24.

Chapter Four

1. See also Berlant and Warner 2000.

2. Motion of Plaintiffs in Hernandez v. Robles, N.Y. App. LEXIS 1836, 29 (2006).

3. See Berlant 1998 for an in-depth discussion of how the marital zone of privacy operates to legitimize citizens.

4. Affidavit of Lauren Abrams, Hernandez v. Robles, N.Y. App. LEXIS 1836 ¶12 (2006).

5. Ibid., ¶18.

6. The argument that individuals disproportionately subjected to state surveillance are considered less worthy or undignified is well established in studies of race and gender in United States welfare policy (see Roberts 1997).

7. Lawrence v. Texas, 539 U.S. 558 ¶525 (2003).

8. Steve Dasbach, "Reject 'Defense of Marriage Act,' " Libertarian Party press release, June 5, 1996, accessed September 20, 2005, http://www.buddybuddy.com/dasbach1.html.

9. Rick Tompkins, "Government Has No Role in Blocking Gay Marriages," Libertarian Party press release, July 1996, accessed September 20, 2005, http://www.buddybuddy.com/tompkin1.html.

10. As Michel Foucault argued in *The History of Sexuality*, the discourses establishing the "homosexual" as a species, or classification of personhood found in nature, produce multiple strategies: those that regulate same-sex eroticism as a perversion as well as efforts to "demand that [homosexuality's] legitimacy or 'naturality' be acknowledged" (1990, 101).

11. Brief of Doctors Richard S. Colman, Rodica N. Meyer, and Lorah Sebastian as Amicus Curiae in Support of Plaintiffs-Respondents and Cross-Appellants, Li and Kennedy v. State of Oregon, LEXIS 144, 7 (2005).

12. Ibid., 7.

13. Ibid., 4.

14. American Civil Liberties Union, "ACLU Message Points on Marriage for Same-Sex Couples and the Federal Marriage Amendment," November 2003, 3,

accessed January 20, 2007, http://www.aclu.org/getequal/ffm/section1/1a2points
.pdf.

15. See Sedgwick 1993, which persuasively argues that grounding gay and lesbian identities in the immutability of nature will not effectively shield queer sexualities from social regulation in the postmodern era of technological manipulations
of nature.

16. Representative Ed Fallon, "Testimony to Iowa General Assembly: Defense
of Marriage Act," February 20, 1996, accessed January 20, 2007, http://www.buddy
buddy.com/fallon-1.html.

Chapter Five

1. As Chet Meeks and Arlene Stein (2006) point out, Michael Warner's (1999)
critique of same-sex marriage as an assimilationist strategy assumes a problematic
model of false consciousness. Bourdieu provides a more accurate model of subjectivity without discounting the normative value of marriage consecrated by the
state action. For Bourdieu, objective social structures are inculcated in people's
understanding of the social world (*habitus*), and structured agents also recursively
structure social relations and objects. Bourdieu's concept of *habitus* provides a way
to understand objective regularities in agents' action without resorting to a calculative rational actor model or assumptions of false consciousness, both overly
deterministic accounts of subject formation (1990b).

2. Affidavit of Daniel Hernandez, Hernandez v. Robles, N.Y. Ct. App. LEXIS
1836 ¶15 (2006).

3. Similarly, filling out forms and checking boxes also become a site for individuals' alienation when they are forced to identify themselves with one racial group
or another (Schor 2005).

4. Affidavit of Cindy Meneghin, Lewis v. Harris, N.J. Super. LEXIS 186 ¶13 (2005).

5. Declaration of Lancy Woo, City and County of San Francisco v. State of
California, Cal. App. 4th LEXIS 669 ¶5 (2005).

6. For foundational feminist theorizations of multiple marginality by race, gender, sexual orientation, and class, see, for example, Anzaldúa 1987; Collins 2000;
Crenshaw 1992; hooks 1984. Also see Leong 1996 for a broad interdisciplinary
discussion of Asian racial identities as they intersect with sexual difference.

7. Affidavit of Karen Nicholson-McFadden, Lewis v. Harris, N.J. Super. LEXIS
186 ¶13 (2005).

8. *Defense of Marriage Act*, 104th Cong., 2nd Judicial Subcommittee (May 15,
1996) (testimony of Nancy McDonald).

9. Brief of American Psychological Association as Amicus Curiae in Support of
Plaintiffs-Respondents and Cross-Appellants, 20, Multnomah County v. Oregon,
338 Ore. 376, 110 P.3d 91, 2005 Ore. LEXIS 144 (April 14, 2005).

10. Tami's concern predated the Patient Protection and Affordable Care Act (PPACA), passed in December 2009, which prohibits the denial of insurance due to preexisting conditions.

11. Baker v. State of Vermont, 170 Vt. 194, 744 A.2d 864, LEXIS 406 ¶39 (1999). The Vermont court based this decision on its state constitution's article 7 "common benefits clause," which differs slightly from the interpretation implied by the federal Constitution's Fourteenth Amendment.

12. See also Moats 2004.

13. Baker v. State of Vermont, 170 Vt. 194, 744 A.2d 864, LEXIS 406 ¶44 (1999).

14. Quoted from Moats 2004 (133).

15. 347 U.S. 483, 74 S.Ct. 686, 98 L.Ed. 873.

16. 163 U.S. 537, 16 S.Ct. 1138.

17. Goodridge v. Department of Public Health, 440 Mass. 309, 789 N.E. 2d 941, LEXIS 814 ¶71 (2003).

18. Ibid., ¶25.

19. Marriage Cases, S147999, 43 Cal. 4th 757 (76 Cal.Rptr. 3d 683, 183 P.3d 384), p. 64 (2008).

20. Ibid., 62–63.

Chapter Six

1. See Jordan 2005 for a comprehensive account of church opposition to same-sex unions in the United States.

2. Hadley Arkes, "The Role of Nature," May 15, 1996, cited in Sullivan 2004 (276).

3. Ibid., 277.

4. For more on moral panics, see Weeks 1981 and 1995 and Epstein 2006.

5. *Federal Marriage Amendment (The Musgrave Amendment)*, 108th Cong., 2nd Judicial Subcommittee, Sess. 90 (May 22, 2004), 39.

6. *Legal Threats to Traditional Marriage: Implications for Public Policy*, 108th Cong., 2nd Judicial Subcommittee, Sess. 76 (April 22, 2004), 21–22.

7. See Gayle Rubin 1993.

8. *Federal Marriage Amendment (The Musgrave Amendment)*, 108th Cong., 2nd Judicial Subcommittee, Sess. 90 (May 22, 2004), 22.

9. It is not true that most animals exist in monogamous pairs, including primates, who are the closest to humans genetically (Fisher 1992; Sperling 1997).

10. Lee Badgett, "Will Providing Marriage Rights to Same-Sex Couples Undermine Heterosexual Marriage? Evidence from Scandinavia and the Netherlands," Institute for Gay and Lesbian Strategic Studies, July 2004, accessed September 3, 2005, http://www.iglss.org/media/files/briefing.pdf#search=%22%22Will%

20Providing%20Marriage%20Rights%20to%20Same-Sex%20Couples%20Under mine%20Heterosexual%20Marriage%22%22.

11. I define romantic, couple love by drawing from Swidler 2001 and Cancian 1987.

12. Affidavit of Lauren Abrams, Hernandez v. Robles, N.Y. Ct. App. LEXIS 1836 ¶9 (2006).

13. Declaration of Lancy Woo, City and County of San Francisco v. State of California, Cal. App. 4th LEXIS 669 ¶3 (2005).

14. Affidavit of Cindy Meneghin, Lewis v. Harris, N.J. Super. LEXIS 186 ¶3 (2005).

15. Goodridge v. Department of Public Health, 440 Mass. 309, 789 N.E. 2d 941, LEXIS 814 ¶58 (2003).

16. Ibid., ¶59.

17. Ibid.

18. Ibid., ¶70.

19. Lewis v. Harris, 188 N.J. 415, 908 A.2d 196, N.J. LEXIS 1521 ¶37 (2006).

20. Ibid., ¶42.

21. Marriage Cases, S147999, 43 Cal.4th 757 (76 Cal.Rptr.3d 683, 183 P.3d 384), p. 79n52 (2008).

22. Ibid., 80n52.

23. Ibid., "Concurring and Dissenting Opinion by Baxter, J.," 17.

24. Baker v. State of Vermont, 170 Vt. 194, 744 A.2d 864, LEXIS 406 ¶3 (1999).

25. Ibid., ¶29.

Conclusion

1. Colin Jones, "Marriage Proposal: Why Not Privatize?" *San Francisco Chronicle*, January 22, 2006, accessed January 20, 2007, http://www.sfgate.com/cgibin/article.cgi?f=/c/a/2006/01/22/ING6FGOLVA1.DTL.

References

Anzaldúa, Gloria. 1987. *Borderlands / La Frontera: The New Mestiza*. San Francisco: Aunt Lute Books.

Armstrong, Elizabeth. 2002. *Forging Gay Identities: Organizing Sexuality in San Francisco, 1950–1994*. Chicago: University of Chicago Press.

Badgett, M. V. Lee. 2009. *When Gay People Get Married: What Happens When Societies Legalize Same-Sex Marriage*. New York: New York University Press.

Bawer, Bruce. 1993. *A Place at the Table: The Gay Individual in American Society*. New York: Poseidon Press.

Beck, Ulrich. 1992. *Risk Society: Towards a New Modernity*. London: Sage Publications.

Berger, Peter. 1963. *Invitation to Sociology: A Humanistic Perspective*. Garden City, NY: Doubleday.

Berlant, Lauren. 1997. *The Queen of America Goes to Washington City: Essays on Sex and Citizenship*. Durham, NC: Duke University Press.

———. 1998. "Live Sex Acts (Parental Advisory: Explicit Material)." In *Feminism, the Public and the Private*, edited by Joan Landes, 277–301. Oxford: Oxford University Press.

Berlant, Lauren, and Michael Warner. 2000. "Sex in Public." In *Intimacy*, edited by Lauren Berlant, 311–30. Chicago: University of Chicago Press.

Bernstein, Mary. 2001. "Gender, Queer Family Policies, and the Limits of Law." In *Queer Families, Queer Politics: Challenging Culture and the State*, edited by Mary Bernstein and Renate Reimann, 420–46. New York: Columbia University Press.

Bourdieu, Pierre. 1984. *Distinction: A Social Critique of the Judgment of Taste*. Cambridge, MA: Harvard University Press.

———. 1986. "The Forms of Capital." In *Handbook of Theory and Research of the Sociology of Education*, edited by J. G. Richardson, 241–58. New York: Greenwood Press.

———. 1990a. *In Other Words: Essays towards a Reflexive Sociology*. Palo Alto, CA: Stanford University Press.

———. 1990b. *The Logic of Practice*. Palo Alto, CA: Stanford University Press.

———. 1991. *Language and Symbolic Power*. Cambridge, MA: Harvard University Press.

———. 1993. *The Field of Cultural Production: Essays on Art and Literature*. New York: Columbia University Press.

———. 1996. *The State Nobility: Elite Schools in the Field of Power*. Palo Alto, CA: Stanford University Press.

———. 1998. *Practical Reasons*. Palo Alto, CA: Stanford University Press.

———. 1999. *Outline of a Theory of Practice*. Cambridge: Cambridge University Press.

———. 2000. *Pascalian Meditations*. Palo Alto, CA: Stanford University Press.

———. 2001. *Masculine Domination*. Palo Alto, CA: Stanford University Press.

———. 2004. "The Peasant and His Body." Translated and adapted by Richard Nice and Loïc Wacquant. *Ethnography* 5 (4): 579–99.

Bourdieu, Pierre, and Loïc Wacquant. 1992. *An Invitation to Reflexive Sociology*. Chicago: University of Chicago Press.

Brown, Wendy. 1995. *States of Injury: Power and Freedom in Late Modernity*. Princeton, NJ: Princeton University Press.

———. 2004. "After Marriage." In Mary Lyndon Shanley, *Just Marriage: On the Public Importance of Private Unions*, edited by Joshua Cohen and Deborah Chasman. New York: Oxford University Press.

———. 2005. *Edgework: Critical Essays on Knowledge and Politics*. Princeton, NJ: Princeton University Press.

Butler, Judith. 1993. *Bodies That Matter: On the Discursive Limits of "Sex."* New York: Routledge.

———. 2002. "Is Kinship Always Already Heterosexual?" *Differences: A Journal of Feminist Cultural Studies* 15 (1): 14–44.

Cahill, Sean. 2004. *Same-Sex Marriage in the United States: Focus on the Facts*. Lanham, MD: Lexington Books.

Cancian, Francesca. 1987. "Love and the Rise of Capitalism." In *Gender in Intimate Relationships: A Microstructural Approach*, edited by Barbara Risman and Pepper Schwartz, 12–25. Belmont, CA: Wadsworth.

Carrington, Christopher. 1999. *No Place Like Home: Relationships and Family Life and Gay Men*. Chicago: University of Chicago Press.

Chauncey, George. 2004. *Why Marriage? The History Shaping Today's Debate over Gay Equality*. New York: Basic Books.

Collier, Jane, Michelle Rosaldo, and Sylvia Yanagisako. 1997. "Is There a Family?" In *The Gender/Sexuality Reader*, edited by Roger Lancaster and Micaela di Leonardo, 71–81. New York: Routledge.

Collins, Patricia Hill. 2000. *Black Feminist Thought: Knowledge, Consciousness, and the Politics of Empowerment*. New York: Routledge.

Coontz, Stephanie. 1992. *The Way We Never Were: American Families and the Nostalgia Trap*. New York: Basic Books.

———. 2005. *Marriage, a History: From Obedience to Intimacy, or How Love Conquered Marriage*. New York: Viking.

Cott, Nancy. 2000. *Public Vows: A History of Marriage and the Nation*. Cambridge, MA: Harvard University Press.

Crenshaw, Kimberlé. 1992. "Whose Story Is It, Anyway? Feminist and Anti-racist Appropriations of Anita Hill." In *Race-ing Justice, En-gendering Power: Essays on Anita Hill, Clarence Thomas, and the Construction of Social Reality*, edited by Toni Morrison, 402–40. New York: Pantheon Books.

Dean, Mitchell. 1999a. *Governmentality: Power and Rule in Modern Society*. London: Sage Publications.

———. 1999b. "Risk, Calculable and Incalculable." In *Risk and Sociocultural Theory: New Directions and Perspectives*, edited by Deborah Lupton, 131–59. Cambridge: Cambridge University Press.

D'Emilio, John. 2006. "The Marriage Fight Is Setting Us Back." *Gay and Lesbian Review* 13 (6): 10–11.

D'Emilio, John, and Estelle B. Freedman. 1988. *Intimate Matters: A History of Sexuality in America*. New York: Harper and Row.

Dizard, Jan E., and Howard Gadlin. 1990. *The Minimal Family*. Amherst: University of Massachusetts Press.

Donzelot, Jacques. 1979. *The Policing of Families*. Translated by Robert Hurley. New York: Pantheon Books.

Duggan, Lisa. 2003. *The Twilight of Equality: Neoliberalism, Cultural Politics, and the Attack on Democracy*. Boston: Beacon Press.

Duggan, Lisa, and Nan D. Hunter. 1995. *Sex Wars: Sexual Dissent and Political Culture*. New York: Routledge.

Eliasoph, Nina. 1996. "Making a Fragile Public: A Talk-Centered Study of Citizenship and Power." *Sociological Theory* 14 (3): 262–89.

———. 1997. "'Close to Home': The Work of Avoiding Politics." *Theory and Society* 26 (5): 605–47.

———. 1999. "'Everyday Racism' in a Culture of Political Avoidance: Civil Society, Speech, and Taboo." *Social Problems* 46 (4): 479–99.

Epstein, Steven. 2006. "The New Attack on Sexuality Research: Morality and the Politics of Knowledge Production." *Sexuality Research and Social Policy: Journal of NSRC* 3 (1): 1–12.

Eskridge, William, and Darren Spedale. 2006. *Gay Marriage: For Better or Worse? What We've Learned from the Evidence*. New York: Oxford University Press.

Esping-Andersen, Gøsta. 1990. *The Three Worlds of Welfare Capitalism*. Cambridge: Blackwell Publishing.

Ettelbrick, Paula. 2004. "Since When Is Marriage a Path to Liberation?" In *Same-Sex Marriage: Pro and Con: A Reader*, edited by Andrew Sullivan, 122–28. New York: Vintage.

Ewald, François. 1991. "Insurance and Risk." In *The Foucault Effect: Studies in*

Governmentality, edited by Graham Burchell, Colin Gordon, and Peter Miller, 197–210. Chicago: University of Chicago Press.

Fetner, Tina. 2008. *How the Religious Right Shaped Gay and Lesbian Activism*. Minneapolis: University of Minnesota Press.

Fineman, Martha. 1995. *The Neutered Mother, the Sexual Family and Other Twentieth Century Tragedies*. New York: Routledge.

———. 2004. *The Autonomy Myth: A Theory of Dependency*. New York: New Press.

Fisher, Helen. 1992. *Anatomy of Love*. New York: Norton.

Foucault, Michel. 1990. *The History of Sexuality: An Introduction*. Vol. 1. New York: Vintage Books.

———. 1991. "Governmentality." In *The Foucault Effect: Studies in Governmentality*, edited by Colin Gordon, Graham Burchell, and Peter Miller, 87–104. Chicago: University of Chicago Press.

———. 1994a. *The Birth of the Clinic: An Archaeology of Medical Perception*. Translated by A. M. Sheridan Smith. New York: Random House.

———. 1994b. *The Order of Things: An Archaeology of the Human Sciences*. New York: Random House.

———. 1995. *Discipline and Punish: The Birth of the Prison*. Translated by Alan Sheridan. New York: Vintage Books.

Fox, Nick. 1999. "Postmodern Reflections on 'Risk,' 'Hazards' and Life Choices." In *Risk and Sociocultural Theory: New Directions and Perspectives*, edited by Deborah Lupton, 12–33. Cambridge: Cambridge University Press.

Fraser, Nancy. 1998. "Sex, Lies and the Public Sphere: Reflections on the Confirmation of Clarence Thomas." In *Feminism, the Public and the Private*, edited by Joan Landes, 314–38. Oxford: Oxford University Press.

Gallagher, Maggie. 1996. *The Abolition of Marriage: How We Destroy Lasting Love*. Washington, DC: Regnery Press.

Gamson, Joshua. 1995. "Must Identity Movements Self-Destruct? A Queer Dilemma." *Social Problems* 42 (3): 390–407.

Gerstmann, Evan. 2004. *Same-Sex Marriage and the Constitution*. Cambridge: Cambridge University Press.

Ghaziani, Amin. 2008. *The Dividends of Dissent: How Conflict and Culture Work in Lesbian and Gay Marches on Washington*. Chicago: University of Chicago Press.

Giddens, Anthony. 1991. *Modernity and Self-Identity: Self and Society in the Late Modern Age*. Cambridge: Polity Press.

———. 1992. *The Transformation of Intimacy: Sexuality, Love and Eroticism in Modern Societies*. Cambridge: Polity Press.

Goldberg-Hiller, Jonathan. 2002. *The Limits to Union: Same-Sex Marriage and the Politics of Civil Rights*. Ann Arbor: University of Michigan Press.

Gordon, Linda. 1994. *Pitied but Not Entitled: Single Mothers and the History of Welfare, 1890–1935*. New York: Free Press.

Graff, E. J. 2004. *What Is Marriage For?* Boston: Beacon Press.

Habermas, Jurgen. 1984. *The Theory of Communicative Action*. Boston: Beacon Press.

Hacking, Ian. 1990. *The Taming of Chance*. Cambridge, UK; New York: Cambridge University Press.

Halley, Janet E. 1993. "The Construction of Heterosexuality." In *Fear of a Queer Planet*, edited by Michael Warner, 82–102. Minneapolis: University of Minnesota Press.

Hays, Sharon. 2003. *Flat Broke with Children: Women in the Age of Welfare Reform*. New York: Oxford University Press.

Heath, Melanie. 2009. "State of Our Unions: Marriage Promotion and the Contested Power of Heterosexuality." *Gender and Society* 23 (1): 27–48.

Herdt, Gilbert, and Robert Kertzner. 2006. "'I Do, but I Can't: The Impact of Marriage Denial on the Mental Health and Sexual Citizenship of Lesbians and Gay Men in the United States." *Sexuality Research and Social Policy: Journal of NSRC* 3 (1): 33–49.

Hochschild, Arlie Russell. 1983. *The Managed Heart: Commercialization of Intimate Feeling*. Berkeley: University of California Press.

———. 1989. *The Second Shift: Working Parents and the Revolution at Home*. With Anne Machung. New York: Viking.

———. 1997. *The Time Bind: When Work Becomes Home and Home Becomes Work*. New York: H. Holt.

———. 2003. *The Commercialization of Intimate Life: Notes from Home and Work*. Berkeley: University of California Press.

hooks, bell. 1984. *Feminist Theory: From Margin to Center*. Cambridge: South End Press.

Hull, Kathleen. 2006. *Same-Sex Marriage: The Cultural Politics of Love and Law*. Cambridge: Cambridge University Press.

Hunter, James. 1991. *Culture Wars: The Struggle to Define America*. New York: Basic Books.

Jackson, Stevi, and Sue Scott. 1999. "Risk Anxiety and the Social Construction of Childhood." In *Risk and Sociocultural Theory: New Directions and Perspectives*, edited by Deborah Lupton, 86–107. Cambridge: Cambridge University Press.

Jordan, Mark D. 2005. *Blessing Same-Sex Unions: The Perils of Queer Romance and the Confusions of Christian Marriage*. Chicago: University of Chicago Press.

Koppelman, Andrew. 2006. *Same-Sex, Different States: When Same-Sex Marriages Cross State Lines*. Ann Arbor, MI: Sheridan Books.

Korteweg, Anna C. 2003. "Welfare Reform and the Subject of the Working Mother: 'Get a Job, a Better Job, Than a Career.'" *Theory and Society* 32:445–80.

Kotulski, Devina. 2004. *Why You Should Give a Damn about Gay Marriage*. Los Angeles: Advocate Books.

Lasch, Christopher. 1977. *Haven in a Heartless World*. New York: Basic Books.

Lemke, Thomas. 2001. " 'The Birth of Bio-politics': Michel Foucault's Lecture at the College de France on Neo-Liberal Governmentality." *Economy and Society* 30 (2): 190–207.

———. 2004. "Disposition and Determinism—Genetic Diagnostics in Risk Society." *Sociological Review* 52 (4): 550–66.

Leong, Russell. 1996. *Asian American Sexualities: Dimensions of the Gay and Lesbian Experience*. New York: Routledge.

Lewis, Oscar. 1959. *Five Families: Mexican Case Studies in the Culture of Poverty*. New York: Basic Books.

Lichter, Daniel T., Deborah Roempke, and Brian J. Brown. 2003. "Is Marriage a Panacea? Union Formation among Economically Disadvantaged Unwed Mothers." *Social Problems* 50 (1): 60–86.

Lichterman, Paul. 2002. "Seeing Structure Happen: Theory-Driven Participant Observation." In *Methods of Social Movement Research*, edited by Bert Klandermans and Suzanne Staggenborg, 118–45. Minneapolis: University of Minnesota Press.

Liebman, Marvin. 1992. *Coming Out Conservative: An Autobiography*. San Francisco: Chronicle Books.

Lupton, Deborah. 1999. "Risk and the Ontology of Pregnant Embodiment." In *Risk and Sociocultural Theory: New Directions and Perspectives*, edited by Deborah Lupton, 59–85. Cambridge: Cambridge University Press.

McLanahan, Sara, and Gary Sandefur. 1994. *Growing Up with a Single Parent: What Hurts, What Helps*. Cambridge, MA: Harvard University Press.

Meeks, Chet, and Arlene Stein. 2006. "Refiguring the Family: Towards a Postqueer Politics of Gay and Lesbian Marriage." In *Intersections between Feminist and Queer Theory*, edited by Diane Richardson, Janice McLaughlin, and Mark E. Casey, 136–55. New York: Palgrave.

Merin, Yuval. 2002. *Equality for Same-Sex Couples: The Legal Recognition of Gay Partnerships in Europe and the United States*. Chicago: University of Chicago Press.

Metz, Tamara. 2007. "The Liberal Case for Disestablishing Marriage." *Contemporary Political Theory* 6:196–217.

———. 2009. "The Future of Marriage and the State: A Proposal." In *Marriage and Family: Perspectives and Complexities*, edited by H. Elizabeth Peters and Claire M. Kamp Dush, 325–44. New York: Columbia University Press.

Mills, C. Wright. 1959. *The Sociological Imagination*. New York: Oxford University Press.

Moats, David. 2004. *Civil Wars: A Battle for Gay Marriage*. Orlando, FL: Harcourt.

Moon, Dawne. 2004. *God, Sex, and Politics: Homosexuality and Everyday Theologies*. Chicago: University of Chicago Press.

———. 2005. "Discourse, Interaction, and Testimony: The Making of Selves in the U.S. Protestant Dispute over Homosexuality." *Theory and Society* 34 (5–6): 551–77.

Moon, Dawne, and Jaye Cee Whitehead. 2006. "Marrying for America." In *Fragile Families and the Marriage Agenda*, edited by Lori Kowaleski-Jones and Nicholas H. Wolfinger, 23–45. New York: Springer.

O'Malley, Pat, and Mariana Valverde. 2004. "Pleasure, Freedom and Drugs: The Uses of 'Pleasure' in Liberal Governance of Drug and Alcohol Consumption." *Sociology* 38 (1): 25–42.

Ortner, Sherry. 1974. "Is Female to Male as Nature Is to Culture?" in *Women, Culture and Society*, edited by Michelle Rosaldo and Louise Lamphere, 67–87. Palo Alto, CA: Stanford University Press.

Phelan, Shane. 2001. *Sexual Strangers: Gays, Lesbians, and Dilemmas of Citizenship*. Philadelphia: Temple University Press.

Philipson, Ilene. 2002. *Married to the Job: Why We Live to Work and What We Can Do about It*. New York: Free Press.

Pinello, Daniel. 2006. *America's Struggle for Same-Sex Marriage*. Cambridge: Cambridge University Press.

Polikoff, Nancy D. 1993. "We Will Get What We Ask For: Why Legalizing Gay and Lesbian Marriage Will Not 'Dismantle the Legal Structure of Gender in Every Marriage.'" *Virginia Law Review* 79:1535–50.

———. 2008. *Beyond (Straight and Gay) Marriage: Valuing All Families under the Law*. Boston: Beacon Press.

Popenoe, David. 1996. *Life without Father: Compelling New Evidence that Fatherhood and Marriage are Indispensable for the Good of Children and Society*. New York: Free Press.

Pugh, Allison J. 2005. "Selling Compromise: Toys, Motherhood and the Cultural Deal." *Gender and Society* 19 (6): 729–49.

Quadagno, Jill. 1994. *The Color of Welfare: How Racism Undermined the War on Poverty*. New York: Oxford University Press.

Rauch, Jonathan. 2004. *Gay Marriage: Why It Is Good for Gays, Good for Straights, and Good for America*. New York: Times Books / Henry Holt and Co.

Richardson, Diane. 2000. "Claiming Citizenship? Sexuality, Citizenship and Lesbian/Feminist Theory." *Sexualities* 3 (2): 255–72.

———. 2004. "Locating Sexualities: From Here to Normality." *Sexualities* 7 (4): 391–411.

———. 2005. "Desiring Sameness? The Rise of a Neoliberal Politics of Normalization." *Antipode* 37 (3): 515–35.

Roberts, Dorothy. 1997. "Punishing Drug Addicts Who Have Babies." In *Critical Race Feminism: A Reader*, edited by Adrien Katherine Wing, 127–35. New York: New York University Press.

Rose, Nikolas. 1987. "Beyond the Public/Private Division: Law, Power, and the Family." *Journal of Law and Society* 14 (1): 61–76.

————. 1990. *Governing the Soul: The Shaping of the Private Self.* New York: Routledge.

————. 1999. *Powers of Freedom: Reframing Political Thought.* Cambridge: Cambridge University Press.

Rose, Nikolas, and Peter Miller. 1992. "Political Power beyond the State: Problematics of Government." *British Journal of Sociology* 43 (2): 173–205.

Rubin, Gayle. 1993. "Thinking Sex: Notes for a Radical Theory of the Politics of Sexuality." In *The Lesbian and Gay Studies Reader*, edited by Henry Abelove, Michèle Aina Barale, and David M. Halperin, 3–44. New York: Routledge.

Schor, Paul. 2005. "Mobilizing for Pure Prestige? Challenging Federal Census Ethnic Categories in the USA (1850–1940)." *International Social Science Journal* 57 (1): 89–101.

Scott, James. 1998. *Seeing Like a State: How Certain Schemes to Improve the Human Condition Have Failed.* New Haven, CT: Yale University Press.

Sedgwick, Eve. 1993. "How to Bring Your Kids Up Gay." In *Fear of a Queer Planet*, edited by Michael Warner, 69–81. Minneapolis: University of Minnesota Press.

Shanley, Mary Lyndon. 2004. "Just Marriage: On the Public Importance of Private Unions." In *Just Marriage*, edited by Joshua Cohen and Deborah Chasman for *Boston Review*, 3–30. New York: Oxford University Press.

Sigle-Rushton, Wendy, and Sara McLanahan. 2002. "The Living Arrangements of New Unmarried Mothers." *Demography* 39 (3): 415–33.

Smith, Anna Marie. 2007. *Welfare Reform and Sexual Regulation.* Cambridge: Cambridge University Press.

Sperling, Susan. 1997. "Baboons with Briefcases vs. Langurs with Lipstick: Feminism and Functionalism in Primate Studies." In *The Gender/Sexuality Reader: Culture, History, Political Economy*, edited by Roger N. Lancaster and Micaela di Leonardo, 249–64. New York: Routledge.

Stacey, Judith. 1990. *Brave New Families: Stories of Domestic Upheaval in Late Twentieth-Century America.* Boston: Beacon Press.

————. 1996. *In the Name of the Family: Rethinking Family Values in the Postmodern Age.* Boston: Beacon Press.

Stacey, Judith, and T. Biblarz. 2001. "How Does the Sexual Orientation of Parents Matter?" *American Sociological Review* 66 (2): 159–83.

————. 2004. "Marital Suitors Court Social Science Spin-sters: The Unwittingly Conservative Effects of Public Sociology," *Social Problems* 51 (1): 131–45.

Stein, Arlene. 2001. *The Stranger Next Door: The Story of a Small Community's Battle over Sex, Faith, and Civil Rights.* Boston: Beacon Press.

Stone, Deborah. 1999. "Beyond Moral Hazard: Insurance as Moral Opportunity." *Connecticut Insurance Law Journal* 6 (1): 11–46.

Stychin, Carl F. 2003. *Governing Sexuality: The Changing Politics of Citizenship and Law Reform.* Portland, OR: Hart Publishing.

Sullivan, Andrew. 1989. "Here Comes the Groom: A (Conservative) Case for Gay Marriage." *New Republic* 28:20–22.

———. 2004. *Same-Sex Marriage, Pro and Con: A Reader*. New York: Vintage Books.

Swidler, Ann. 2001. *Talk of Love: How Culture Matters*. Chicago: University of Chicago Press.

Thistle, Susan. 2006. *From Marriage to the Market: The Transformation of Women's Lives and Work*. Berkeley: University of California Press.

Tronto, Joan. 1993. *Moral Boundaries: A Political Argument for an Ethic of Care*. New York: Routledge.

———. 2001. "Who Cares? Public and Private Caring and Rethinking Citizenship." In *Women and Welfare: Theory and Practice in the United States and Europe*, edited by Nancy J. Hirschmann and Ulrike Liebert, 65–83. New Brunswick, NJ: Rutgers University Press.

———. 2004. "Marriage: Love or Care?" In *Just Marriage*, edited by Joshua Cohen and Deborah Chasman for *Boston Review*, 37–40. New York: Oxford University Press.

Valverde, Mariana. 2003. "Police Science, British Style: Pub Licensing and Knowledges of Urban Disorder." *Economy and Society* 32 (2): 234–52.

Wacquant, Loïc. 2001. "The Penalisation of Poverty and the Rise of Neo-Liberalism." *European Journal on Criminal Policy and Research* 9 (4): 401–12.

———. 2002a. "Gutting the Ghetto: Political Censorship and Conceptual Retrenchment in the American Debate on Urban Destitution." In *Globalization and the New City: Migrants, Minorities and Urban Transformations in Comparative Perspective*, edited by Malcolm Cross and Robert Moore, 32–49. Hampshire, UK: Palgrave.

———. 2002b. "Taking Bourdieu into the Field." *Berkeley Journal of Sociology* 46:180–86.

———. 2007. "French Working-Class *Banlieue* and Black American Ghetto: From Conflation to Comparison." *Qui Parle* 16 (2): 1–33.

Waite, Linda. 2000. "Trends in Men's and Women's Well-being in Marriage." In *The Ties That Bind: Perspectives on Marriage and Cohabitation*, edited by Linda Waite, with Christine Bachrach, Michelle Hinden, Elizabeth Thomson, and Arland Thornton, 368–92. New York: Aldine de Gruyter.

Walder, Andrew G. 2009. "Political Sociology and Social Movements." *Annual Review of Sociology* 35:393–412.

Walters, Suzanna Danuta. 2001. "Take My Domestic Partner, Please: Gays and Marriage in the Era of the Visible." In *Queer Families, Queer Politics: Challenging Culture and the State*, edited by Mary Bernstein and Renate Reimann, 338–57. New York: Columbia University Press.

Warner, Michael. 1999. *The Trouble with Normal: Sex, Politics, and the Ethics of Queer Life*. New York: Free Press.

Weeks, Jeffrey. 1981. *Sex, Politics, and Society: The Regulation of Sexuality since 1800*. New York: Longman.

———. 1995. *Invented Moralities: Sexual Values in an Age of Uncertainty*. New York: Columbia University Press.

Weeks, Jeffrey, Brian Heaphy, and Catherine Donovan. 2001. *Same-Sex Intimacies: Families of Choice and Other Life Experiments*. New York: Routledge.

Weston, Kath. 1991. *Families We Choose: Lesbians, Gays, and Kinship*. New York: Columbia University Press.

Whitehead, Barbara. 1996. *The Divorce Culture: Rethinking Our Commitments to Marriage and Family*. New York: Vintage Books.

Whitehead, Jaye Cee. 2007. "Feminist Prison Activism: An Assessment of Empowerment." *Feminist Theory* 8 (3): 299–314.

Wilkinson, Iain. 2001. *Anxiety in a Risk Society*. London: Routledge.

Wilson, William J. 1996. *When Work Disappears: The World of the New Urban Poor*. New York: Random House.

Wolfson, Evan. 2004. *Why Marriage Matters: America, Equality, and Gay People's Right to Marry*. New York: Simon and Schuster.

Index